CD-ROM Technology

for

Information Managers

Ahmed M. Elshami

AMERICAN LIBRARY ASSOCIATION

Chicago and London 1990

Designed by Heidi Osterhout

Composed in Baskerville on
Alphatype Multiset III by
E.T. Lowe Publishing Company

Printed on 50-pound Glatfelter,
a pH-neutral stock, and bound
in 10-point Carolina cover stock
by Braun-Brumfield, Inc.

The paper used in this publication meets the minimum requirements of American
National Standard for Information Sciences—Permanence of Paper for Printed Library
Materials, ANSI Z39.48-1984. ∞

Library of Congress Cataloging-in-Publication Data

Elshami, Ahmed M., 1936-
    CD-ROM technology for information managers / by Ahmed M. Elshami.
        p.   cm.
    Includes bibliographical references.
    ISBN 0-8389-0523-4 (alk. paper)
    1. Optical disks—Library applications.   2. Optical storage devices—Library applica-
tions.   3. Library science—Technological innovations.   4. Information technology.
5. CD-ROM.   I. Title.
Z681.3.O67E43   1990
025.3—dc20   89-37880
                                                                             CIP

Contents

Figures

Tables

Preface

CD-ROM (Compact Disc–Read Only Memory) belongs to a group of discs called *optical discs*. The information on this type of disc is written, then read, by means of a laser beam. Although CD-ROM technology is very new, it has generated a great deal of interest because of its high storage capability, transportability, and data retention.

In the last two decades computers have dominated the publishing industry; however, the final product of the computer has remained printed matter. In the case of optical discs, the final product is quite revolutionary, and the shift from paper and microform to CD-ROM will have an impact on the library as an information provider. As the quantity of published materials on CD-ROM increases, the habits of both librarians and users will change.

Understanding the dimensions of this new technology is essential to librarians in order for them to participate effectively in products and application decision-making. Hardware manufacturers and software developers need to receive comments, criticisms, and suggestions from librarians to produce the type of information products and services needed by libraries. This book attempts to simplify and demystify optical discs, CD-ROM specifically, not only for librarians and archivists, but also for the general reader.

Chapter 1 explains the optical technology and the types of optical discs, including Videodiscs, CD-Audio, CD-ROM, DVI (Digital Video Interactive), CD-I (Compact Disc Interactive), VDI (Videodisc Interactive), WORM (Write-Once Read-Many), Erasable Optical Discs, and others.

Chapter 2 deals with the issue of standards. Unless there are some CD-ROM standards, the technology will suffer greatly as a result of the retardation of purchasing initiatives by librarians and other consumers. Standards form the basis for the compatibility between software and hardware.

Chapter 3 covers the steps of producing a CD-ROM disc along with different types of indexing and searching techniques. The premastering operation is explained, and some costs are provided with each step.

Chapter 4 deals with document storage systems and the use of optical discs for archival storage. Issues and problems associated with long-term storage are indicated, and interactive systems such as (Interactive Videodisc) and CD-I are discussed.

During the 1970s, while optical technology was still in the experimental stage, some major advances were developed, including online networks and COM (computer output microfilms). The number of online databases has risen to almost 3,000 worldwide. Microcomputers have linked these databases with government offices, homes, service facilities, libraries, educational institutions, businesses, and corporations. Although telecommunications have broken geographical barriers and distances, the major limitation in using online networks is the high cost involved. CD-ROM, on the other hand, has brought the end user in direct contact with many online databases. Before the advent of CD-ROM, such databases seemed remote. Chapter 5 deals with the issue of CD-ROM and online services and the related role of online searchers. Other media, such as COM, CD-I, and the Erasable Optical Disc (released during the last quarter of 1988), are also discussed in relation to CD-ROM.

Chapter 6 covers hardware issues, including an explanation of Microsoft Extensions software, which lets the computer deal with a CD-ROM disc drive as if it were another computer disk drive. Also explained in this chapter are the multi-access approach, "daisy-chaining," and local area networks (LANs).

Using many CD-ROM databases at a workstation requires the user to type a different command for each database. If there is a menu, the user would select a number or a letter from the menu in order to load a specific database. Chapter 7 provides a step-by-step approach to creating menus for loading different CD-ROM databases.

Because of their limited financial resources, libraries must purchase consistently useful products. However, there are certain features that a library should look for in any product, for example, speed, ease of use, compatibility, system output, and overall performance. Chapter 8 deals with issues that the industry should approach seriously when producing a CD-ROM product. Other topics such as hypertext and hypermedia are explained.

While research is the main source of new technologies, marketing is instrumental in transforming these technologies into products and services. While the success or failure of products and services cannot be accurately predicted, there is no group better than librarians, information specialists, and archivists to guide the industry when developing or evaluating the new technology. They are, after all, the chief end users. There is a variety of CD-ROM products that support some library operations, such as current and retrospective cataloging, circulation, interlibrary loan, union catalogs, and public access catalogs. These products are described in chapters 9 through 11.

Chapter 12 highlights available titles for full-text, governmental, statistical, Macintosh, and audio applications.

Since the introduction of the first CD-ROM products in late 1985, many new products have hit the market at a steady rate. There were about 90 titles available in 1986, and almost 260 titles in 1987. By 1988, this number reached well over 500 titles. As of this writing, the exact number of available CD-ROM titles, including private databases on CD-ROM, is not exactly known. Appendixes A and B list some 480 titles covering a wide range of subjects produced by almost 200 developers (listed in Appendix C).

Alas, CD-ROM remains an elusive and volatile market. Just when the product list was thought to be stabilized, some developers no longer supported their products and others had dropped their CD-ROM programs. Despite such failures, all indications endorse the notion that optical technology has established a foothold in the marketplace.

NOTE: The use of photos of any product, or the reference to any manufacturer, does not imply endorsement by the author or by the American Library Association.

Acknowledgments

The author would like to express his personal gratitude to Roger Strukhoff, Editor-in-Chief of *CD-ROM Review* (published by the International Data Group, Peterborough, N.H.) for reading the first draft of this book. His comments and directions were more than helpful.

Special thanks are extended to the many people and companies who provided the author with useful materials:

Darcy R. Cook, Marketing Director, Library Systems, General Research Corporation, Santa Barbara, Calif.

Terri L. Duer, Marketing Administration Manager, Brodart Automation, Williamsport, Pa.

Richard N. Fletcher, Director/Product Research, Database Products, Inc., Dallas, Tex.

Joel M. Lee, Marketing Manager, Auto-Graphics, Inc., Pomona, Calif.

William W. Liu, Marketing, Custom Design Technology, Inc., San Jose, Calif.

Eva Marsh, Cygnet Systems, Inc., Sunnyvale, Calif.

Rose M. McElfresh, Marketing Support Representative, Marcive, Inc., San Antonio, Tex.

Judith Michaelson, Manager, Marketing Services Department, OCLC, Dublin, Ohio

Diane K. Rangel, Vice-President, Product Development, Quantum Access, Houston, Tex.

Natalie Tanner, Sales Administrator, SilverPlatter, Wellesley Hills, Mass.

Teresa J. Wagner, Product Manager, Gaylord Information Systems, Syracuse, N.Y.

Bowker Electronic, New York, N.Y.

BRS Information Technologies, Latham, N.Y.

Dialog Information Services, Palo Alto, Calif.

EBSCO Publishing, Birmingham, Ala.

FABS International, DeFuniak Springs, Fla.

Grolier Electronic Publishing, Danbury, Conn.

Information Access, Foster City, Calif.

Library Corporation, Washington, D.C.

Meridian Data Corporation, Capitola, Calif.

Oxford Electronic Publishing, New York, N.Y.

TriStar Publishing, Fort Washington, Pa.
University Microfilms International, Ann Arbor, Mich.
Utlas International, Overland Park, Kans.
Western Library Network, Olympia, Wash.
H.W. Wilson Co., Bronx, N.Y.

1 Optical Disc Systems

Technology

Optical systems refer to the group of media that utilizes laser optics during recording and reading processes. Systems such as CD-ROM (Compact Disc Read-Only Memory) and videodiscs are optically sensitive devices that are used to store and distribute information. The significance of optical systems is in their tremendous storage capability. Combining the high storage capacity of optical systems with the high performance of present and future microprocessors and very high-density memories will revolutionize the ways people deal with information. Optical systems use different types of lasers; typically small diode semiconductors, infrared lasers, or gas lasers. Most current drives use small gallium arsenide semiconductor lasers, which produce oval beams of near-infrared light. Such systems utilize a variety of flat discs that are manufactured in different sizes (3.5″, 4.72″, 5.25″, 8″, 12″ and 14″). While recording, a laser beam is focused on the surface of the master disc and etches or burns the data in microscopic holes, or *pits*.

There are two techniques to lay out these microscopic pits. The first method is known as the Constant Angular Velocity (CAV), in which the pits are laid on the disc in concentric tracks resembling the tracks on floppy diskettes. The second method is known as the Constant Linear Velocity (CLV). In this method, the pits are laid out in one spiral track.

The difference between the CAV method and the CLV method is that on a CAV disc, each ring has the same amount of information on the sectors on the outer portion of the disc as the inner portion (Figure 1.1). In this case, the rotational speed of the disc is kept constant; but the information on the outer rings is more spread out than on the inner rings, since the number of the sectors per ring is constant.

On a CLV disc, data are arranged sequentially (Figure 1.2). Each sector or block of data takes up the same amount of physical space on the spiral, resulting in more sectors on the outer part of the spiral than the inner part. Thus a CLV disc holds more information than a CAV disc. A CLV drive must spin at constantly changing speeds to ensure that the amount of data passing under the reading head is constant. It spins faster on the inside part of the spiral than on the outside; hence, the access time in optical systems—the time that the access mechanism

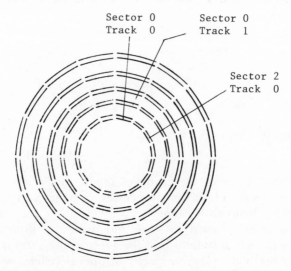

Figure 1.1 Tracks on a CAV disc are laid out in concentric rings. The sectors on the outer rings are longer and their number is equal to the sectors on the inner rings.

takes to be positioned at a specific location on the disc—is quite slow by computing standards. Access time is 500 milliseconds for CD-ROM compared to the average 30 milliseconds for hard disks (a millisecond is one thousandth of a second). Concerning the performance, a CLV disc drive is slower in accessing information than a CAV disc drive, due to the continuous rotational speed change.

During the recording process, the laser writing mechanism is set to its high-power mode, which is seven to ten milliwatts (.007 to .01 watts).

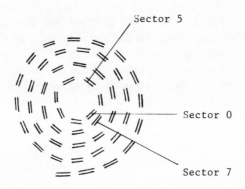

Figure 1.2 Spiral format of CLV disc. All sectors are the same length, resulting in more sectors on the outer tracks.

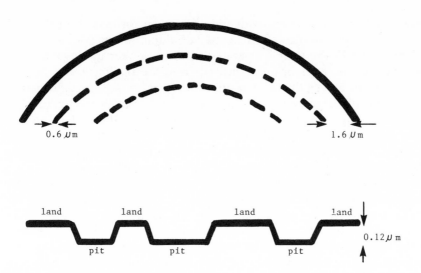

Figure 1.3 Pits and lands.

When the laser emitted from the writing head hits the surface of the disc, it melts a specific area in the recording layer. The result of this process is an oblong depression called a pit. However, unlike a phonograph record, the track is neither a groove nor a continuous line but only marks forming a spiral of a broken line (Figure 1.3).

The oblong pits are 0.12 microns (i.e., micrometers or millionth meters) deep and about 0.6 microns wide. Along the spiral, the spaces between the pits are called *lands*. The minimum length of a pit, or the land between two pits, is 0.9 microns. The maximum length is 3.3 microns.[1]

The distance between the tracks in the spiral is 1.6 microns forming 16,000 tracks per inch (tpi), compared to 96 tpi on a floppy diskette. The number of pits is almost two billion on the recording surface of the disc. This combination of very close tracks and microscopic pits generates the compact and huge storage capacity for all members of the optical media.

Reading Optical Discs

If you magnify part of the spiral you will see dark marks of optical contrast with respect to the unmarked areas on the mirror surface of

1. M. G. Carasso, J. B. H. Peek, and J. P. Sinjou, "The Compact Disc Digital Audio System," *Philips Technical Review* 40(6): 151–56 (1982).

the disc. The disc is read with the laser beam focused from the back side of the disc on the reflective layer of aluminum or gold. Generally, during a read, the laser is operated in its low-power mode (about one milliwatt). The laser beam is focused from the reading mechanism in the form of a very tiny spot of light onto the track. The light is then reflected off the shiny surface of the disc to a photodetector (a light-sensitive gadget), according to the contrast between the dark marks and the shiny areas. The continuous illumination of the track will vary as the disc rotates according to the difference in reflectivity due to the pits and lands on the track.

Because the disc rotates, the duration of the photo signal will vary according to the marks along the spiral. This contrast causes the reflection to change along the broken line. When the laser hits a dark spot, the reflected light scatters out and the photo signal decreases. The change in reflection is picked up by the reading mechanism—this mechanism replaces the stylus of the conventional phonograph—which converts it into an electrical signal. The read head interprets the change in the recording surface as a binary one, while the unchanged recording surface is interpreted as a binary zero. (The binary system is composed of two digits, 0 and 1, in contrast to the decimal system, which is composed of ten digits, 0 through 9.)

When the light strikes a flat area between pits, it is "reflected" into the lens, but when it strikes a pit, it is "diffracted" (scattered), and the photo signal decreases so that very little light finds its way back into the lens (Figure 1.4). The information signal changes along the tracks

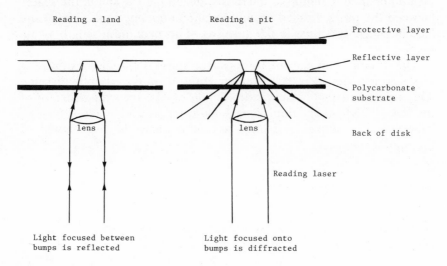

Figure 1.4 Reading the pits and lands. Reading is done through the back of the disc.

according to these diffractions and reflections from weaker to stronger light signals. The amount of light reflected back from the spiral track is measured. This signal is converted to digital data (0 or 1), that is picked up by the computer. The optical read-out system generates a detector signal, which is a reliable copy of the original recorded signal on the disc. This photo signal includes the "information" that is transformed into audio, video, or data signals. The speed at which the disc spins is carefully coordinated with the position of the lens.

Because environmental factors such as dust particles, fingerprints, and minor scratches lie outside the focal plane of the laser beam in the read head, they have little effect on playback quality.

Types of Optical Media

In an evolving technology such as optical media, it is not easy to categorize the types of optically sensitive materials according to their capabilities and features since these are continually being changed. Nor is it possible to accurately predict their potential because of their elusive market. It is inappropriate to distinguish between optical systems according to their optical recording technology, because the techniques used in data recording and reading are almost the same among various optical systems. In addition, it is improper to divide the media according to its consumer uses (entertainment, creative leisure, and general reference such as dictionaries, newspapers, magazines, etc.) and professional applications (scientific, engineering, legal, libraries, archival storage and records management, medicine, government, etc.) since professional characteristics are intrinsic in both applications. The data storage function approach, however, seems appealing since it distinguishes between the various applications according to the use of the optical medium as a memory device.

A data storage unit can function as: read-only; write once and read always; or write, erase, and read many times. Accordingly, there are at least three memory devices:

1. Read-Only Memory refers to any memory that is programmed at the time of its manufacture. The user cannot delete or alter its content, since the content can only be read.
2. Write-Once Memory refers to that memory to which the user, not the manufacturer, is able to write information. However, once the information is stored in this memory, there is no way to erase or alter its content.
3. Erasable Memory, on the other hand, is a memory that can be read, written to, or altered by the user at any time.

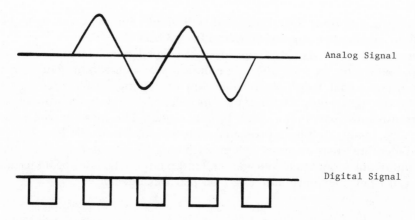

Figure 1.5 Analog is a continuous method, but digital is discrete or discontinuous.

Each type can be either analog (information is recorded on disc as video signals), digital (information is recorded on disc as binary notation, represented by 0s and 1s), or a combination of analog and digital.

In computing terminology, *analog* means data represented by means of a signal that is of a continuously variable physical quantity (often expressed as a wave), such as voice, music, or electrical voltage. An analog signal does not have a fixed value. It always fluctuates between a lower limit and an upper limit, thus having a continuously valid interpretation from the smallest to the largest value that it can achieve.[2] Analog data are often graphically represented as a sine curve. Such a curve bears some physical relationship to the original quantity (Figure 1.5).

This is in contrast to digital recording where data is generated as or translated into a series of discrete, fixed values, such as digits (0 to 9) or

2. In a watch with a sweep second hand, it is not easy to determine the exact time, as the time fluctuates between lower and upper values. It is not correct to say that the time is 2:37 exactly because the time is a continuous variable and not fixed. The time is a function with a lower value and an upper value. So, we can say that the time falls between 2:37:01 and 2:37:59, which is a continuous function that has upper and lower limits. Also, temperatures on a mercury thermometer have analog values, since at any time the temperature fluctuates between a lower and an upper value.

In the analog recording process used to record sound on phonograph records, an analog (likeness) of the original sound waves is stored in the form of jagged waves in a spiral groove on the surface of a plastic disc. As the disc rotates on the phonograph, a stylus (needle) rides along the groove. The waves in the groove cause the stylus to vibrate. These vibrations then are transformed into electric signals that may be converted back into sound by speakers.

In contrast to a watch with a sweep second hand, a digital watch displays the time as a fixed, or discrete, value.

other characters. Digital information is usually recorded in a series of binary notations and has only a discrete number of interpretations, usually two. In binary notation each signal is either 0 or 1; 0 means negative (or *off*) and 1 means positive (or *on*). For example, the capital letter *B* is equal to 00100010 in binary notation. Each signal (0 or 1) in the binary notation is called a *bit*. A pattern of eight bits is known as a *byte*, and a number, typically two or four bits, is called a *word*.

In the optical digital recording used to record sound on a compact disc, an analog-to-digital converter (Figure 1.6) is used to transform the audio signal into digital (numerical) information (0s or 1s). This signal is stored in digital code in the form of tiny pits or depressions on the surface of the disc. During the read-out, the light of a laser beam is reflected from the spinning disc. As the laser beam is reflected, the pits break it up into pulses of light. These pulses of light then are converted into electrical signals. The electrical signals are decoded and strengthened before they reach the speakers.

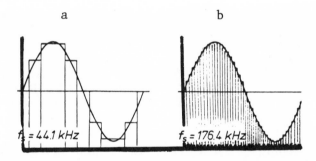

Figure 1.6 (a) Signal sampled at a rate of 44.1 KHz. (b) Same signal sampled at a rate of 176.4 KHz. The curve is approximated more closely to the analog wave form, which will result in a more accurate representation of the sound.

Read-Only Memory

Read-Only Memory (ROM) contains pre-written data or programs stored in the memory by the manufacturer. The content of such memory is permanent, i.e., nonerasable. This type of memory can only be read, and the user has no control over the content of such memory. Thus, the user cannot alter, update, or erase the content in any way. Such memory is suitable for publishing materials that do not require input from the user, for example, movies, games, training and educational materials, and reference works and services (indexes, directories, dictionaries, encyclopedias, almanacs, maps, etc.). Figure 1.7 enumerates some of the media included in this category.

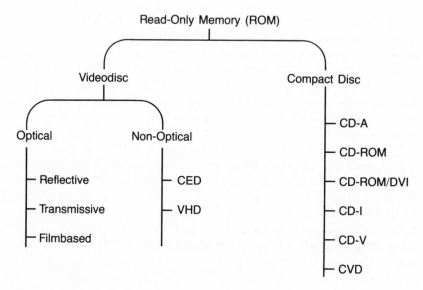

Figure 1.7 Types of Read-Only Memory discs.

Videodiscs

Videodisc, synonymous with LaserVision and also loosely termed "laser videodisc," is a generic term referring to different types of discs that have been developed by different manufacturers such as N. V. Philips (Netherlands), Radio Company of America (RCA), Vector Company of Japan (JVC), Thomson/CSF of France, and McDonnell-Douglas Electronics Company. These types of videodiscs are manufactured according to different techniques and processes. In general, a videodisc is an optical disc that has the capability of storing color video pictures and two-channel sound along a spiral track. The plastic double-sided disc is 30 centimeters (12 inches) in diameter with a central spindle hole. The most common types have either a shiny surface or a surface enclosed in a caddy for more protection. The program information is recorded on the disc in analog signals (like the data transmitted for television), while the control information is recorded in digital, usually in binary notation.

LaserVision is a high-quality audio-video communication system that stores NTSC (National Television Systems Committee) composite signals in an FM (frequency modulation) format on the videodisc. This FM signal modulates the laser beam on the recorder. Generally, a blue argon laser beam is used to write the pits on a master glass disc, while a low-power laser beam, such as the helium neon, is used in a videodisc player. The pits are a mechanical representation of the FM signal.

The optical videodisc technology is traced to James Logie Baird, a television pioneer who began experimenting on mechanical scanners and display devices in 1923. By 1926, Baird was able to transmit human faces using a disc both to scan the subject at the transmitter and to scan a modulated neon bulb at the receiver.[3]

Early in 1961, several engineers at 3M Company, including Wayne Johnson, Paul Gregg, and Dean DeMoss, were studying ways of developing home video systems. In March 1961, 3M approached Stanford Research Institute (now SRI International) seeking assistance in determining the feasibility of recording full-band-width television signals on a disc that could be replicated using electron-beam machining. Because gas lasers had not yet appeared on the scene, high-pressure, short-arc mercury and xenon lamps were used in the recording process. By 1963, 3M was able to record several 16-millimeter movies on discs, and by 1964, it was possible to make 15-minute television recordings and design several home disc players. High-quality silver halide recording discs were produced. By 1965, efforts were directed at reducing the cost of the final discs. Between December 9, 1960, and January 7, 1966, about 19 patents were granted to 3M pertaining to videodisc development.[4] However, experiments continued during the 1970s, and in 1978, 3M used Zenith laser equipment to develop its own videodisc.

Other experiments were conducted at Philips Research Laboratories early in 1970 to develop the videodisc. Philips used some kind of microfilm pictures arranged spirally on the surface of the disc. But it became clear that this was not a practical method due to control problems (focusing and timing). Soon an alternative method was applied (Figure 1.8)—a spiral track of depressions (pits). The information, coded as the length of the pits and spaces between the pits, known as lands, was read out optically by means of a laser beam.[5]

The engineers thought of using some form of phonograph record as an inexpensive medium to disseminate visual information, and the scheme was taken up by a research group from Philips. By mid-1971, the first experiments with a spiral track of pits were accomplished, but improvements were required to reduce the snow on the screen. On September 5, 1972, N. V. Philips held a press conference at the Philips Research Laboratories to demonstrate the first video long play (VLP) system. The player used in this demonstration was equipped with a tracking and focusing system. The playing time was thirty minutes of color picture and sound recorded on a glass plate. The VLP record could be produced simply, and in quantity, by the normal pressing

3. Philip Rice and Richard F. Dubbe, "Development of the First Optical Videodisc," *SMPTE Journal* 91(3): 277–84 (Mar. 1982).

4. Ibid., p.284.

5. K. Compaan and P. Kramer, "The Philips VLP System," *Philips Technical Review* 33: 177–93 (1973).

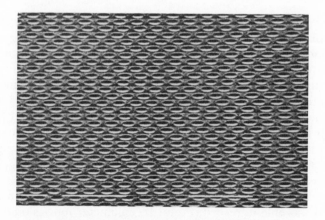

(Source: *Philips Technical Review* v.41, no.11/12 (1983).)

Figure 1.8 Micrograph of a pattern of pits in recorded video information as it appears through a scanning electron microscope. The slight differences in length and in the spacing between the pits are typical of video recording.

techniques. In this system a television picture was recorded as a succession of short grooves, or pits, of variable length.

After 1975, Philips changed the light source from a large gas laser to a smaller semiconductor laser, which improved the control system. At that time it became possible to produce the laser videodisc (LV) player commercially. By 1976, videodiscs had reached the U.S. market.

In order to distinguish between VLP and other videodisc systems based on non-optical pick-ups (heads), the name was changed from VLP to LaserVision.[6] Almost at the same time, RCA developed SelectaVision, a nonlaser capacitance electronic disc system (CED). The CED used a non-optical pick-up with a stylus that came in actual contact with the videodisc's surface. Capacitance metal discs record programming as varying electrical charges on the disc surface. In 1984, RCA discontinued SelectaVision, leaving laser videodisc as the only standard.

In the Philips laboratories there were some other experiments on control problems such as light tracking of the spiral and other effects such as stability of the disc, external disturbances, wobbling, disc errors, and vibrations. In 1976, research resulted in three important developments. The first was a reading light pen that was very compact and light. It could accurately follow the bouncing and wobbling track on the surface of the disc. The second development resulted in the current

6. D. McCoy, "The RCA Developed SelectaVision Videodisc System," *RCA Review* 39: 7 (1978).

audio compact disc (CD) from which CD-ROM was devised. The third development was the use of an LV disc as a computer storage medium, digital optical recording (DOR).[7]

During the 1960s, MCA planned to develop a videodisc using a process similar to that used in making a phonograph record that could be read by an optical stylus using a light source.[8] The first public demonstration of MCA's videodisc was in December 1972, three months after Philips announced its videodisc. Philips and MCA then decided to work out a technological standard that resulted in the LaserVision standard. MCA decided to produce the videodisc while Philips concentrated on producing the player. The first videodisc mastering and replication plant in the United States was built in Carson, California, by MCA. The plant produced its first videodisc in December 1978.[9] Today the Carson plant is run by Pioneer.

Videodisc Characteristics   Videodiscs are capable of carrying dual-channel audio and video information. The two audio channels can be played simultaneously (stereo sound) or individually (monaural sound). If the stereo is not needed, each channel is capable of carrying different types of information, such as two different languages. Discs are formatted in accordance with the television standards. In the United States, the standard contains either 54,000 or 108,000 frames of program per side (allowing one-half hour or one hour of playing). In Europe, formats contain 47,000 frames per side.

Videodiscs have the capability of sequential playback of video and audio programming, slow motion, fast forward or backward, scanning, and freeze frame. Not all these capabilities are supported by all types of videodiscs. In contrast to videotapes—generally known as videocassettes—videodiscs have the ability to play in non-sequential mode, thus accessing any frame regardless of its location on the disc. This random-access capability suits individual needs of users, especially in training applications, simulation, military training operations, interactive situations such as handling medical emergencies, and language training.

Types of Videodiscs   Not all videodiscs use laser optics in the playback mode. Based on this fact, videodiscs can be divided into two groups: optical videodiscs and non-optical (or capacitance) videodiscs.

Optical Videodiscs   Optical videodiscs use optical techniques in the form of a laser beam or other light source for data recording and

7. G. Bouwhuis and others, *Principles of Optical Disc Systems* (Bristol, England: Adam Hilger Ltd., 1985).

8. Mark Magel, "The LaserVision Standard ODC Begins the Teaching Trail," *Optical Information Systems* 6(2): 132–44 (Mar.-Apr. 1986).

9. Ibid.

playback. The nature of this process does not allow the read head to touch the surface of the disc, thus extending the life of the disc and the read mechanism. There are three types of optical videodiscs: reflective optical videodiscs (ROV), transmissive optical videodiscs (TOV), and film-based optical videodiscs (FOV).

CAV, the standard-play laser videodisc format, is most commonly used for interactive applications, whereas a videodisc player is interfaced with a computer. In this format, the 12-inch disc holds 54,000 video frames. The disc rotates at a constant speed of 1,800 revolutions per minute (rpm), one frame per revolution. Each frame can be addressed and presented individually within a few seconds with most videodisc players.

CLV, the extended-play laser videodisc format, is most commonly used for linear applications such as movies, concerts, etc. The rotation speed varies from 600 to 1,800 rpm while maintaining a constant track length for each frame. This format allows for recording up to sixty minutes of motion video on each side of a 12-inch disc. However, this prohibits addressing or displaying specific frames by location. This format is not applicable for interactive applications, since its searching capabilities are limited.

Reflective Optical Videodiscs The reflective optical videodisc (ROV) has an opaque shiny surface, and it is the most dominant technology. During playback, a laser beam is reflected off the surface of the disc onto a mirror, then into a decoder, where the signal is translated by the system into information. The predominant videodisc format in this group is LaserVision, now a trade name of Philips, Hitachi, Pioneer, and others. LaserVision has become the de facto industry standard. When a videodisc cannot be played on LaserVision, it is described as "nonstandard."

In the LaserVision system, which records video information, the signal is recorded on the disc in the form of a spiral track consisting of a succession of pits and lands. The information is presented in the track in analog form, like a television signal. Each transition from land to pit and vice versa marks a zero crossing of the video signal. Reflective optical videodiscs include the following three types: interactive videodisc (IVD), 8-inch videodisc, and the "instant jump."

The merging of motion video and audio with interactivity of the personal computer has been combined in the IVD systems. This interaction is accomplished through the use of a laser videodisc player and a computer interface. The 12-inch videodisc is capable of storing 54,000 still frames of video, or up to half an hour of full-motion video and audio per side. IVD is used for training in medical and industrial settings, and for information terminals and learning stations in schools. Because it needs a sophisticated graphics display subsystem, IVD is expensive.

Another version of the 12-inch LaserVision videodisc is an 8-inch disc, developed by Pioneer, which can hold either 14 minutes of motion video or 25,200 still-frames and 28 minutes of audio on two channels on each side of the disc. This 8-inch disc can be played on a 12-inch disc player, since playing starts in the middle of the disc and moves outward.

Some videodisc players have the ability to perform the so-called instant jump, a random access over a few hundred tracks between 100 to 250 frames forward or backward from a particular point. With this feature it is possible to create lively video scenes without the visual interruption, or screen blanking. This technique is used in video games. Current manufacturers of this technique include Philips, Hitachi, and Pioneer.

Transmissive Optical Videodiscs   Transmissive optical videodiscs (TOV) are made of flexible translucent material. This type of videodisc allows the laser beam to pass through the transparent disc to a decoder on the other side. Each side of the disc can be read without turning the disc by adjusting the focus of the light so that it shines through the disc to access the lower surface. TOV are produced by Thomson/CSF of France and distributed in Europe.

Film-based Optical Videodiscs   At the end of 1985, McDonnell-Douglas announced the production of film-based optical videodiscs (FOV). This system, developed by ARDEV (an Atlantic Richfield company that became the Videodisc Division of the McDonnell-Douglas Electronics Company), is a transmissive videodisc made of Mylar-based photographic film. It is inscribed with a low-powered laser in the mastering process. This type of videodisc is capable of having built-in compressed audio. A laser-film disc is single-sided and can hold 18 minutes of motion video, or 32,000 still-frames per disc, or 40 hours of compressed audio. The player of this film-based videodisc is manufactured by Sansui of Japan.

Non-Optical or Capacitance Videodiscs   Capacitance videodiscs are non-laser systems. These non-optical systems have the ability to store information in the form of electrical charges. They use a mechanical stylus-like device similar to that of a phonograph. Capacitance discs record programs as varying electrical charges on an electronically conductive metal disc surface covered with a layer of insulating plastic. The information is read as capacitance variations, which are decoded to television images. There are two types of capacitance videodiscs: the grooved capacitance electronic disc (CED) and the grooveless video high density (VHD).

Capacitance Electronic Disc   CED, a grooved videodisc format developed by RCA, was a non-laser system that used a stylus that rides in the spiral groove track. CED systems did not support either random access or freeze frame. At maximum information density, both sides of the disc could store two hours of motion picture. RCA abandoned CED in 1984.

Video High Density   VHD is a grooveless capacitance videodisc format that uses a broad stylus to pick up data. VHD was developed by the Vector Company of Japan (JVC), an affiliate of Matsushita. The General Electric Company and Thorne EMI Ltd. also used this technology. It was introduced to the American market in the fall of 1985. The VHD disc, which supports still frame, can accommodate an hour of motion programming per side. There is less wear on the grooveless capacitance disk than on the grooved disk because the stylus movement is not governed by the physical tracking of the groove. The system supports random access of individual frames. Although VHD workstations are used for education and training applications, this type of disc is not well suited to the storage of large quantities of digital data.[10]

Compact Discs

Compact Disc—Audio   The compact disc (CD) is a trademark name for an aluminized disc, 4.72 inches (12 cm) in diameter. It is made of polycarbonate, a very tough, clear plastic used in bullet-proof windows. The information is recorded on the surface of this layer. On the top of the polycarbonate is an extremely thin layer of aluminum that follows the contours of the pits. The layer reflects light from the laser beam used to read the disc. A layer of clear resin protects the top of the disc and carries the disc's label. The study of the possibility of recording audio signals optically on a disc through the use of a laser beam started in 1974 at Philips Research Laboratories, in close cooperation with the Philips Audio Division. At that time, it became clear that a method would have to be used different from the LaserVision system: digital signal coding (binary) instead of analog (video) signal methods.[11] On the CD the signal is recorded in a similar manner, but the information is presented in the track in digital form. Each pit and each land represents a series of bits called *channel bits*.[12] After each land/pit or pit/land transition there is a *1*, and all the channel bits in between are *0* (Figure 1.9).

The CD was originally designed to store high-fidelity music for which compact disc digital audio (CD-DA) now is a world standard

10. Judy McQueen and Richard W. Boss, *Videodisc and Optical Digital Disk Technologies and their Applications, 1986 Update* (Chicago: American Library Association, 1986), p.7–22.

11. "Compact Disc Digital Audio," *Philips Technical Review* 40(6): 149–80 (1982).

12. M. G. Carasso, J. B. H. Peek, and J. P. Sinjou, "The Compact Disc Digital Audio System," *Philips Technical Review* 40(6): 151–56 (1982).

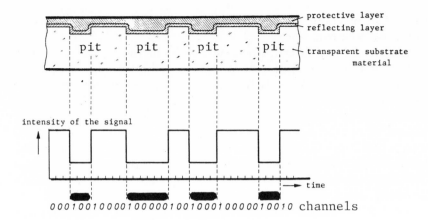

(Source: *Philips Technical Review*, v.40, no.6 (1982).)

Figure 1.9 Cross section of a compact disc. The intensity of the signal read by the optical pick-up is plotted as a function of time.

format, sometimes called the Red Book standard.[13] The Red Book is not available to the public but only to compact disc manufacturers who contract with Philips and Sony. After an agreement in principle had been reached with Sony of Japan in 1979, extensive technical discussions were started, mainly about the signal processing. The standard for this new technology was introduced in 1980 by Philips and Sony. The digital audio compact disc and its player are designed according to this worldwide standard. Audio compact discs were developed in the laboratories of N.V. Philips, and the first compact disc digital audio players were introduced in 1982.

CD-DA is considered an optical medium for playback of audio signals. In this system, binary notations are read by a low-power laser beam and processed digitally to regenerate the actual sound. This process does not involve any physical contact between the reading mechanism and the medium itself (the compact disc). This results in an extremely low rate of distortion, while producing a high-fidelity sound superior to that of traditional record players (where the stylus touches and runs along the spiral groove on the surface of the record, resulting in the wear of the record as well as the reading mechanism). In the case of the CD, there is no sound distortion during playback. In order to protect the CD against possible scratching and damage, the surface of the disc is covered with a transparent film. A CD audio needs a drive

13. The Compact Digital Audio Disc System Document, Technical Committee no.60A. The Central Office of the International Electronical Committee 3, Rue de Varembe, Geneva, Switzerland.

(player) to function. This player is designed to perform without being connected to a computer.

Compact Disc Read-Only Memory   In the literature, the terms CD-ROM, CD ROM, CDROM, or CD/ROM are found. However, the form CD-ROM is now used widely. The Compact Disc Read-Only Memory is based on CD-audio technology. It is a version of compact disc standard used primarily to store general-purpose digital data for personal computers. The CD-ROM standard is the result of the cooperation between Philips and Sony, who announced this new technology in 1983. The standard that describes the physical format for the storage of digital data on a compact disc has been documented in the Yellow Book Standard, which was released in its final form in 1985.

A CD-ROM is capable of holding about 543 megabytes (or Mb; mega = one million) of digital information on one side, the equivalent of 1,500 5.25-inch or 800 8-inch floppy diskettes or 10 60-megabyte computer magnetic discs. It can hold roughly 275,000 pages at 2,000 characters per page, or 15,000 page images at 36 kilobytes per image.

The storage capacity of the CD-ROM is overwhelming. You can store all the telephone directories in the United States on five CDs. The ability to store large amounts of data on the 4.72-inch single-sided disc, which is relatively heat- and scratch-resistant, makes CD-ROM the perfect candidate as a storage and distributing medium for textual information such as reference works, manuscripts, technical bulletins, journals, telephone directories, parts catalogs, manuals, maps, almanacs, census data, tax and legal codes, product information, archives, computer databases, and statistical and financial data. This capability—which may lead the information age into a new era, much as did papyrus in ancient Egypt more than 4,000 years ago—was the main reason that Steve Lambert and Suzanne Ropiequet selected the title *CD-ROM: The New Papyrus* for their classic work published by Microsoft Press in 1986.[14]

CD-ROM can store still and/or moving images in black and white or color; stereo or two separate sound tracks, integrated with and/or separate from the images; digital program files such as word processors or spreadsheets; and digital information files such as documents, records, or catalogs.

A CD-ROM disc needs a drive to function. Unlike the CD audio player, the CD-ROM drive cannot stand alone to perform; it has to be connected to a computer. Since CD-ROM is a computer peripheral, which means it operates only in conjunction with a computer, its abilities are in part a function of the host computer. In practice,

---

14. *CD-ROM: The New Papyrus: The Current and Future State of the Art,* ed. by Steve Lambert and Suzanne Ropiequet (Redmond, Wash.: Microsoft, 1986).

CD-ROM is designed according to the capabilities of the computer. For example, if the computer is capable of displaying graphics, CD-ROM can be designed to do the same. In addition, CD-ROM can be interfaced (connected) with all existing and future computer systems. It is limited only by the capabilities of the operating system and the microprocessor in the connected computer.

Because of this relationship between CD-ROM and computers, any computer advances will have a positive impact on CD-ROM. With this in mind, CD-ROM is expected to become more absorbed within the computer architecture. This dependency on the host computer is reflected in the design of CD-ROM drives. The most recent drives from Philips, Sony, Panasonic, JVC, Denon, and Taxan USA can be fitted in the personal computer (PC) as a half-height drive. This drive can be seen as a super hard-disc drive. However, the concept of ROM is still applied, meaning that the medium is not recordable (i.e., the end user cannot record data directly on it). Data has to be stored on the disc only by a manufacturer that is usually the publisher of the CD-ROM.

CD-ROM discs cannot be played on musical CD players. Like CD-audio, a CD-ROM cannot be copied, erased, or altered, a feature that will protect software developers against unauthorized or illegal copying. Magnetic fields, such as those found in some book-circulation terminals in libraries, cannot alter or destroy the data recorded on a CD-ROM. Compared to a floppy diskette, which must be handled with special care, a CD can take some abuse without damage to the disc or the data.

The differences between CD-ROM and videodiscs are:

1. Information is stored on a videodisc in analog signals (video signal) while a CD-ROM stores data in digital format (binary notation).
2. Videodisc can store motion video information.
3. Physical dimensions: CD-ROM is 4.72 inches while a videodisc is either 3.5, 5.25, 8, 12, or 14 inches in diameter.
4. CD-ROM is a trademark standard, licensed through Philips and Sony.

The similarities are:

1. Both are read-only memories.
2. Their archival life is at least ten years (according to laboratory tests).
3. Both store digital information, audio, and still-frame video.
4. Although both can be used as multimedia information devices, neither is perfect yet in that respect.

The differences between CD-ROM and CD-audio are:

1. Although both require the same correction technique, CD-ROM requires a higher level of error correction than a CD-audio (see Chapter 2).
2. Although both CD-ROM and CD-audio players use the same control and display systems, a CD-ROM works in concert with a computer, while a CD-audio works without a computer. One can, however, hook up CD-ROM drives with CD-audio capability to a computer and control the audio through inexpensive, commercially available software.
3. A CD-audio player has a built-in digital-to-analog processor in order to send analog sound signals to the stereo amplifier, while the CD-ROM player sends digital information to the computer. For this reason a CD-audio player is not capable of running a CD-ROM disc.

The similarities are:

1. Both have the same dimensions, 4.72 inches or 120 millimeters in diameter, 1.2 millimeters in thickness, and the diameter of the programmed area on both is 50–116 millimeters.
2. Both have a shelf life of at least ten years (according to laboratory tests).
3. Both can be remotely controlled.
4. Both can be replicated at the same facility, since the software is recorded on both by the same techniques. The huge success of the CD-audio industry has resulted in massive replication facilities worldwide, where CD-audio and CD-ROM can be replicated at the same facility.

Compact Disc Interactive   Compact Disc Interactive (CD-I), on the other hand, is a technical specification for a multimedia system capable of simultaneously handling audio, video, data, text, executable codes, graphics, and computer programs. It offers high data capacity combined with television-quality image on a standardized player that includes sophisticated graphic processing capabilities. Once more, Philips and Sony devised the standard for CD-I (the Green Book Standard). Philips/Sony's CD-I standard is based on the CD-ROM format (Yellow Book Standard). The CD-I standard was announced on February 24, 1986, and later at the March 1986 First International Conference on CD-ROM sponsored by Microsoft in Seattle, Washington.[15]

Unlike CD-ROM, CD-I is not a computer peripheral, but a self-contained system or a videodisc player. It is designed to work

15. D. Rosen, "History in the Making: A Report from Microsoft's First International Conference on CD ROM," *Educational Technology* 26(7): 16–19 (July, 1986).

independently from the computer since it has a built-in microprocessor for interactive applications. Because maturation of this new technology has been slower than anticipated, it is not possible to speculate on its availability in the market. CD-I is a specific application of CD-ROM based on a single media concept, where information as well as software will be stored on one bootable disc with a readable function.[16] (A bootable disc is one that includes the operating system required to start or boot the machine.) CD-I players will be able to play all audio compact discs, as well as CD-ROM discs.

A functional CD-I system was demonstrated during Microsoft's Third International Conference on CD-ROM in Seattle on March 3, 1988.

Digital Video Interactive   Digital Video Interactive (DVI) was announced and demonstrated by General Electric/RCA during the March 1987 Second International Conference on CD-ROM sponsored by Microsoft in Seattle. DVI provides the means to display up to an hour of full-screen, full-motion video, as well as high-resolution still images, computer animation, three-dimension graphics and video images, and multitrack audio with CD quality combined with foreground video objects, text, and dynamic graphics—all under user control, from highly compressed digital data stored on a single, standard CD-ROM disc that runs on a standard CD-ROM drive. DVI, as was demonstrated in Seattle on March 3, 1988, provides capabilities for the user to interact with applications featuring full-motion and multichannel audio.

Producing digital-based video is a complex process that requires large amounts of data. When the information in a standard screen of analog video measuring 512-by-400 pixels—a pixel is the smallest picture element in a video display, represented by a point that can be independently assigned color and intensity—is converted into digital form, it takes about 600 kilobytes of data per image or frame. In order to portray full-motion effect, a television screen must display about thirty frames of video every second. Although the capacity of a CD-ROM is very high (543Mb), using the figures above will show that a CD-ROM can hold only 30 seconds of digital video. The reading speed of a CD-ROM is 150 kilobytes per second, meaning that the CD-ROM is a slow medium to show video at its real-time speed. In fact, the 30-second digital video will be displayed in more than one hour.

RCA solved this problem by compressing the data before a master is manufactured. The data is stored on the disc in its compressed format. Each time the disc is played, the data is decompressed. To decompress the data RCA uses a very large-scale-integration (VLSI) chip set to

16. Robert J. Moes, "The CD-ROM Puzzle: Where Do the Pieces Fit?" *Optical Information Systems* 6(6): 509–11 (1986).

perform this process. RCA's Video Display Processor (VDP) is a two-chip set that consists of a pixel processor (VDP1) and an output display processor (VDP2). The VDP includes a computer bus interface—a link that allows the conductor used for transmitting signals to establish communication between the computer and the chips—which allows the chip set to be used in a variety of system architectures, including the IBM PC-AT.[17]

DVI has been developed by General Electric at the David Sarnoff Research Center, RCA's historic central laboratory in Princeton, New Jersey. Research into the project began in 1984, and in 1988 the DVI venture was sold to Intel. The existing prototypes are mostly in training, higher education, and customer information applications. Although DVI is similar to the CD-I concept, and much like a videocassette recorder, each has a different technical approach.

Compact Disc Video Compact Disc Video (CD-V) is produced by Philips and Sony. This 4.72-inch disc stores video as analog signals (like a television signal), though CD digital video storage also exists. CD-V uses standard LaserVision production equipment. It supports full-screen motion video for five minutes playing time at 2,700 rpm. It is capable of holding up to 9,000 still frames, and it can be accompanied by audio tracks. The hardware includes a stand-alone player. Intended for the home entertainment market, CD-V combines sight and digital sound but is not compatible with CD-audio players. Think of CD-V as MTV on disc. It has nothing to do, in terms of applications, with CD-ROM, CD-I, or DVI.

Compact Video Disc Compact Video Disc (CVD) is a hybrid analog/digital system invented by Lowell Nobel and Ed Sandberg. It is not part of Philips/Sony CD development. It uses standard LaserVision analog production equipment and custom modulation hardware for additional digital processing. At a speed of 900–1,800 rpm, it is capable of running twenty minutes of full-screen motion video using the Constant Linear Velocity technique (CLV), and ten minutes if Continuous Angular Velocity (CAV) is used. It can hold up to 18,000 still frames per side. It has sound capability. The hardware involved includes a stand-alone player with a built-in computer. CVD is not commercially available, but when manufactured it will be intended for the home entertainment market.

17. "New Integrated Video and Graphics Technology: Digital Video Interactive." An article based on the text of the document released at the Microsoft Second Annual CD-ROM Conference, March 1987. *Optical Information Systems* 7(6): 412–15 (Nov.-Dec. 1987).

Write-Once Memory

Write-Once Memory, usually referred to by the industry as Write-Once Read-Many (WORM), is an optical disc technology in which the user may record information on the disc as well as read from it, but not erase or change it. Sometimes it is referred to as OD3, or OD-Cubed, for Optical Digital Data Disc; or WOOD (Write-Once Optical Disc).

Write-Once systems are more expensive than Read-Only. However, these systems are able to directly read after writing information. Write-Once discs allow the user to write information on them at any time on site or from a remote location—using a telephone line and a modem. Once the information is recorded, the system does not allow any alteration in the recorded data. Hence, WORM systems are appropriate for archival storage and transaction recording, since tampering with the data is inhibited.

The WORM system until now is not a replacement for magnetic disks, although it is seen as a link between magnetic media and the erasable optical systems. Like CD-ROM, the media used in Write-Once technology are said to be stable for ten years or more.[18] WORM discs cannot be read on CD-ROM drives, nor can CD-ROM discs be used with WORM drives. However, the Compact Disc Programmable Read-Only Memory system (CD-PROM), which Philips and Sony specified in the Blue Book more than four years ago, now called CD-Write Once, is necessarily a WORM system. It will play CD-ROMs, and the higher-priced systems will play audio discs as well.

WORM discs come in a variety of sizes—3.5, 4.7, 5.25, 8, 12, or 14 inches, but the most common sizes are 5.25 and 12 inches. The 5.25-inch discs are used on personal computers; the 12-inch discs are used for archiving mainframe and minicomputer data. Standards have not been developed to control disc construction, data formatting, or the layout of the WORM disc. At present, the capacity of WORM discs ranges between 200 megabytes and 1.2 gigabytes (1 gigabyte = 1 billion bytes).

Three WORM technologies are used in industry: phase change, dye polymer, and ablative. Of the three, the ablative approach is currently used most often.

Ablative technology uses a laser to burn a permanent pit into the surface of the WORM disc, exposing the layer underneath. This lower layer differs in its reflectivity from the top layer. The fluctuation of light reflected from the surface due to the pits is read as information by the computer. Because forging information on a WORM disc is

---

18. Leonard Laub, "What Is CD ROM?" in *CD-ROM: The New Papyrus,* p.42–71.

highly unlikely, it is best suited to extensive archival and records management activities.

Optical Read-Only Memory

In anticipation of the development of high-performance writable optical disc systems, some companies have prepared Read-Only versions of these discs. 3M Company refers to this disc as OROM, for Optical Read-Only Memory, while Sony calls it DataROM. This type of media supports on-site data recording. OROM can be any size but is typically 5.25 inches (13 cm) in diameter. Faster access to data can be achieved due to the tracks being laid down in a concentric CAV, which is a nonstandard format, i.e., a non–Philips/Sony standard.

Digital Optical Recording

Digital Optical Recording (DOR) is an implementation of videodisc as a computer storage medium that was a large computer memory used in combination with a semiconductor laser. Some ten billion bits (corresponding to 500,000 pages) can be stored on one disc. In this system, information is stored in the form of holes burned into a thin metal layer on the disc.[19]

Philips Research Laboratories in Eindhoven (Holland) and the United States contributed to the development of this technology. It was presented to the press in November 1978 while still in the experimental stage. DOR discs are used now on the professional equipment market. DOR discs are composed of an alloy of tellurium and other substances such as selenium, antimony, and sulphur. The aging process of this alloy is said to be very slow. A DOR disc consists of a glass substrate coated with an ultraviolet photopolymerized lacquer layer and a recording layer. The lacquer layer is pregrooved for tracking purposes and provided with information for addressing and synchronization. The recording layer consists of a material in which a laser beam can easily write holes with a significant difference in contrast on read-out.

In digital optical recording on discs, the data are recorded and read by means of a laser beam with a diameter of 1 micron. The DOR system differs from the Videodisc and Compact Disc systems, where the information is prerecorded on the disc by the manufacturer. In DOR, the information is written by the user.

Direct Read After Write

Direct Read After Write (DRAW) is an optical storage technique used in WORM systems in which an optical medium can be locally recorded

19. L. Vriens and B. A. J. Jacobs, "Digital Optical Recording with Tellurium Alloys," *Philips Technical Review* 41(11/12): 313–24 (1983/84).

but not erased.[20] Actually the term DRAW refers to a technique in error control, in which the machine continuously reads the data after it is written in order to verify the accuracy of each data block by comparing it with the data input stream. If an error is detected, the data are immediately corrected and rewritten on another location on the disc (instead of waiting until all data have been recorded). This process of recording is called real-time recording; unlike CD-ROM, it produces a videodisc in one pass without copying from a master. Since the information becomes ready the instant it is recorded, no processing is required. It seems that the term DRAW is now being used in the literature as one of the videodisc technologies.

DRAW is a good technique for archival purposes.[21] However, the effects of aging of the media must be taken into consideration when using such systems. In analog video recording, deterioration of the video signal results in "dropouts." These dropouts, or the loss of signals on the recorded medium, usually are caused by environmental contamination (dust, fingerprints, accumulated dirt, etc.) or the aging of the medium. Technically, it is very difficult to accurately predict the point at which it becomes impossible to read and interpret the picture information. If we compare this medium with magnetic tapes, we will find that the information on the tapes has to be refreshed on an average of every two years. Deterioration of the digital data can be restored through error correction techniques.

There are some DRAW systems on the market. They include Optical Disc Corporation's Recordable Laser Videodisc (RLV), a standard system (compatible with LaserVision); Panasonic's Optical Memory Disc Recorder (OMDR), a nonstandard system (not compatible with LaserVision); and Hitachi's DRAW, a nonstandard system marketed in Japan.

Optical Memory Card

Optical Memory Card (OM-Card) or LaserCard (a trademark), also known as Write-Once Card, has been developed and patented by Drexler Technology Corporation of Mountain View, California, for data recording and storage. This optical storage device, the size of a credit card, is capable of storing up to two megabytes (the equivalent of 800 pages of text) in either a Read-Only or Write-Once format. Applications for this optical recording technology include medical card systems, financial/bank cards, electronic publishing, data collection and

20. A. Huijser, "Material for On-line Optical Recording," in G. Bouwhuis and others, *Principles of Optical Disc Systems*, p. 210–27.

21. A. Huijser, "Applications," in G. Bouwhuis and others, *Principles of Optical Disc Systems*, p. 262.

distribution, air travel cards, driver's licenses, and vehicle/equipment maintenance records.[22] Expected future applications of the LaserCard include medical history records, hardware maintenance records, security access codes in high-security areas, and personnel information such as training status of employees in multilevel training programs.[23] A LaserCard optical memory is writable (recordable), i.e., the end user can store data directly on it rather than have to ask a manufacturer to process it.

Erasable Memory

An erasable memory is a memory whose contents can be modified (read, written, or erased) by the user, like a hard disk. However, in contrast to hard disks, erasable cartridges are removable with storage capacity ranges between 500 megabytes and 1 gigabyte. Erasable products began to ship to the consumer market at the end of 1988. Many companies such as Sony, Advanced Graphics Applications, Canon, and Alphatronix have produced erasable drives. These manufacturers (all except Canon) have adopted an ISO (International Standards Organization) standard for erasable drives. This assures that erasable discs will work on any erasable drive produced by any manufacturer. However, this has to be tested in order to be proven correct. The capacity of ISO drives is 650 megabytes with an average access time of 80 milliseconds.

The magneto-optic technique is the most dominant method used to alter data on the erasable disc. In this technique, media data is written via a high-powered laser beam that creates a blister or bubble in the metallic layer of the disc. To change data, the laser fires high-intensity light onto a microscopic area on the disc, heating the surface of the blister (roughly 300 degrees Centigrade). At this point, it is easy to change the magnetic property of the heated portion. This is done through a magnetic coil that emits a weak magnetic field that changes the magnetic properties of the surface of the disc. This is done the same way a computer changes the surface of a magnetic disk to the corresponding binary 0 or 1. Once the laser shuts off, the surface cools down and the data cannot be easily altered unless the surface is heated again.

The Magneto-Optic (M-O) disc, which is an erasable disc, is in fact a magnetic medium. It is written by a magnetic field and read optically

22. "Two New U.S. Patents Strengthen Drexler Technology's Position in Compact Memory Marketplace," *Optical Information Systems* 6(2): 97–98 (Mar.-Apr. 1986).

23. Robert B. Barnes and Frank J. Sukernick, "The Optical Memory Card's Role in the Distribution of Technical Information," *Optical Information Systems* 6(6): 504–8 (Nov.-Dec. 1986).

by sensing the rotation of polarization of light reflected from the surface. To read data, a low-intensity laser is fired onto a spot on the disc. When the light is reflected, its waves rotate in one of two directions, depending on its polarization. A light detector senses the reflected light and interprets its polarization as 0 or 1.

The erasable media can be written thousands of times. They can be described as Write Many Read Always (WMRA), which allows the user to continuously overwrite (delete old data and record new data on the same spots) and read the disc as often as floppy diskettes and hard disks are used today. This media is very new, and little is known about its problems with long-term physical stability. Prices of erasable drives range between $4,000 and $6,000, while erasable discs cost between $200 and $250.

2 CD-ROM Standards

CD-ROM is best described as an optical distributing medium for large volumes of programs and/or machine-readable data that have a low rate of updating.[1] Because of its capability in holding large amounts of data in different forms such as text, illustrations, graphs, and computer programs, it can be used in areas such as:

1. The publishing industry for mass-produced materials
2. Office applications for the preservation of records and archival storage
3. Data processing in computer backup systems
4. Simulation and interactive applications in such settings as training and education
5. Dissemination of information through Local Area Networks (LANs) or in the office environment

There are more than 500 CD-ROM products on the market today, but the inability to run them on just any CD-ROM drive was of concern to all users. Such was the situation before the approval and implementation of the standard for CD-ROM volume and file structure. Before agreeing on any standards, the majority of CD-ROM systems did not allow the transportability (transportation of a disc from one CD-ROM system to another) or interchangeability (exchange of information between two systems) due to the lack of standards. This alone was enough to raise doubts about what users should buy or at least consider acquiring in the future. The lack of standards slowed down the procurement of CD-ROM systems in libraries.

Because of the high price of CD-ROM products, it was impossible to run a product developed by different producers with similar contents (such as a database produced by different CD-ROM publishers) on one drive for comparability and evaluation before acquisition of the product. The lack of standards before 1988 was a major flaw in the CD-ROM industry and the stumbling block between the technology and the end user. Unlike a CD-audio, which could be played on almost any CD-audio player, a CD-ROM disc had to be accessed by a specific

---

1. M. A. O'Connor, "CD-ROM versus Erasable Compact Disc," *Videodisc and Optical Disk* 5(6): 454–60 (1985).

drive. Because of their importance, standards were considered an evaluative criterion for CD-ROM.[2]

The incompatibility issue seems to fade away as a result of the adoption of the International Standards Organization to the High Sierra Group specifications (ISO 9660) and the development of Disk Operating System Extensions MSCDEX by Microsoft (see Chapter 6). It seems that libraries may always "have to insist that producers create software that will be compatible with their competitors, make it possible to disarm the device driver installation instructions, or else warn purchasers that each program will probably need its own dedicated PC and player."[3] (Device drivers act as a bridge between the application program and different hardware, such as printers, monitors, and CD-ROM drives.) Standards will supposedly allow running of a CD-ROM product with any microprocessor, no matter what operating system is used by the processor, be it VMS, UNIX, IBM-DOS, Apple DOS, OS/2, or MS-DOS. In other words, at one stage of the CD-ROM industry, it was unrealistic for a library to acquire three different systems or workstations to run three different CD-ROM products.

Theoretically, any CD-ROM disc will physically run on any CD-ROM drive, and any CD-ROM drive can be read by any microcomputer "so long as volume and file system and drivers software corresponding to the operating system of the host computer has been installed in the computer's memory."[4]

There are many standard levels that should be addressed by the industry in order to achieve compatibility among CD-ROM drives, discs, interface with microcomputers, and operating systems. There is a universal standard, that is, the Philips and Sony standard. However, this standard covers only the physical specifications of the disc.

Compatibility cannot be achieved without an agreement by the CD-ROM industry on the following standard levels:

1. Disc physical standard
2. Disc logical standard
3. Drive standard
4. Operating system software
5. Application standard
6. Device drivers

2. David C. Miller, "Evaluating CDROMs: To Buy or What to Buy?" *Database* 36–42 (June 1987); and Nancy Herther, "A Planning Model for Optical Product Evaluation," *Online* 10(5): 128–30 (Sept. 1986).

3. Karla J. Pearce, "CD-ROM: Caveat Emptor," *Library Journal* 113(2): 37–38 (Feb. 1, 1988).

4. Julie B. Schwerin and others, *CD-ROM Standards: The Book* (Pittsfield, Vt.: Learned Information, 1986).

Disc Physical Standard

This level of standard has been addressed by Philips and Sony. Its development goes back to 1978, when Philips devised a specification for digital audio recording. In 1979, Philips and Sony agreed on a standard to record music on compact disc and published their scheme in a book known as the Red Book. A year later, in 1980, the Red Book was accepted by the Japanese Digital Audio Disc Committee. In 1983, this standard was followed by another standard for the CD-ROM, published in the Yellow Book. The CD-ROM standard is based on the CD-audio standard. Julie Schwerin et al. emphasize the fact that the Philips and Sony standard is a medium standard rather than a hardware design standard. They argue that although "it would be an advantage if the access or seek time could be improved, perhaps by using a CAV track format...it would not be possible to deviate from the situation of the spiral tracks (CLV) without going outside the standard and creating a non-standard product....However, it is possible to improve on the servo-mechanisms and read head mechanism in the drive, and thus improve the performance of the CD-ROM in access time while still remaining within the standard."[5]

The servo-mechanism mentioned here refers to focus and tracking servos that continuously receive values from their environment, then adjust themselves by maintaining a constant rate in relation to focus and tracking operations.

The physical standard deals with the track and block (known also as *sector*) layout, data density, the content area of each block, and error checking encoding. The Yellow Book and the Red Book address these physical and recording levels as follows:

The physical dimensions of a compact disc are 12 centimeters in diameter, 1.2 millimeters thick, 15 millimeters center hole. The compact disc is single-sided, and its recording density is 16,000 tracks per inch (tpi). The diameter of the program area is 50 millimeters to 116 millimeters. The Constant Linear Velocity (CLV) format is used. Access time ranges between a half and a full second (500 and 1,000 milliseconds), which is considered very slow compared to the access time of a typical Winchester disk drive (30 milliseconds). The data-transfer rate is 150 kilobytes per second. The capacity is 75 minutes per side.

5. Ibid., p.15–16.

Data Structure

Definitions:
1 byte = 8 bits
1 kilobyte = 1,024 bytes
1 block = 2,048 user data bytes
1 second = 75 blocks = 150 kilobytes
1 minute = 60 seconds × 150 kilobytes = 9,000 kilobytes
1 hour = 60 × 9,000 = 540,000 kilobytes = 552,960,000 bytes

The structure of data on the spiral track on CD-audio and CD-ROM is the same. Data spiral starts at the inside and runs towards the outside. Data are grouped in blocks or sectors. A block, 2352 bytes, is the smallest addressable unit of a CD-ROM. A block is composed of 98 frames (Figure 2.1). The frame is 24 bytes and is considered the basic information storage unit of a CD-ROM.

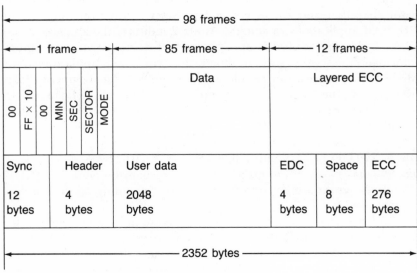

Figure 2.1 A CD-ROM data block is 2352 bytes.

Each block starts with 12 bytes (1 byte of 00, 10 bytes of FF, 1 byte of 00). The CD-ROM drive keeps track of its location on a disc by tallying the number of bytes it passes and by looking for sync information. Header data are used to identify the block. The first 3 bytes contain the block's address, which is used by the disc drive to locate the block. Addresses are expressed in terms of playing time. The Philips/Sony standard provides for 75 minutes (MM) of playing time, while CD-ROMs

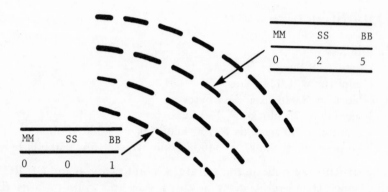

Figure 2.2 Physical addressing scheme.

utilize 60 minutes of the full capacity. Each minute is divided into 60 seconds (SS), and every second is divided into 75 blocks (BB) (Figure 2.2).

The fourth byte is called the *mode*. Mode 1 indicates the presence of error detection and correction codes (EDAC), which are needed in CD-ROM applications in general. Mode 2 indicates the absence of the EDAC codes, and is used in applications that do not require maximum information integrity such as home and consumer applications. In Mode 2, more space can be allocated to the user data segment (2336 bytes) due to the absence of the EDAC codes (Table 2.1). The user data is the data stored on the CD-ROM as information, such as text, video, sound and graphics, etc.

Thus, a standard 60-minute disc contains: 60 MM $\times$ 60 SS $\times$ 75 BB = 270,000 blocks; and 270,000 blocks $\times$ 2048 bytes per block = 552,960,000 bytes of user data, or 553 megabytes on a CD-ROM. (Different figures are given in the literature depending on the amount of time used.)

The Error Detection Code (EDC) is added to determine whether the user data on the CD-ROM disc is different from the original data. An 8-byte space is left unused between the EDC and the next segment, the Error Correction Code (ECC). The ECC is used to correct the user data if an error is detected. This code is a highly sophisticated algorithm based on the Reed-Solomon code.[6]

These levels of error detection and correction are more essential to CD-ROM, where data retrieval is involved, than to CD-audio. Even the slightest error on CD-ROM will terminate the program, while an error on CD-audio might go undetected by the listener.

---

6. For a good article on ECC see H. J. Hoeve, J. Timmermans, and L. B. Vries, "Error Correction and Concealment in the Compact Disc System," *Philips Technical Review* 40(6): 166–72 (1982).

Table 2.1 Track Structure

Designation	Byte Order	Byte Count	
		Mode 1	Mode 2
Synchronization data	0-11	12	12
Header data	12-15	4	4
Minute	12		
Second	13		
Block	14		
Mode	15		
User data	16-2063	2048	2336
Error detection code	2064-2067	4	—
Unused space	2068-2075	8	—
Error correction code	2076-2351	276	—
		2352	2352 bytes

Modulation

Pits and lands (the spaces between pits) do not correspond to 1s and 0s as one might think. The transition from a pit to a land or from a land to a pit is represented by 1 (channel 1), while the length between pits is represented by 0s (channel 0s). To understand this pattern, let us use an example.

The binary notation equivalent to decimal 3 is 00000011. There is no conceivable way to represent the adjacent 1s, as they are represented in this number as pits on the disk. This led to computation of the EFM Modulation Code (Eight to Fourteen Modulation system) that will convert the 8 bits to 14 bits by using a special conversion table. This assures that no two channel 1s follow each other. Also, it separates adjacent 1s with zero channels. In this system, data bits are translated 8 at a time into 14 channel bits (CB) using a look-up table (Table 2.2). Three additional merge bits are added to the 14-bit modulation code to separate the start and end of each 14-bit symbol, so each 8-bit data (byte) is represented by 17 CBs. In this system, each frame is composed of 588 bits as follows:

1. A synchronizing pattern composed of 24 bits plus 3 channel bits for proper separation, i.e., 27 CB.
2. A control and display code composed of 14 bits plus 3 bits for proper separation, i.e., 17 CB.

Table 2.2 8- to 14-Code Conversion Table for 0 through 10

	DATA BITS	CHANNEL BITS
0	00000000	01001000100000
1	00000001	10000100000000
2	00000010	10010000100000
3	00000011	10001000100000
4	00000100	01000100000000
5	00000101	00000100010000
6	00000110	00010000100000
7	00000111	00100100000000
8	00001000	01001001000000
9	00001001	10000001000000
10	00001010	10010001000000

(Source: *CD-ROM: The New Papyrus*, vol. 1, p. 66, fig. 6.)

3. 24 bytes of user data are transformed into 17 CB each, i.e., 408 CB.

4. An error correction code composed of 8 × 17, i.e., 136 CB.

This tells the master recorder to start a pit edge when 1 is received and continue forming a land when zeroes are received. The land continues as long as there are zeroes until another 1 CB is received. When a 1 is received, the land ends and a pit edge is formed (Figure 2.3), and so on.[7]

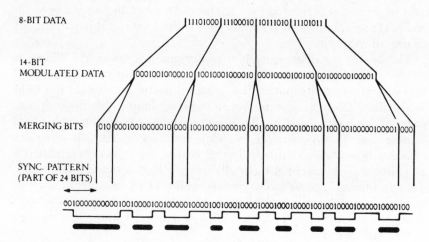

(Source: *CD-ROM: The New Papyrus*, vol. 1, p. 67, fig. 8.)

Figure 2.3 Modulation.

7. J. P. J. Heemskerk and K. A. Schouhamer Immink, "Compact Disc: System Aspects and Modulation," *Philips Technical Review* 40(6): 157–64 (1982).

Disc Logical Standard

The disc logical standard covers data representation on the disc: volume and file structure, directories, and paths organization. The industry has been trying to fill in this gap since 1985. In the High Sierra Hotel at Lake Tahoe, Nevada, a voluntary industry group composed of Reference Technology, LaserData, TMS, Xebec, Digital Equipment Corporation, Apple, Hitachi, Microsoft, Philips, 3M, VideoTools, and Yelick gathered for its first meeting on October 31 and November 1, 1985. The purpose of the meeting was to address the problem of the disc logical structure that the Yellow Book and the Red Book left out. This group was later known as the High Sierra Group (HSG). The HSG is also known as the CD-ROM Ad Hoc Committee or the CD-ROM Group. The HSG addressed the volume, directory, and file structures that are common among operating systems. This would result in the development of a single version of the data that would work on different operating systems.[8] The logical standard will necessarily build on the Philips/Sony physical standard. The work of the HSG was supported by the CD-ROM Standards Committee formed by the Information Industry Association (IIA) in November 1985. In January 1986, the American Library Association (ALA) was invited to participate in the group along with the European information industry. A monthly meeting was held from November 1985 to May 1986. In June 1986, the group issued its proposal, which was then submitted to the National Information Standards Organization (NISO).

On October 14, 1986, NISO CD-ROM Standards Committee (SC-EE) concluded its work on "The Volume and File Structure for Compact Read-Only Optical Discs for Information Interchange," Z39.60-19-8x. All references to CD-ROM were replaced by "Read-Only Optical Media." The draft was approved, and it is expected to be followed by standards for the structure of those fields provided in the basic structure of bibliographic records. It is also expected to produce standards for the exterior labeling and documentation, with a compliance symbol to be used by publishers of CD-ROM to identify their products. An equivalent standard is being considered by the International Standard Organization (ISO 9660). NISO contributed to the U.S. review and balloting to the ISO 9660. The standard was approved in December 1987.

The ISO 9660 is not yet in its final format. Many issues are still under investigation, especially in the area of bibliographic citations (e.g., the contents and format of publisher, data preparer, copyright,

---

8. The HSG-proposed standard is published as Appendix A in *CD-ROM Standards: The Book.*

abstract, and bibliographic file identifiers). ALA is involved on that level of standards along with the ISO Technical Committee (TC 46). The first draft is expected to be available from NISO in the first quarter of 1990.

Volume Structure

A single CD-ROM disc is called a *volume*. If a file resides on a collection of discs, the discs are called a *volume set*, such as a database recorded on more than one disc. Eventually, any volume will be able to hold one or more files. The volume structure designs the relationships among a volume set.

The information on this level tells something about arrangement of data on a CD-ROM, such as physical addresses and logical sectors; volume space that is organized into logical blocks; volume structure standard identifier; volume set identifier; date and time of the creation of a volume; volume expiration date; publisher identifier; data preparer; application identifier; copyright file identifier; and abstract file identifier.

File Structure

The size of a volume set is limited to 65,535 volumes. The length of a record may be up to 32,767 bytes. The information recorded would include date and time of file creation, file modification, file expiration, and file effectiveness; record format; and record length and record attributes.

Directory Structure

The directory is just the table of contents of a volume set. It includes the contents in the main directory (root directory) and the subdirectories. Directory structure specifies the exact locations of the files on the disc. It specifies the directory hierarchy, depth of directory hierarchy, path table, order of path table contents, and directory length. The directory structure is a hierarchical directory tree providing up to 65,535 directories.

Drive Standard

The physical and the logical disc standards did not specify how a drive should perform in order to cope with the disc physical and logical standards. This is in contrast to the CD-audio, where any audio disc can be played on almost any drive. This issue requires some attention in order for a disc to run on almost any drive. Part of this problem has been solved by the Disk Operating System Extensions developed by Microsoft Corporation.

Operating System Software

The operating system (OS) deals with the host computer. OS such as IBM/DOS, MS/DOS, UNIX, OS/2, and Apple DOS should have the flexibility to accommodate CD-ROM, i.e., designed to access CD-ROM drives. Present operating systems have trouble accessing files greater than 32 megabytes. Microsoft's Extensions make the computer "believe" that it is accessing another computer drive.

Application Standard

This level addresses the user directly, and it is concerned with issues such as bundling retrieval software with the CD-ROM disc, the use of Boolean logic in search strategies, the use of artificial intelligence for system-user interaction, and the application of menus and sub-menus in a specific product. Application standard is supposed to facilitate the interpretation of information prerecorded on the volume for reasons of interchangeability. (Among the organizations involved at this level is the American Library Association.) Application software refers to the access and retrieval of data needed by a user. There are many applications software on the market. These are offered by their producers on a license, or Original Equipment Manufacturer (OEM), basis to information providers for integration into their CD-ROM products.

Device Drivers

Device drivers are program codes that deal with peripherals such as printers, floppy disk drives, and CD-ROM drives. These can be separated or loaded through the operating system software, or they may be in application software. Device drivers' incompatibility makes it impossible to have more than one active device driver working at a time—the system has to be rebooted every time the CD-ROM title is changed. This could become a problem in places such as reference departments, where multiple CD-ROM titles are used. Device drivers produced by different companies for different titles for the same CD-ROM drive are not compatible. Some of these drivers reside in memory while some do not. Drivers are transparent to the user since they are used only by the application programs. A device driver functions as a bridge between the application program and different hardware components. When an application program needs to access a disc, it does that through a device driver that sends instructions to the specified drive. When information is found, the drive sends it back to the application program through the device driver. Then the application program displays the information to the user.

To overcome this problem, Microsoft Corporation developed MS-DOS CD-ROM Extensions (MSCDEX). MSCDEX work together with the Microsoft Disk Operating System (MS-DOS) to provide transparent access to CD-ROM discs in a standard PC environment. The Extensions allow reading any High Sierra–format CD-ROM disc. The transparent implementation ensures that existing software can work with CD-ROMs. The High Sierra–format, together with the Extensions, ensure disc interchangeability—allowing the user to use many different CD-ROM discs with a single CD-ROM drive. Most CD-ROM manufacturers have licensed the MSCDEX. The list includes Hitachi, Philips, Sony, Sanyo, and Toshiba. (Microsoft has produced a version of the MSCDEX for the Apple computers.) MSCDEX are available through major drive manufacturers and marketers. MSCDEX are licensed and not sold directly to consumers.

Interface

No standard exists for the bus structure (interface) that connects the CD-ROM drive and the computer. A system whose interface "speaks" differently than the drive or the disc will not establish communication. In system structure, it is imperative to have an intelligent interface to support systems integration. Any interface should be able to permit the addition of mass storage, optical storage, Local Area Networks (LANs), printers, plotters, modems, and other devices. Interfaces are of two types: single-user system interface, such as that of workstations; and multiuser system interface, such as that of LANS. Both types can also be distinguished as single- or multi-drive systems.

There are many interfaces on the market, including Shugart Associates System Interface (SASI) and Small Computer Systems Interface (SCSI). SASI provides a low level of intelligence, while SCSI (pronounced "scuzzy") provides a rich set of commands and supports services to multiple hosts as well as devices. It also directs the output to printers, plotters, and other storage devices. It can be assumed that SCSI is emerging as the de facto microcomputer CD-ROM drive interface standard. The SCSI controller can support as many as eight logical units, such as a host computer and seven peripherals, seven hosts and one peripheral, or a mixture.[9] It is used for interfacing hard disk drives by Apple and IBM. There are other proprietary interfaces used on systems produced by specific manufacturers, such as Panasonic, Hitachi, Philips, and Sony. However, most CD-ROM drives produced by these companies will work with SCSI interface.

9. Carl Warren, "SCSI Bus Eases Device Integration," in *CD-ROM: The New Papyrus*, ed. by Steve Lambert and Suzanne Ropiequet (Redmond, Wash.: Microsoft, 1986), p.85–89.

3 CD-ROM Production

Producing a CD-ROM involves many steps and different hardware and software applications. Depending on the amount of information and design, the process of developing a CD-ROM can be quite complex.

Components

The basic components of a simple system configuration may involve the following:

1. An IBM PC, XT, AT, or compatible; a Macintosh; or any microcomputer that can support a hard disk and a 9-track magnetic tape drive through an interface such as an SCSI bus.
2. A hard disk unit with a capacity twice the size of the processed data files is recommended. (300, 600, 900, 1200, 1500, 1800, 2100, and 2400 megabytes are available on the market.)
3. Magnetic tape drive (½-inch, 9-track, 1600 bits per inch (bpi)).
4. System software utility programs for text editing, directory managers, file format converters, indexer, utility input/output for disk-to-tape data transfer, and a file location generation utility.
5. Microsoft MS-DOS Extensions or MAC Extensions.

CD-ROM Developing Steps

Developing a CD-ROM disc involves many steps. Time and cost reported here are approximate.

Step 1. Product Design

Product design includes the selection of an application. The average time is four months.

Step 2. Content Licensing for Copyrighted Data

This phase is the longest, depending on the parties involved. Some developers report twenty-four months.

Step 3. Indexing and Retrieval Software

There are many ways to develop retrieval software:

a) *Finished products.* The commercially available retrieval software programs require minimal developing time and cost—$5,000 to $10,000 plus royalties. Production, which can be done in-house, needs understanding of databases and text files.

b) *Tool kits.* A tool kit will provide the user with control over the design and implementation. Such kits have been tested by their developers. A tool kit has the advantage of shortening the development time. Cost ranges between $10,000 and $50,000 plus royalties, and there might be a licensing support.

c) *Service bureaus.* Service bureaus will develop the retrieval software for a specific database. The customer does not own the source program. The cost ranges from $25,000 to $100,000 for development plus royalties, while the time ranges between a month and four months.

d) *Hiring a specialist.* Hiring a specialist, in order to customize the retrieval software to deal with a specific database, can be costly—from $75,000 to $250,000 plus royalties. In addition, it is time-consuming, between two months and a year. Specialists are few in this field. The specialist might insist on becoming the owner of the source code.

e) *In-house development.* The most costly and time-consuming approach for the developer is to develop personal routines. The advantage is that the developer will own the source code, and no royalties are paid. At least one excellent programmer is needed. The cost ranges between $200,000 and $400,000, while the time involved ranges between six months and two years.

A retrieval package includes the following components:

a) *Formatter.* A formatter (optional) arranges the raw data and formats it, so that it can be used by the indexing program.

b) *Indexer.* This is the engine that creates the pointer table for the data in a data file.

c) *Retrieval engine.* This is a main part of the retrieval software. It searches the indexes, locates the data, and then finds the matching records in the data file.

d) *User interface.* This is a main part of the retrieval software. After the retrieval engine finds the data in the data file, the user interface takes the found data to the output device (screen, printer, hard disk, etc.).

e) *Screen designer.* The software should allow the developer to tailor the screens for a specific application.

A retrieval package includes most of the following:

a) *Search.* It provides phrase searching and keyword lists to the end user; supports thesaurus and synonym look-ups, Boolean connectors, and different data formats; searches a range of dates, numeric ranges, and alphabetical ranges; supports proximity and adjacency searches, the use of natural language, and wild cards; displays query history; supports mixed-mode-fixed-field databases, free text, and graphics; provides high index speed; and accepts many formats such as ASCII, EBCDIC, etc.

b) *Display.* It displays number of hits, and statistical information about multiple word query; supports modification of the screen by the user; highlights keywords, runs under windows, and provides page and record scrolling; displays data record by record; and offers selective display of specific fields.

c) *Output.* It has the capability to direct output to a printer, a floppy disk, or a hard disk; format the output; and sort by record or any field in the record.

(For a list of retrieval software developers, see Appendix G.)

Step 4. Content Capture or Data Preparation

Data preparation can be thought of as the process of transforming existing data from their current form, such as books, microforms, magnetic media, etc., to one ready for publication on CD-ROM. Data can be of different formats including text, images, video images, or audio.

Since the majority of CD-ROMs on the market are text-oriented products, such as databases, reference works and services, or products of technical processes, a publisher cannot produce a CD-ROM disc unless the data are captured in machine-readable format. Machine-readable data are data that are transformed into binary digits or bits (in the form of 0s and 1s). Each letter should be transformed into its equivalent binary form.

a) If the data are in machine-readable form, on a computer, a word processor, or a typesetting system, the data can be captured from the storage medium (floppy diskettes, hard disks, magnetic disks, or tapes) and then used.

b) Data can be collected through Optical Character Recognition (OCR) scanners, which accept a printed document as input. As the printed document passes through the scanner, a bit-mapped image (*vector*) of the document is produced. In this case the user will be able to retrieve a copy of the document, as in the archive and record systems. Some readers identify the characters by their shapes and store them in digital form, i.e., binary representation, or character-coded text (*raster*), such as text files created by a word processor. In this case the user will be able to search individual words and retrieve specific sections of the text.

c) If the data are not in machine-readable form, they have to be entered through the keyboard and stored in ASCII codes (an expensive and time-consuming operation).

d) Audio signals also can be converted from their analog representation into digital format through an analog-to-digital processor.

e) Artwork, photographs, and other graphs also have to be digitized through special scanners (digital cameras). The scanners break the graph into pixels, and the pixels into digits.

f) Data can also be transferred from WORM systems or other optical media into CD-ROM discs.

Step 5. Editorial Correction and Reformatting

This phase of the operation takes about six months. It involves finding and correcting errors; adding necessary hierarchy information; and marking special sections such as tables, cross-references, headers, and footnotes. Non-printing information should be removed. Files are to be broken into logical segments and file names added. "Stop words" (such as prepositions, insignificant words, definite and indefinite articles) are to be identified. All codes and markups used by a specific word processor or typesetting software should be replaced by Standardized Generalized Markup Language (SGML), which is used as an electronic markup to identify parts of a document, such as chapter heads, tables, footnotes, etc. The data are to be compressed by eliminating redundant or unnecessary data as well as empty and repetitive areas. Compressing text data includes replacing repetitive words with binary representation or any other codes. This includes definite articles and words that have little content meaning. In image data, levels of contrast will be eliminated. At this level of processing, the text of the file should be clean and identified by file name. This step might require networked PCs with large, hard-disk file servers.

The arrangement of data is to be determined. The location of the indexes should be defined. The logical format is to be communicated to the originating software in order to create a directory. Creating a directory for a small number of files is an easy operation. The complexity of the problem grows when a directory is needed to be built for thousands of files embedded in hundreds of directories and subdirectories. In this case a system utility program is used to scan the files and create all the directories, subdirectories, and the names of the files. This step is crucial because the software should be able to read such directories and locate all the files. In some applications the directory is placed in the middle of the file structure to minimize the average seek time.[1]

Step 6. Indexing

Searching millions of bytes linearly on a CD-ROM disc (from the first byte to the last byte) is a very long process. At the current CD-ROM transfer rate of 150 kilobytes per second, reading 450 megabytes of text requires 3000 seconds (or 50 minutes). Compressing the data results in improved search time but will not eliminate the problem. Indexing the file is one solution.

To facilitate data search and retrieval, an index should be created on the CD-ROM. The index is a list of addresses (locations) where the data can be found. The size of the index is determined by the application of the CD-ROM. An index that contains every word in the file may become larger than the file itself. There is special indexing software that will create the index automatically. The resulting index is designed to work only with a specific search and retrieval software.[2]

Types of Indexes and Searching Techniques

The simplest type of index is the *key index*. During an actual search, the key index is searched first. Data are accessed by either a key value of a data field (author, title, subject, etc.) or by the record number. Each key index holds a copy of the key value associated with the address of the data record on the spiral track. So, every searchable field on the record (author, title, subject, etc.) is assumed to have a key index (author index, title index, subject index, etc.). To locate a specific record, the search begins by matching the request with the specific key value index. If there is a match, then the address of the record is used to access the specific record in the data file. (A data file is that which holds the user's data, such as a database.) Key indexes can work with ordered data files or unordered data files.

Ordered Data Files   In ordered data files, data files and their indexes are kept sorted (Figure 3.1). In general, this type of index is inefficient at the time of updating since much data in the data file, as well as the index, must be moved around when records are added,

---

1. Don Rodgers, "Data Preparation for CD-ROM," *Optical Information Systems* 6(3): 209–13 (May–June 1986).

2. *CD-ROM Optical Publishing*, Vol. 2, ed. by Suzanne Ropiequet and others (Redmond, Wash.: Microsoft Press, 1987), p.103–17.

DATA FILE			KEY INDEX
Rec#	Name		Name
0	Anderson	——	Anderson
1	Blake	——	Blake
2	Carl	——	Carl
3	David	——	David
4	Edwards	——	Edwards
5	Gale	——	Gale

Figure 3.1 In ordered data files, data files are kept in the same order as the key index. Each record has a number and can be accessed through its position in the data file.

deleted, or changed, or when updating any key field in the data file. The key index does not include record numbers because the position of the key in the index corresponds to the position of the record in the data file, a minor advantage. At some point, a search can be done directly in the data file without going through the key index. Since bibliographic citations include many searchable fields, records in the main data file are organized on one key only (author field, title field, etc.). This key is called the *primary key*. Other secondary key indexes must use record numbers.

Unordered Data Files   In the unordered data file, records are arranged in the order in which they are added to the file, while the key index is sorted (Figure 3.2). When the data file is updated, a minimum of data movement is required. Each time the data file is updated, the program updates the key indexes as well.

Inverted Index   This method is ideal for full-text fields. Essentially the indexes are created by a special indexing program using a process known as *full inversion*. In this method, the whole text is scanned for

DATA FILE		KEY INDEX			RECORD POINTER
Rec#	Name	Rec#	Name		
0	Edwards	5	Anderson	——	5
1	Carl	3	Blake	——	3
2	Gale	1	Carl	——	1
3	Blake	4	David	——	4
4	David	0	Edwards	——	0
5	Anderson	2	Gale	——	2

Figure 3.2 In unordered data files, data are kept in the same order in which they are added to the file while the key field index is sorted. Each record has a number and can be accessed through its pointer.

keywords. The keywords are sorted and counted. The keyword has to be listed once, while a pointer will be assigned for each occurrence of the word in the file. Such a pointer will refer to the location of each record in the file (Figure 3.3). The resulting index is called an *inverted index*. The only words not included in the index are "stop words" —words deliberately omitted because they occur so often or have so little meaning as to be useless in a search. These would include *a, an, the, this, that,* and others. Inverted indexes best suit Boolean and relational operations.

KEY INDEX

OCCURRENCE LIST

Word	Count	Pointer		Record #
Activenture	1	1		3
Apple	1	2		4
Borland	3	3		1
		4		8
		5		10
Faxon	2	6		2
		7		6
Libraries	2	8		5
		9		8
Wilson	1	10		7

Figure 3.3 Inverted index.

Methods of Searching

Index files can be searched in many ways.

Sequential Search   In the sequential search, entries are searched sequentially from the first record until a match is found or until the end of the file is reached. The performance of this type of search is appreciated when used with very small files.

Binary Search   The second type of search is the binary search, assuming the entries in the index file have a constant length. In the binary search, the first search range includes every entry in the index from *A* to *Z*. If an index file contains *n* records, a maximum of $\log^2(n) + 1$ and an average of $\log^2(n) - 1$ comparisons are required to find a particular record. The search program determines the size of the index file and calculates the number of records it contains, then inspects the middle record in the search range. If the middle record is a match, the search ends and the record is located on the spiral track. If there is no match, the program determines which half includes the requested item, depending on its relative location to the middle record (before or after the middle record). Usually, the middle record in every search range is examined first to see if there is a match. If there is none, the program determines which half should be searched next. The search keeps narrowing the search range in halves and compares the requested item with the middle record in every search range until a match is found.

There is no doubt that binary search is superior to sequential search. As is, binary search is not considered fast enough to be used in CD-ROM when indexes include millions of entries. This is due to the fact that in real life, entries in many indexes are distributed unevenly. If names or titles are clustered around specific letters of the alphabet, search time will not be uniform and it will increase considerably when searching such clustered entries. Another problem occurs when trying to find multiple matches. In this case the search program might have to exclude the unmatched records and pull out the matched records. This is not quite right since records have to be inspected for matching and mismatching from both directions of the original match (before and after the middle record). There are some structured search methods that overcome these problems. They are used with indexes such as the binary tree index, the balanced binary tree index, and the hash table index.

Binary Tree Index In the binary tree index, each entry in the index is considered a node consisting of a key value (author, title, subject, etc.), a record number, an address to the record, and a linkage to a left and right subtree (Figure 3.4). The first node is the head of the tree structure. The first record in the data file constitutes the root node of the index. This first node has a left link to all the lesser keys in the subtree, for example, *A–N*, and a right link to all the greater keys, for example, *O–Z*. If the keys are not well distributed, the tree might become asymetrical, which will affect search time. A study should be conducted to identify the lesser keys and the greater keys in a specific index, depending on the distribution of letters in the index. For instance, if names appear to cluster around letters, such as *A, D, E, M,* and *N*, these will then be the greater keys.

Balanced Binary Tree Index This type of index is known also as the B-Tree Index. In B-Tree indexes, keywords from a specific field (author, title, etc.) are placed in key records. These key records are then placed in keyword blocks, which are file blocks (a file block is 2048 bytes). If each record in the keyword block is 32 bits long, each block is created from the keyword blocks. The new index will hold only the first record from the keyword block and the block number. The retrieval software will determine which keyword block to search (Figure 3.5).

During a search, since *A* falls before *E*, the search is directed to the

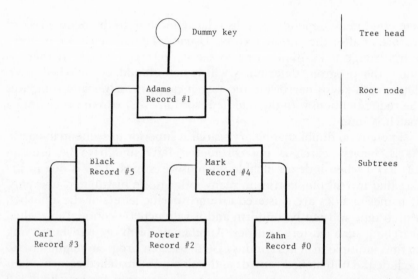

Figure 3.4 A binary tree index. Two subtrees may be used with each block; the one on the left holds the lesser keys, while the one on the right holds the greater keys.

first keyword block, while a search for T will be directed to the fourth block. There is no need to index the first keyword block since A comes before E naturally. This system saves search time. Balanced trees utilize the space on the disc efficiently, leaving no wasted blocks. They suit exact and partial match applications since they allow the index to be ordered by key value.

Hash Table Index *Hashing* is an indexing method that uses the value of the key to compute its location within an index file. Indexing algorithm tables are used to replace, for example, the alphabetical

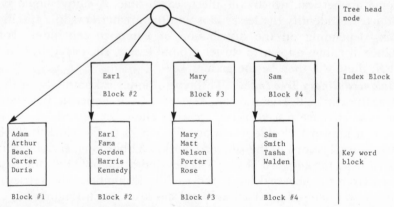

Figure 3.5 Balanced binary tree index.

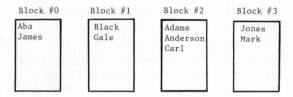

Figure 3.6 Hash table index. Alphabetical letters are converted into their equivalent numbers. Carl = $3 + 1 + 18 + 12$ = 34/4 blocks = 8, remainder 2. So, Carl will be placed in Block #2.

characters *A–Z* with numbers 1–26. The values are added then divided by the number of index blocks. The remainder will determine the block where the keyword is located (Figure 3.6).

Most hashing techniques use the hexadecimal values of the ASCII codes. For instance, if the record key is CARL, the sum of its ASCII code in hexadecimal will be (C = 43h, A = 41h, R = 52h, and L = 4Ch), yielding 122h. The sum is divided by the number of the records in the file and the remainder is multiplied by the record size to obtain the offset of the record in the data file. In this method, the data file is ordered by the hash code.

Another method is to consult a hash table containing record numbers and then locate the record in a separate data file. If the same hash code is assigned to more than one record, a linking field containing the record number is added to the hash table in order to access the record in the data file.

Step 7. Data Structure

Data structure is the operation of building the text on magnetic tape in a similar structure as it would be represented on a CD-ROM disc. The data within a file is identified by name, size, and location, so that a CD-ROM drive can recognize each piece of information. File structure will affect the access to data.

Physical tape formatting refers to the way individual bytes of data are written physically onto the magnetic tape. It deals with issues such as format of data in a file. The record size is equal to the CD-ROM user data block, 2048 bytes. Some mastering facilities such as 3M recommend using a tape block size of 8192 bytes.[3] Block sizes greater than 8192 can also be handled. Mastering facilities recommend the use of .5-

3. 3M Optical Recording Department, "CD-ROM Data Input Specification," Version 3.1, Oct. 1988.

inch, 9-track computer tape. To maximize storage per reel, tape length should be 2,400 feet on 10.5-inch magnetic tape reels.

Tape density—the number of bytes per inch (BPI) recorded on the tape—is usually specified by the mastering facility. It is best to follow the facility's tape-density specification. There are different capacities, however. The most-used tape density is phase-encoded (PE) 1600 BPI, with 45 megabytes the average capacity, or group-encoded (GCR) 6250 BPI, with 180 megabytes as average capacity.

The magnetic tape is designed according to the ANSI X3.27-1978 standard (American National Standards Institute) (Figure 3.7).[4]

Beginning of Tape Marker	BOT	Marks the beginning of writable area on a volume
Volume Label	VOL1	Identifies the volume
File Header 1–3	HDR1 HDR2 HDR3	Identifies and delimits each file
Tape Mark	TM	End of file mark, it separates file section from header labels
File Section	DATA	Contains user data
Tape Mark	TM	Separates file section from trailer labels
File Trailer Labels	EOF1 EOF2 EOF3 EOV1 EOV2 EOV3	Describes and delimits files. When a file is continued, EOV labels are written instead of EOF labels
Tape Mark	TM TM	Indicates the logical end of volumes Two consecutive tape marks are always written after the trailer labels of the last file on a volume
End of Tape Marker	EOT	Marks the beginning of the end of the writable area

Figure 3.7 The ANSI standard (ANSI X3.27-1978) for labeled magnetic tape.

4. The ANSI X3.27 "Magnetic Tape Labels and File Structure for Information Interchange" publication may be acquired from: American National Standards Institute, 1430 Broadway, New York, NY 10018.

Step 8. Simulation/Disc Imaging and Testing

Once the size of files is determined along with their layout and directory specification, and once the blocks of information are constructed and the indexes are developed, the creation of the disc image would be the next step. Because the CD-ROM disc will be an exact copy of the disc image, a test should be conducted for functionality, access speed, and reliability in order to see if the performance of the disc image is exactly what the developer expects. The overall performance of the image should meet the original design.

The disc image should be stored on a large computer such as the VAX, but a PC/AT could also be used. No matter what computer is used, it is important that the application software should be able to run the disc image in conjunction with the retrieval software. At this point any problems should be detected and corrected. These tests will check the accuracy of indexing, the suitability of the retrieval program, and user-system interface in connection with screen menus and layout, search argument prompts, and overall system performance. The final file directory should conform with the CD-ROM format.

Step 9. Premastering

Premastering is the process of adding the 288 bytes of EDC and ECC (the error correcting and error detecting bytes), 12 synchronization bytes, 3 sector address bytes, and 1 mode byte to each 2048-byte block. The premastering process usually creates a standard .5-inch 9-track magnetic tape that is 1600 bits per inch (or a rigid disk). This tape or disk is used by the CD-ROM mastering facility to produce the master disk. The data are recorded on the tape in ASCII.

There are many premastering facilities such as:

> Alde Publishing, Minneapolis, Minn.
> Brodart, Library Automation Division, Williamsport, Pa.
> Denon Digital Industries, Madison, Ga.
> Digital Equipment Corp., Malboro, Mass.
> Meridian Data, Inc., Capitola, Calif.
> Optical Media International, Los Gatos, Calif.
> Quantum Access, Houston, Tex.
> SilverPlatter, Wellesley Hills, Mass.

Step 10. Mastering and Replication

Once the premaster tape or rigid disk is created, and the Sync, Header, EDC, and ECC bytes are added, its data are transferred into a computer then moved into an encoder interface, where they pass through a CD-ROM encoder. The data are then transferred into a laser beam recorder (laser data drive cutter), where data bits are transformed into microscopic pits and lands along a spiral track on a glass master disc. This process is called *writing* or *etching*. Generally, writing is done by using a "write pulse" generated by a laser diode. The main function of the diode is to permit the electrical current to flow in one direction and inhibit its flow in the opposite direction. When the energy emitted from the diode in its high-power mode (7 to 10 milliwatts, or .007 to .01 watt) hits the surface of the disc, it melts a specific area in the recording layer forming an oblong depression on the recording layer.

The glass master disc is covered with a "photoresist" coating comparable to a photographic film. The data are transferred to a modulator (a fast shutter such as that used in a camera). The modulator controls a powerful short-wavelength laser beam as it passes through a lens. As the beam hits the photoresist coating, it forms a spot. During the creation of the master, the glass disc spins while the lens moves radially to form the spiral track. (The laser works from the center of the disc to the outer edge.) After the photoresist is "developed," the exposed areas are turned into pits while the unexposed areas form the lands. After the master is covered with a thin silver coating, it is used to produce stampers for disc replication.

The master is transferred by either electroplating or photopolymer replication (Figure 3.8) onto a negative nickel shell (or *father*). When the nickel copy is separated from the master, the information in the relatively soft resist on the master is destroyed. This negative shell is used to create a number of positive impressions (*mothers*) onto several other shells (Figure 3.9). From each mother, a number of stampers (*sons*) are created and used for subsequent replication using injection molding techniques.[5] The information-bearing surface of these replicas is physically sealed off from contact with the environment by a reflective aluminum layer, enabling the CD-ROM drive to read the data by a low-power laser beam. The surface of the disc is then coated with a protective lacquer to protect the disc against environmental effects such as minor scratches, dust, and fingerprints. Each replica is then punched at the center, tested for evaluation, labeled, and packaged. At the mastering facility, each disc is inspected and subjected to quality-control tests (Figure 3.10). Such tests ensure that all the data are on the disc,

5. J. Pasman, "Mastering," in G. Bouwhuis and others, *Principles of Optical Disc Systems* (Bristol, Great Britain: Adam Hilger Ltd., 1985), p.189–209.

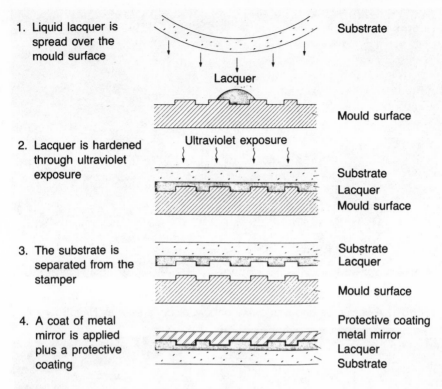

1. Liquid lacquer is spread over the mould surface

    Substrate

    Lacquer

    Mould surface

2. Lacquer is hardened through ultraviolet exposure

    Ultraviolet exposure

    Substrate
    Lacquer
    Mould surface

3. The substrate is separated from the stamper

    Substrate
    Lacquer

    Mould surface

4. A coat of metal mirror is applied plus a protective coating

    Protective coating
    metal mirror
    Lacquer
    Substrate

(Source: *Philips Technical Review*, v.40, no.10 (1982).)

Figure 3.8 Replication process. Two such discs are glued together to form the final double-sided disc if needed.

the disc does not contain any uncorrectable errors, and disc labeling/packaging meets customer requirements.

At this point any typographical errors or omissions cannot be corrected once the discs are made. Producing a CD-ROM can be a long project, but the replication process is straightforward. It may take between 5 and 20 days. Some replicators offer turnaround in 3 to 5 days, while some offer express service, 24-hour turnaround. The updating processes should be faster and are done the same way.

There are many mastering and replication facilities, such as:

Denon Digital Industries, Madison, Ga.
Hitachi America Ltd., San Bruno, Calif.
JVC America Disc, Inc., Irvine, Calif.
Philips/Du Pont Optical, Wilmington, Del.
Philips Subsystems & Peripherals, Knoxville, Tenn.

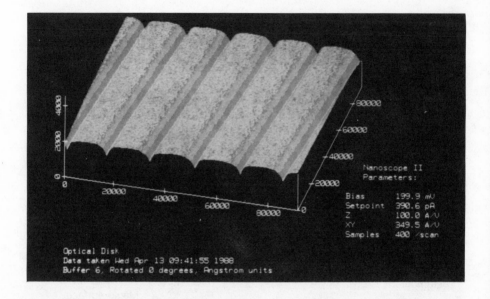

PHOTO 1. A SERIES OF GROOVES ON AN OPTICAL DISC, AS SEEN BY NANOSCOPE II.

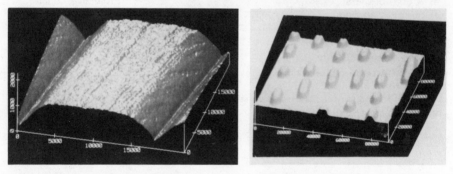

PHOTO 2. SUPER MAGNIFICATION OF
ONE OPTICAL DISC GROOVE.

PHOTO 3. ACTUAL PITS AND LANDS FROM
A CD STAMPER.

(Reprinted with permission from *CD-ROM Review*, IDG Communications.)

Figure 3.9 A dramatization of actual pits and lands. Photos were taken at Digital Instruments in Santa Barbara, Calif., in 1988 through NanoScope II, a scanning, tunneling microscope, developed by Digital.

Quantum Access, Inc., Houston, Tex.
Sanyo, Little Ferry, N.J.
Sony, San Jose, Calif.
3M, St. Paul, Minn.

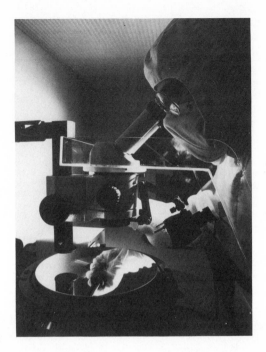

(Reprinted with permission from *CD-ROM Review*, IDG Communications.)

Figure 3.10 Microscopic inspection of a CD-ROM disc at Shape Optimedia, Inc., a replication factory in Sanford, Me.

Production Time

On the average, producing a new product on CD-ROM may take one year as follows:

Media selection	4 months (1–6)
Application development	6 months (2–12)
Data preparation	
Disc mastering	1 month (.5–2)
Disc replication	
Distribution	

Costs

The price of developing a CD-ROM is high, due to long planning, data preparation, and copyright problems. In addition, the whole operation

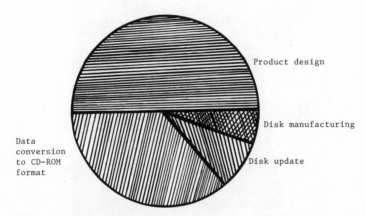

(Source: Philips and Du Pont, CD-ROM Developers Seminar held by Meridian Data, Inc., of Capitola, Calif. in New York, June 14, 1988.)

Figure 3.11   Cost of application development.

depends on precision equipment and a clean environment. Cost will differ depending on the size of data and their availability in machine-readable format. For instance, the total development cost for the Library of Congress's first optical disc was $250,000, while the total cost of replication and printing was only $20,000.[6] Manufacturers charge on the average $250 per hour for data premastering service, while mastering prices are between $2,000 and $4,000 based on turnaround and volume. The cost of one disc is between $2 and $10 based on turnaround and volume. For any CD-ROM product, almost 50 percent of the budget will be allocated for the design of the product, 35 percent for data conversion to CD-ROM format, 10 percent for disc manufacturing, and 5 percent for disc update (Figure 3.11).

6. Patti Myers, *Publishing with CD-ROM: A Guide to Compact Disc Optical Storage Technologies for Providers of Publishing Services* (Westport, Conn.: Meckler Publishing, 1986), p.65.

4 Applications of Optical Storage Systems

Mass storage technology has contributed to the popularity of personal computers. The hard disk as a mass storage device has transformed the PC into an essential tool that is capable of storing millions of bytes of data. It was not until the advent of optical storage devices that a new frontier had to be explored.

There are many types of optical media, and each type is meant for a specific application. While CD-ROM is expected to be an appropriate long-term archiving medium and an effective tool in the publishing industry for nonvolatile data, Write-Once Read-Many (WORM) systems are most appropriate for archival storage. The absence of the capability of writing on CD-ROMs is not a disadvantage—as some might see it—in areas of entertainment, training, and informational and reference services and programming. These prerecorded materials do not require updating by the user. Updating is best left to a publisher for better quality and control of the data. However, the situation is different in records and archival storage where data, which are owned by an office or an organization, must be recorded on site for reasons of confidentiality and sensitivity of the materials to be stored in the system. Unless a WORM system is used for the storage of inactive records, the lack of erasability (the ability to erase data written on the medium and to write new data in their place) might constitute a problem. There is some concern as well with WORM systems in the area of archivability (archival stability).

Document Storage Systems

Office filing and document storage systems have been used as early as 1980. Some of these systems are geared to the storage of digitized image data (storage of an exact image of the document, known as *vector*) than to recorded character-encoded digital data (storage of data in a document as characters in ASCII format such as files created by a word processor or a spreadsheet, known as *raster*). However, many of the existing systems accept data input from a keyboard or data transferred from a computer system or from remote facsimile units over telecommunications lines. Scanned materials are stored in the system as

(Courtesy of TAB Products Co., Palo Alto, Calif.)

Figure 4.1 Laser Optic Filing System, series 2000, includes a scanner, 19-inch screen, optical disc (12-inch or 5.25-inch), and a laser printer.

digitized images of the original documents (Figure 4.1). These documents are indexed before the actual recording on the optical disc is done. The DRAW recording technique (see Chapter 1) used in most of these systems enables errors to be identified immediately after data have been recorded. Correction is done by rewriting the data on a new sector on the optical disc. A new address is established for the corrected data, then the old address is erased. (The old data stay on the disc, but the computer will not be able to access it since its address has been erased.)

A standard letter (8.5 by 11 inches) can be stored in some systems in fewer than 10 seconds, and it can be retrieved in no more than 3 seconds. These systems have high-density storage—for example, the Megadoc system of Philips has a capacity of storing 500,000 pages per disc side. They provide total integrity since they capture all of the information, thus maintaining the quality of documents. It is suggested that the cost of storing such documents on 48X reduction microfiche (hardware is excluded) would be $253,000. The cost of storing the

same number of document images on a juke-box unit would be $64,000.[1]
There are essentially three types of systems on the market:

1. Large-capacity systems are designed for handling hundreds of millions of documents. They are usually custom-configured systems. Prices for such systems exceed $300,000.
2. Medium-capacity systems are typically stand-alone systems. Juke-boxes can be added to enhance the capacity of the system. These systems have the capability to be accessed through remote-control workstations. They can store as few as 50,000 documents. Prices for such systems vary between $100,000 and $300,000.
3. Low-capacity systems are those using 5.25-inch discs. These systems have data capacities approaching 100 megabytes per side. Prices range between $20,000 and $100,000 for a complete system. Many systems available today are manufactured in different sizes and capacities. Among the companies that manu-facture optical filing systems are Philips, FilNet Corporation, Panasonic, Toshiba, Hitachi, Sharp, Sanyo, Canon, Mitsubishi, and TAB Products.

Write-Once Read-Many

WORM systems are used in applications requiring that data be saved and maintained permanently by the user, for example, engineering drawings. The drawings are scanned, the images converted into vectors (an exact copy of the document), and then stored on WORM discs. Later, the drawings can be accessed, displayed, and converted to hard copy.

In a desktop publishing system, WORM discs can be used to store data sheets, catalogs, and reference manuals, then produced by a computer and a laser printer.

In the medical industry, WORM systems can be used to store medical records, many of which are required by law to be stored for twenty years. These could include lab test results, X-ray data, patient progress reports, and many others.

In computer retail stores, many software packages can be saved on WORM discs for demonstration purposes, thus saving the time of loading discs and installing software into the computer's memory.

1. Judy McQueen and Richard W. Boss, *Videodisc and Optical Digital Disk Technologies and Their Applications in Libraries, 1986 Update (Library Technology Reports* Monograph) (Chicago: American Library Association, 1986), p.97.

The large capacity of WORM discs makes them ideal for storing statutes, depositions, and legal documents.

Distributing corporate databases on WORM discs from one site to another is also feasible, since WORM discs can be updated at remote locations.

Physical Features

Both CD-ROM and WORM use a solid-state laser to read data stored as pits and lands on a reflective metallic-surface disc made of polycarbonate. However, WORM discs cannot be read on CD-ROM drives. WORM discs, manufactured by companies such as 3M, Maxell Corporation of America, and Plasmon Data Systems, are twice as thick as a CD-ROM, measuring about two millimeters. A layer of tellurium, a metallic substance, is deposited by a vapor-plating process on the surface of the disc. Other layers of polycarbonate are deposited to protect the recording surface. These layers are very thin and appear to be transparent. Recording is done on both sides of the disc, which is housed in a hard case protected by a sliding metal shutter. In order to record on the reverse side, the disc has to be removed then flipped over. Once data are recorded on the WORM disc, data become unalterable. They can neither be deleted nor can they be changed. For this reason, WORM systems are better used for historical and inactive archives.

Two different types of tracking schemes are used in the industry. The first type, called *pregrooved*, has tiny, V-shaped grooves pressed into the disc during manufacture. These grooves are used as tracks, and data are written into them and read by the laser.

The second type is called *sampled servo* and uses tiny holes on the surface of the disc to supply tracking information. These holes are spaced at fixed angular distances, with the space between them being used to store data. Each time that the tracking holes are encountered by the laser, any deviation in the position of the laser is corrected by a servo mechanism.

File Storage

File storage is the layout or arrangement of the files on the disc. According to the file layout, WORM drives can be divided into two types:

1. *Sequential storage drives.* In the sequential layout, files are arranged one after another in an order much like a magnetic tape. However, this layout does not allow files to be updated or

extended, but only copied. When updating a file, the system flags the old file as obsolete and writes the new file at another location on the disc. The advantage of the sequential storage is that data retrieval is fast.

2. *File linking drives.* The linked layout WORM systems allow files to be stored and updated on a block basis, much like the way a disk operating system (DOS) stores files on floppy diskettes. In file linking, the system records the file in a sequential order, however a space is left between each data block for a pointer that refers to a new data block if one is to be added later. This assures the efficient use of the space on the disc, but access time for the information is increased. If a file is updated, the link has to be changed from the old block number to the new block number. These pointers are stored and maintained in file allocation tables.

Issues and Concerns

1. WORM systems lack a common physical and logical standard. However, since these systems are not widely disseminated like CD-ROM, it seems that standards are not a crucial issue or a severe problem.[2]
2. The life expectancy of all optical storage media is questionable because not enough is known about the physical and chemical characteristics of these materials. It is suggested that the user check the disc periodically to keep track of the bit error rate to know when to copy data to a fresh disc. Manufacturers claim a 10-year life (Sony claims it has developed a 100-year disc) for the medium. However, with "so little known about the medium in its early developmental phase, optical digital disc is not recommended as a long-term storage medium at this time."[3]
3. Through the lifetime of the disc, the surface tension could widen the pits, thus affecting the integrity of the information. With excessive heat build-up in the drive due to high angular velocity or cumulative energy from repeated readings, the disc might expand or shrink depending on the temperature and humidity. For these reasons, a backup disc is desirable.
4. When tellurium or a tellurium alloy is used, the greatest problem is oxidization in a humid environment. Humidity reduces the sensitivity of the surface of the disc, thus disrupting the formation of new holes and leading to loss of old data.

2. Linda W. Helgerson, "Optical Storage Peripherals," *Inform* 1(2): 14–19 (Feb. 1987).
3. Alan Calmes, "To Archive and Preserve: A Media Primer," *Inform* 1(5): 17 (May 1987).

5. Electrochemical corrosion may also be initiated by local dust particles in the office environment.

6. The main application of WORM systems is in long-term archival data storage. *Archivability* refers to the length of time that data stored on a medium will remain stable without deterioration. Archival stability is a major factor when considering recording media for long-term storage. Since optical storage systems have not been in use that long, more research on archivability should be done. The information stored on a disc made of tellurium or tellurium alloys might be affected by the aging of the sensitive layer and its substrate. Aging occurs in the form of small localized defects such as pinholes and tiny cracks, called "drop-outs," in the storage layer.[4] Blisters (Figure 4.2) may also be formed and cause flaking of the surface.[5] Accelerated aging is known to be performed in laboratories in

(Source: *Philips Technical Review,* v.41, no. 11/12 (1983).)

Figure 4.2 A scanning electron microscope micrograph of a severely blistered recording layer after 100 days of test. Blistering is attributed to cyclic and shrinking of the lacquer. This condition is exceptional and will not occur in normal office use. However, imperfections in the substrate, the lacquer layer, or the recording layer could cause blisters to develop.

4. A. Huijser and others, "Aging Characteristics of Digital Optical Recording (DOR) Media," *SPIE Proceedings* p.270–75 (1983).

5. L. Vriens and B. A. J. Jacobs, "Digital Optical Recording with Tellurium Alloys," *Philips Technical Review,* 41(11/12): 313–24 (1983/84).

simulated environments, yet the translation of accelerated life into real life remains an uncertain step.[6]

Characteristics

Unlike microfilm, which has remained readable over the last 50 years, optical recording is still an unreliable long-term storage medium.

Because of their great storage capacity, WORM discs may be used to create huge databases, preserve records and archives, or document projects. However, due to their high cost, their popularity and acceptance are moving very slowly. The average price for a WORM system is $3,000 for capacities up to 240 megabytes and $10,000 for 800 megabytes. While the average price of a single-sided disc is $150, the average price of a double-sided disc is $200. They may be expensive, but they are cost-effective for large information files.

The number of tracks on the disc differs from system to system. While, for example, Optotech disc format calls for 18,000 tracks with 22 sectors of 512 bytes each on each side, the Information Storage format has 14,900 tracks with 34 sectors of 256 bytes each on each side.

WORM drives are five to ten times slower than hard disk drives in seek time (moving their heads between random tracks). While the access time for CD-ROM ranges between 500 and 1,000 milliseconds, it is 150 to 300 milliseconds for WORM systems. The transfer rate is 50 to 200 kilobytes compared to 150 to 200 kilobytes in CD-ROM.

During the mounting process, optical files become accessible to DOS through a file allocation structure into a DOS-compatible format. Once a file is mounted it becomes accessible by any application software that is DOS compatible.

Communicating or downloading can be done using telecommunication systems in local area networks (LANs). Transmission of the data is done through a modem onto hard magnetic disks. WORMs in a large corporation can be updated centrally then distributed to local offices to incorporate the updated information into their WORM drives. Using ROMs instead of WORMs in this respect for distributing data is a very costly operation.[7]

While the 5.25-inch discs are ideal for a workstation in some locations, a typical archive department would want to create a centralized filing and retrieval system or a LAN using a multiple 12- or 14-inch WORM storage filing disc in a juke-box for use by different departments.

6. Huijser and others, p.270.
7. Andrew D. Roscoe and Philip M. Parker, "Online Optical Disk: Database Distribution Strategies," *Inform*, 1(5): 12, 47 (May 1987).

Such configuration will allow for multi-user, multi-tasking activities.[8]

The storage capacity of WORM discs on the market varies from system to system depending on the size of the disc, ranging from 250 megabytes for a 5.25-inch disc to more than 6 gigabytes for a 14-inch disc. For organizations having sensitive personnel or financial materials, or classified documents, WORM can be used on location to develop the required filing system rather than sending these materials to an outside CD-ROM developer. WORM systems can be used in the library to store such collections as urban archives, special collections, or pamphlets.

Available WORM Systems

There are many WORM systems already on the market, including:

ISI 525WC, produced by Information Storage, Inc., requires 35K RAM, one floppy-disc drive, one half-length slot, DOS 3.0 or later, 122-megabyte disc capacity per cartridge side, ESDI (Enhanced Small Device Interface) or SCSI interface. Files are arranged in sequential order. Cost: $2,795.

Maximum Storage APX-3000, produced by Maximum Storage, Inc., requires 256K RAM, one floppy-disc drive, one half-length slot, DOS 3.0 or later, 122-megabyte disc capacity per cartridge side, ESDI interface. Files are arranged in a linked format. Cost: $3,495.

Micro Design LaserBank 800, produced by Micro Design International, Inc., requires 384K RAM, hard-disk drive, DOS 3.0 or later, 400-megabyte disc capacity per cartridge side, SCSI interface. Files are arranged in a sequential format. Cost: $9,995.

Optotech 5984, produced by Optotech, Inc., requires 128K RAM, one full-length slot, DOS 3.0 or later, 200-megabyte disc capacity per cartridge side, Optotech or SCSI interface. Files are arranged in a linked format. Cost: $2,950.

H/Hance 525 Optical Disk System, produced by Symphony Systems, Inc., requires 256K RAM, one floppy-disc drive, one half-length slot, DOS 3.0 or later, 120-megabyte disc capacity per cartridge side, ESDI interface. Files are arranged in a sequential format. Cost: $2,950.

Franklin Telecomm FLD-200, produced by Franklin Telecommunications Corporation, requires 512K RAM, DOS 2.1 or later, 200-megabyte disc capacity per cartridge side, Optotech interface. Cost: $4,995.

8. Helgerson, p. 14–19.

(Courtesy of Cygnet Systems, Inc., Sunnyvale, Calif.)

Figure 4.3 A Cygnet juke-box series 5000 for 5.25-inch optical drives supports one or two drives and two auxiliary drives that can be loaded and unloaded manually. The system accommodates 28 to 32 optical disc cartridges and provides up to 31 gigabytes of storage.

Other WORM systems include the $13,000 Alcatel GM1001 drive produced by Alcatel Thompson Gigadisc, Inc., which uses a 12-inch disc with capacity of 1 gigabyte per side; the $8,000 LaserDrive 1200, produced by Laser Magnetic Storage International, which uses a 12-inch disc with capacity of 1 gigabyte per side; the $3,000 LD800W drive, produced by Laserdrive Ltd., which uses a 5.25-inch disc with capacity of 405 megabytes per side; the 1000S model of Optimem (Shugart), which uses a 12-inch disc with capacity of 1 gigabyte per side; and the $18,975 WDD-3000 drive, manufactured by Sony Corporation of America, which uses a 12-inch disc with capacity of 1.6 gigabytes per side.[9] (See Appendix E for a list of WORM drives.)

9. For an evaluation and reviews on WORM systems see Winn L. Rosch, "Worms for Mass Storage," *PC Magazine* 6(12): 135–66 (June 23, 1987); and Frank Bican, "The Worm Turns," *PC Magazine*, 7(6): 199–224 (March 29, 1988).

Interactive Videodiscs

The ability of a system to run linearly in sequence in response to a request from the user is considered a very simple level of interactivity. The degree of interaction might become complicated when a computer is connected to the videodisc and used as a peripheral. In higher levels of interaction the Interactive Videodisc system (IVD) might include a computer, videodisc player, input devices such as touch screens, light pens, speech recognition devices, etc. IVD is a special arrangement that utilizes the visual impact of video and the power and management capabilities of the computer. The ability to integrate sound into the IVD system makes it a live tool for self or group training and learning. Since IVD offers design flexibility, it can be used as an informational system to serve specific functions.

Levels of Interaction

Interactivity can be of different levels. In 1979 the Nebraska Video Design/Production Group identified four levels of interactivity based on player/system sophistication. There has since been no agreement on the number of levels or the specifics of certain levels.[10]

Level Zero

This basic level includes systems that present videodisc program information in a linear sequence. Still- or freeze-frame display is not supported at this level. CED players and CLV videodiscs fall under this level.

Level One

Level one encompasses very simple play modes such as forward and reverse play, fast play and slow motion, freeze- or still-frame, and the ability to go directly to any frame. Most consumer players fall under this category, including the Magnavox 8000 and the Pioneer VP-1000.

Level Two

Level two systems allow automatic branching and simple answer analysis based on single-key input. Feedback from the system on correct/incorrect answers, question response, and menu support are available at this level. This is made possible through the use of a

10. Judy McQueen and Richard W. Boss, op. cit.

programmable microprocessor and small memory buffers. The memory capacity of the microprocessor is almost 1 kilobyte. Videodiscs used for training fall under this category, including the Discovision Associates PR-7820, the Sony LDP-1000, and the French Thomson-CSF CED disc player (available outside North America).

Level Three

This level provides more flexibility by interfacing one videodisc system or more with an external computer. Program potential and capability are enhanced at this level. The interactive program can be stored on the external computer or digitally encoded on the disc (in this case data will be recorded in analog while the program is recorded in digital). The input capability is great. It can be done through a keyboard, keypad, light pen, paddle, joystick, touch screen, voice recognition, or other input devices. Sound and graphics can be integrated into the system. At this level the systems can be described as "intelligent" systems.

At a highly sophisticated level, the program might change based on its interactivity and "experience" with the user.[11]

The four levels of interactivity are in fact different degrees of control over the IVD systems. Linking a microcomputer to a videodisc adds sophistication to the degree of interactivity and leads to more flexible communication between the user and the system. While the control in level one lies with the viewer, it lies in level three with an external computer.

Screen Burn-Ins

It has been noticed that if a monitor displaying the same frame is left on undisturbed for extended periods of time, a state of burn-in develops on the screen. Interactive systems that have still-frame capability are vulnerable to screen burn-in. There are two ways to overcome this problem:

1. Viewing systems that are not operated tend to shut off automatically and operate only when sensors indicate the presence of a user.

2. The program displays the caption of each introductory frame on a different line on the screen at different times.

---

11. Diane M. Gayeski, "Making Interactive Systems More Interactive: New Approaches to Software Tools," *Optical Information Systems* 7(4): 297–300 (July/Aug. 1987).

Fields of Application

Computer-assisted learning (CAL) has great limitations since it is predominantly in text or in diagrams. CAL lacks the visual and aural elements. IVD on the other hand is considered a multimedia system with text, graphics, diagrams, audio, video, and programming capabilities. For this reason many areas have already benefited from IVD, for example, health care, employee training, military training, education, special education, and others.[12] Many schools are using IVD to supplement their courses, where IVDs are placed in computer laboratories or media centers. IVD seems appropriate for situations when repetition is necessary to gain proficiency in a topic. In addition, very complex simulations with feedback capability resulting from psychomotor choices and operations, such as that used in flight simulations, are available on IVD.[13]

The importance of IVD in education has been emphasized since it "provides an especially promising resource for addressing higher order learning within the cognitive/developmental/gestalt psychological tradition."[14] It may give rise to more learning theory research, since a broad range of cognitive and affective behavioral operations can be advantageously designed and tested together. The practicality of IVD as a training medium has been recognized by companies such as General Motors, Ford, and Sears.

Interactive videodisc seems to be effective as an alternative to traditional teaching techniques in many areas such as biomedical education. It is also appropriate for applications where it can substitute for animal experiments in institutions and countries where such experimentation has been eliminated, usually under pressure from humanitarian groups.[15]

IVD is also used in training activities by the U.S. Army. *Screen Digest* reports that IVD has been adopted by the U.S. military as its future training delivery medium. In a five-year period it is expected that 50,000 interactive systems will be installed for military training.[16]

While Kearsley and Frost assert that credible evidence is needed as proof of the effectiveness of IVD, Young and Schlieve found that

---

12. A. D. Evans, "Interactive Video Research: Past Studies and Directions for Future Research," *International Journal of Instructional Media* 13(4): 241–48 (1986).

13. David Deshler and Geraldine Gay, "Educational Strategies for Interactive Videodisc Design," *Educational Technology.* 26(12): 12–17 (Dec. 1986).

14. David Deshler and Geraldine Gay, p.17.

15. Charles E. Branch and others, "The Validation of an Interactive Videodisc as an Alternative to Traditional Teaching Techniques: Auscultation of the Heart," *Educational Technology* 27(3): 16–22 (Mar. 1987).

16. *Screen Digest*, Feb. 1986, p.38.

trainees who used videodisc simulators did not show any difference in their ability to operate complicated communication equipment.[17]

Finally, IVD can be used in the library as a community referral service to provide information on health, social, and human services.

Available IVD Systems

The Pioneer LD-V6000 series (6000, 6010, and 6200) is capable of running level two and level three applications. It has a three-second maximum search time, utilizing 7 kilobytes of RAM, a built-in Z80 microprocessor, and an RS-232 interface for serial communication. Cost: $1,500–$2,000.

Sony LDP-2000 is capable of running level two and level three applications. It has the fastest access time: 1.5 seconds, utilizing 7 kilobytes of RAM, an optional IEEE-488 parallel port, and an RS-232 interface for serial communication. Cost: $1,900–$2,500.

All full-size players can read both 8-inch and 12-inch videodiscs. Some have the capability of an instant jump, where the player can access any frame within 200 frames in either direction of the current location without any noticeable interruption on the screen. All IVD players can read any LaserVision disc regardless of manufacturer. LaserVision has become the default standard with 60 minutes per side.

Compact Disc Interactive

While CD-ROM is directed to the vertical market (business and specialized applications), Compact Disc Interactive (CD-I) is directed to the consumer horizontal market, especially the entertainment, training, education, and informational/reference markets. An example of the informational CD-I product under way is the "Treasures of the Smithsonian," which will put 300 items from the Smithsonian Institution on CD-I. The difference between CD-I and IVD systems is that the CD-I is designed to work independently from the computer. The CD-I drive is equipped with a built-in microprocessor for interactive applications, while IVD requires a computer as a peripheral on level three for interaction.

Unlike the passivity of a user watching a program or a show, CD-I allows the user to exercise a degree of interactivity with a program or

17. G. P. Kearsley and J. Frost, "Design Factors for Successful Videodisc-Based Instruction," *Educational Technology* 25(3): 7–13 (Mar. 1985); and J. I. Young and P. L. Schlieve, "Videodisc Simulation: Training for the Future," *Educational Technology* 24(4): 41–42 (Apr. 1984).

course of instruction in which the content of the program is controlled to some degree by the viewer. Interactivity might include the viewer entering choices according to defined options, thus gaining more motivation. Studies have shown that "adult learners are more motivated and learn better if they are given control over the sequence and pace of training."[18] Since education or training is based largely on one-on-one communication, a CD-I can be used to enhance the abilities of the user through self-learning and on a self-pace basis.

Philips and Sony published the CD-I standard in its final format in the Green Book in February 1987. The Green Book includes the specifications of the required operating system and the data format for the CD-I. On March 3, 1988, a functional CD-I system was displayed in the Third Annual Microsoft CD-ROM Conference in Seattle, Washington. The CD-I player is equipped with a Motorola 68,000 series microprocessor and audio and video processing circuits. The company claims that the system integrates and interleaves audio, video, and text/data functions in a real-time playback (interactive format: text, video, and audio show up at the same time). Furthermore, it can display full-motion video at 12 frames per second with a maximum resolution of 720 by 480 pixels. However, the demonstrated system featured interleaved audio and limited full-motion video. Playing time is 72 minutes with speeds between 200 and 500 rpm. It has video still-frame capability of up to 5,000 natural pictures per disc. Like a CD-audio, which can be played on any player, it is assumed that all CD-I discs will be able to run on any CD-I drive. The computer operating system is stored in a ROM chip in the player. The operating system for CD-I is called *CD-RTOS* (Compact Disc Real-Time Operating System), based on a real-time multitasking system called *OS-9.*

The difference between CD-I and CD-ROM is in the area of data format for audio and images. CD-I is expected to include four audio and three image formats. The sound levels that will range from super hi-fi music mode to speech mode (equivalent to AM broadcast quality) will deliver the maximum 16 channels of sound. Each channel is capable of delivering 72 minutes (19 hours altogether of mono "speech quality" sound, 16 channels by 72 minutes/60), or they can all be used in parallel (72 minutes) for stereo sound or multilanguage programs. Video stills, RGB (Red-Green-Blue) graphics, and color look-up table (CLUT) graphics are included.[19]

---

18. Michael DeBloois, "Designing Interactive Videodisc Training Materials," in *Proceedings of the Third Conference on Interactive Construction Delivery* (Warrenton, Va.: Society for Applied Learning Technology, 1985).

19. Bryan Brewer, "CD-ROM and CD-I," *CD-ROM Review* 2(2): 18–25 (May/June 1987).

Applications

Bruno and Mizushima identified five application categories of CD-I:[20]

1. In the car: maps, navigation, tourist information, real-time animation, and diagnostics.
2. Education and training: do-it-yourself, home learning, interactive training, reference books, albums, and talking books.
3. Entertainment: music, action games, strategic games, adventure games, activity simulation, and "edutainment" (education-entertainment).
4. Creative leisure: drawing, painting, filming, and composition.
5. Work at home or while traveling: document processing and information retrieval and analysis.

In fact, very little is known about CD-I. However, DeBloois advises prospective authors of CD-I–based materials to study the variety of ways users wish to receive information and subsequently apply the capabilities of the new CD-I.[21] Selecting the right media is important for the success of any project. In some projects, the dominant media might be the text; for another, audio may be dominant. CD-I products are expected to reflect an understanding of the impact of the market forces.

Because of CD-I's capability to run data, text, graphics, software, video, and sound with greater interactivity, and because of its ability to interface with external computers, its applications are unlimited. The sophistication of CD-I makes it appealing to library applications in areas such as basic library orientation tours, directions and floor plans, departments and personnel names and their expertise, art and rare collections, and bibliographic instruction.

Eventually, the information desk stationed in many public and university libraries could be replaced by a CD-I station.

20. R. Bruno and M. Mizushima, "New Developments in Optical Media: An Outline of CD-I," *Optical Information Systems* 6(4): 318–23 (July/Aug. 1986).

21. Michael DeBloois, "Anticipating Compact Disc Interactive (CD-I): Ten Guidelines for Prospective Authors," *Educational Technology* 27(4): 25–27 (Apr. 1987).

5 A Comparison between CD-ROM and Other Media

CD-ROM and Online Databases

The ability to access remote online databases since the early 1970s has brought libraries in direct contact with vast amounts of information. Now CD-ROM is bringing the databases themselves into the library. Given its capability, many are concerned whether CD-ROM will bring an end to online databases or, at the least, create a state of rivalry between CD-ROM and online services.

The available public online services are huge in number and capacity. Their services are extremely broad, ranging from databases and communications to videotext and business transactions. The number of existing databases in these categories exceeds 3,000 worldwide, covering a very wide spectrum of topics. Their sizes range from 1000 kilobytes to more than 1000 megabytes—millions of pages of information. Online vendors have invested billions of dollars to keep these services operational, and they are not going to abolish online services in favor of distributing their databases on CD-ROM, just because the technology is there.

According to Holmstrom, the distribution of online databases in connection with their size seems to be bimodal, with a peak in the 100 to 300 megabytes range (Figure 5.1).

Databases falling in this region seem to be appropriate for publication in CD-ROM format. Generally, criteria for selecting a medium for data distribution include ease-of-use, durability, longevity, cost to the manufacturer and the user, usability, speed of access, and portability. Vendors use criteria when they consider publishing a database not only on CD-ROM but on any other medium. For example, when durability, copy protection, large capacity, portability, and/or ease-of-use are critical, the CD-ROM may be more appropriate as a publishing medium. On the other hand, when a limited amount of data is sent to one or many users, the floppy diskette is most cost-effective. Other criteria include the amount of data and its growth over time in order to select the delivery technique, the expected number of users who will buy and benefit from the product, and the timeliness of data and updateness. Almost every database is updated by data being added continuously to the historical base. (It seems that the completely static (non-updatable) database does not exist.)

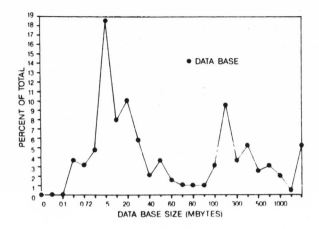

(Source: *Reference Services Review* v.16, no.3 (1988).)

Figure 5.1   Distribution of databases according to size.

The frequency of updating these databases differs from a few seconds to more than a year. While financial information must be updated once an event takes place, other information such as bibliographic data may be of a more historical nature and need to be complemented as new information emerges and becomes available. Users, for instance, expect to receive information on stocks and commodities a few seconds after posting of the transaction at an exchange. This type of data is not recommended for distribution on CD-ROM. Perhaps when the transactions become historical, and are compressed in the form of a summary that includes highs, lows, volumes, etc., they can be distributed on CD-ROM. Historical databases that do not require instant updates may be distributed on CD-ROM. However, not every single online database is a good candidate for distribution on that medium.

Database services store mostly bibliographical data which are targeted at business, education, or academic researchers. Major online databases include:

BRS (Bibliographic Retrieval Services) from BRS Information Technologies, Letham, New York, offers access to more than 150 databases aimed at business and education users.

DIALOG, from Dialog Information Services, Inc., Palo Alto, California, offers access to more than 250 databases aimed at business, education, and professional users. Dialog has published some of its most used bibliographic databases on CD-ROM. It supports electronic mail among its users and offers gateways to stand-alone services such as *Official Airline Guide*.

Infomaster, from Western Union Telegraph Co., Upper Saddle River, New Jersey, pulls data from such vendors as Dialog, NewsNet, Vu/Text, and BRS as well as its own databases. It supports as many as 700 databases, and is directed at business, library, and information specialists.

Vu/Text, from Vu/Text Information Services, Philadelphia, is mainly a newspaper database comprising the full texts of 31 newspapers or news services. However, it also has an online electronic calculator function. It is geared at government, business, and professional users.

NewsNet, from NewsNet, Bryn Mawr, Pennsylvania, is directed at business and professional users. There are 12 databases available through NewsNet, including United Press International (UPI), Associated Press (AP), *USA Today,* and a number of newsletters.

Wilsonline, from H. W. Wilson Co., New York, is targeted at business, library, and information specialists, and academic researchers. Necessarily an index service, it provides access to indexes such as *Applied Science and Technology, Art Index, Education Index, Readers' Guide to Periodical Literature, Cumulative Book Index,* and *Business Periodical Index,* among many others. Wilson has published many of its indexes on CD-ROM.

Communications services offer electronic mail, bulletin boards, and some gateway services that are targeted to business users. Communications services include: *MCI Mail* from MCI; *Dialcom* from Dialcom, Inc.; *EasyLink* from Western Union Telegraph Co.; and *AT&T Mail* from AT&T Customer Assistance Center.

Videotext services support a variety of databases, communications, shopping, game, and miscellaneous services usually targeted to home or education. Most online services in this group are basically consumer-oriented information utilities, such as *The Source,* from Source Telecomputing Corporation; *CompuServe,* from CompuServe; *GEnie* (General Electric Network for Information Exchange), from General Electric Information Services; *Dow Jones News/Retrieval,* from Dow Jones & Co.; and *Delphi,* from General Videotext Corporation, which stores more than 70 databases and allows users access to *Dialog* and networks such as Grouplink and Global Venture Network.

With the advent of CD-ROM, decision making for librarians is becoming more complex in areas of choosing and exploiting new information resources. While librarians are open to opportunities to broaden their services to users, the selection of a service or a medium by a library depends on vital criteria such as cost, update ability, convenience, effectiveness, and acceptance. Because CD-ROM is a read-only medium, an individual disc cannot be updated (though this might be changed in the future). Some CD-ROM products have the capability of combining a CD-ROM search with free online access such as *Wilsondisc* and *Dialog OnDisc*. Thus CD-ROM can be categorized as a supplementary product to online services. Some producers are frequently updating their databases on CD-ROM (quarterly updates are common).

The archives of any information network hold historical, stable, and huge databases. Whether these databases provide bibliographic services, union catalogs used for catalog retrospective conversion, interlibrary loan (ILL) operations, or shared public catalogs, their back-files are good candidates for publication in optical format. In that respect, CD-ROM could again be seen as a complementary tool to online databases. Activities such as sending messages, updating bibliographic records, adding the library's own records, or sending requests for ILL require an online network. Thus there is no indication that optical technology will replace online services. The spread use of CD-ROM however, will probably reduce the cost of online services. This situation might result in online services reaching a large number of small libraries and individual searchers as well.

Another important factor is cost. While the use of a professional database during business hours can cost anywhere from $20 to $300 an hour, the cost of telecommunications and search charges does not persist with CD-ROM. This affords unlimited access to very large volumes of data. The cost factor that is of major concern in online systems seems to improve through the one-time payment over the online system. While databases on CD-ROM, which are leased on an annual basis, impose a persistent annual cost for updates, most archival CD-ROM volumes require one-time payment. However, the fixed and predictable cost in both cases is less than the variable and unpredictable online cost. In contrast to the average cost of online searching, which tends to increase as the volume of users increases, the average cost of a CD-ROM search tends to decrease with every additional search. Considerations to stop searching an online database might be directed to the infrequently searched databases in favor of their CD-ROM versions.

A library that searches only one or two databases all the time can use the CD-ROM version instead of the online service. Added to the cost of the CD-ROM is staff time spent in training the end user on the operations and techniques of the workstation and in preparing effective documentation. In addition, at some point a user may need an intermediary to perform a complex search. Thus, the intermediary involvement cannot be entirely eliminated from the library.

An important question is, Who pays for the CD-ROM search? Many libraries have rebudgeted their online search expenditures to absorb expenses for CD-ROM. Other libraries pass on the cost of using CD-ROM workstations to the user by imposing a cost based on use time or the number of citations printed out. Collecting fees might involve time, paper work, and effort on the staff plus the problem of collecting exact change. Vendacard or coin machines are other considerations, and some college and university libraries have asked for allocations for online services in tuition, which will eventually cover the expenses of CD-ROM workstations.

The size of a database is of major concern. Large databases that can be stored in a single online file may require two, three, or more CD-ROMs. Exchanging discs at a workstation is an inconvenience to the user. A LAN or a juke-box that holds dozens of CD-ROM discs that can be accessed through terminals from remote sites is an appealing system, since the user will unlikely deal with individual discs. A daisy-chain configuration is also a solution to search multiple volumes of a database where each volume is housed in a separate CD-ROM drive connected to one host computer (see Chapter 6).

For an information broker, CD-ROM is considered slow since the broker has to search a large number of databases. In a busy information brokerage firm, exchanging discs, loading databases, and entering same-search statements with every database are time-consuming compared to online services, especially when complex searches are required. LANs or jukeboxes are ideal for a busy brokerage firm.

The ease-of-use of many CD-ROM databases through menus, help screens, and documentation has assisted many users to do their own searches without the help of an online searcher. However, some of the existing databases on CD-ROM, such as *BiblioFile*, require dedicated separate workstations, thus preventing the use of the workstation to run other CD-ROM products. In addition, many software applications do not have the capability to perform a cross-search through different databases installed at one workstation or even save the search strategy for later use, whereas in an online system the user has access to hundreds of databases upon signing in.

One of the major concerns to libraries is the search time. While a complex search on a CD-ROM using Boolean operators (*and, or, not* ...) and truncations takes as much as 30 minutes to complete, the same search can be done online in less than two or three minutes using the power of the mainframe.

Services that sort the data on a specific field or zoom into any field are offered by some online vendors, but they are not feasible on most CD-ROM databases. Many CD-ROM products have the capability of downloading, but of course, downloading a large number of records can require significant time.

Some CD-ROM systems provide a truncation feature, thus allowing the user to enter part of the keyword to search all other forms of the word. For example, a search using "psych*" (* is the truncation symbol on some CD-ROM products) will retrieve: psychic, psychoanalysis, psychologists, psychology, etc. If a product lacks this capability, the user has to enter each term individually.

Among the reasons reported in the literature for buying CD-ROM products are the following:

Cost to access information is fixed.
Search cost is reduced compared to online search cost.
Unlimited access to data.
Reduction of the intermediary role that is required for online search, thus saving staff time.
Introducing new technologies and services to patrons.

At this point, it seems that CD-ROM is not the sole information delivery medium. A hybrid service is emerging in many libraries including one or more of the following: mediated searching, end-user searching done online by the user (in libraries that permit their users to search online), CD-ROM searching, and databases in microform or paper-copy format. The result of utilizing CD-ROM searching is that more users have been introduced to the concept of computerized literature searching than could be accomplished by online services.

Just as online services have never ended manual searches, optical disc technology will unlikely replace online networks in the library environment. The focus here is not on whether CD-ROM should replace online services. Rather, it is on providing an environment in which CD-ROM and other media, including online services, can be used effectively to provide the user with the most efficient retrieval system.

The Role of Online Searchers

In their study of the Evans Library of Texas A&M University, Vici Anders and Kathy Jackson noticed that online connect time had decreased sharply once patrons were aware of laserdiscs. The users who moved from online to laserdiscs were the users of the *BRS/After Dark* and Dialog's *Knowledge Index* services. In the meantime, the users who were using mediated services seemed to still prefer mediated searches, though in smaller numbers. The number of users of *ERIC*, *PsycLIT*, and *Agricola* online had decreased significantly after the installation of the laserdisc (Figure 5.2). This pattern was not so evident with *Dissertation Abstracts* especially when students were heavily engaged in preparing thesis proposals. Anders and Jackson noted that a significant portion of the population of CD-ROM users were undergraduates. The next user segment was composed of graduate students. Faculty and staff having some sort of funding generally preferred mediated searches. Limitations of CD-ROM searching include: response time is slow, data files on a laserdisc are limited in size, and a CD-ROM workstation can

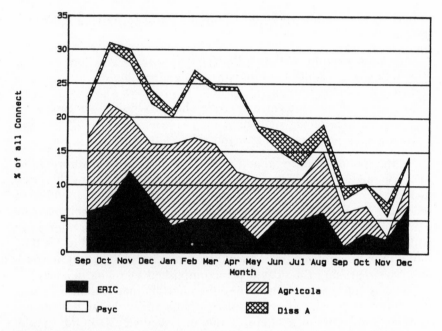

(Reprinted by permission from *Online*, Nov. 1988, p.25.)

Figure 5.2 Online connect time had decreased sharply for *ERIC*, *Psychological Abstracts*, *Agricola*, and *Dissertation Abstracts* during the 16 months from September 1986 until December 1987.

accommodate only one user at a time, thus creating a queue in the reference area. In addition, many CD-ROM workstations are used only as CD-ROM workstations, diminishing the value of the microcomputer.

A major feature of any CD-ROM product is that it creates some kind of physical contact between the user and the medium that contains the data. This is in contrast to online services where the user searches a database through an information intermediary who is trained to design search strategies and perform the actual search. Whether the search results contain all the background information that supports a particular search depends on many factors. These factors include using the right online database or databases; the capability of the searcher in designing the search strategy; and making decisions during a search session when encountering such search problems as not enough information, too many results, or irrelevant information. Sometimes during a search session, the searcher has to expand or limit the search or even to search another database or do a cross-search. All these activities and awareness of any existing problems are part of the background, training, and experience of the searcher.

Contrary to what some might consider a dim future for information intermediaries as more online databases become available on CD-ROM, the role of a well-trained intermediary becomes indispensable. A well-trained intermediary is needed to assist the end user in designing a better search strategy and selecting the right database to fulfill a specific query. Many libraries hold training sessions for their end users, offer orientations, and in some cases educate their users on a one-to-one basis. More reference librarians and paraprofessional staff who were not involved in previous online searching are now acquainting themselves with CD-ROM systems in order to be able to help their users.

Education and training on the use of a CD-ROM product must keep pace with the real marketplace. The present CD-ROM products use the same material in training both end users and librarians. Existing training materials include on-screen tutorials, documentation, summary cards, and videotapes. This is in contrast to online training sessions, which are offered by information vendors and cover a wide variety of databases. These training sessions are rarely offered to the public; they are designed for librarians and information specialists.

However, CD-ROM training materials are not all read and understood by every user. There will always be a need for someone who can answer users' questions. CD-ROM products will positively redefine the role of the information intermediary. Although the user might have a better understanding of his or her topic and search terminology, the librarian has a good understanding of the nature of the database context and search techniques. A librarian is needed to decide whether the CD-ROM searches are adequate or online searches are required. So the formal role—interview, prepare strategy, run search—of an information intermediary and his or her informal role (advising and answering questions) will correlate to the number of online databases published in CD-ROM format. A librarian is also needed to decide what CD-ROMs to include in the library.

CD-ROM and COM

Computer Output Microfilm (COM) refers to the technology of recording information from magnetic tape or directly from a computer on film or fiche using a high-speed interface at speeds up to 26,000 lines per minute. At 48X reduction, COM is able to compress 512 cubic feet of 11-by-14-inch sheets of paper into merely one cubic foot of COM microfiche (or 270 pages on one fiche).

COM systems use different techniques to process the film. Some COM units produce silver-gelatin emulsion film, which requires that the film be removed from the unit and processed in a separate darkroom. Some COM units process the film internally, using either silver-gelatin emulsion film within self-contained chemical baths and drying apparatus, or dry-silver film that is produced by heat without any chemicals inside the COM unit. These types of COM units can be operated offline or online. In the offline process the tape is prepared by a mainframe, then delivered by hand to the COM unit. In the online setting, the data are downloaded from a mainframe by another computer such as a minicomputer, which acts as a front-end computer with the COM unit.

Retrieving the data is accomplished in different ways, such as random filming plus external sorted index; sequential filming in a logical order, either alphabetical or numerical; image control through the use of "blips" (image markers) and a suitable computer-assisted retrieval (CAR) system; and the binary-coding system, which uses bar codes along the edge of the film beneath each image.

COM technology has been used for more than a decade. It is well established in large and small corporations for selected applications. It is used wherever duplication and distribution of vital data are needed daily in different locations until such data are available on the online computer system. While the number of fiche produced daily in a corporation depends on the volume of transactions, some firms produce between 20 and 30 fiche, the equivalent of almost 2,000 pages a day.

In some corporations, there exist situations where data migrate after a period of time from the costly direct-access storage devices to much cheaper and slower media, such as offline COM, tapes, and paper. However, the apparent weakness of COM systems is that they do not allow for data manipulation. Once COM is generated, data cannot be used in different contexts or for different functions. This contrasts with optical disc technology, which can restructure the data to the way the user wants them to be utilized. Freeing the online system from historical data by placing such data on optical media and placing the optical discs themselves in a juke-box or a daisy-chain configuration can prolong the existence of data online for long periods of time.

Applications of COM in libraries are geared more to indexes, manuals, directories, and card catalogs. A number of newsletters, out-of-print titles, unpublished special reports, back-files of newspapers and periodicals, as well as documents and books have been published in COM format.

As a computer output, COM is considered an effective medium that can be produced faster and cheaper than CD-ROM or any optical disc. Although the image quality of COM is inferior to that of CD-ROM, the latter is considered unsuitable for computer output since it is expensive and slow to produce. Also, despite the excellent capability of online systems for solving problems in real time (the response of these systems is very fast), computer output applications online are too expensive and lack distribution capabilities. (WORM systems also cannot be duplicated or distributed in a timely manner, thus they are not suitable for computer output.)

Although records on CD-ROM are more durable and easier to handle than microforms, the life span of optical discs in general is questionable. Unlike CD-ROM, duplication of COM can be easily done online. In contrast to COM, CD-ROM and optical discs in general are fast in connection to online retrieval from large databases where frequent searching is required. Since optical discs have the capability to store information in the form of computer-readable data and in graphics format, their potential uses for computer-aided design (CAD), computer-aided manufacturing (CAM), computer-aided engineering (CAE), and technical manuals and parts catalogs are greater than COM fiche. Because of their large capacity and complexity of development, optical discs are not the right choice to store short-lived information or small jobs. COM systems, on the other hand, are able to handle jobs as small as one page.

In sum, COM is best suited for wide distribution of short-lived information for small and large jobs.

For large volumes of source documents where access to information is done infrequently, optical discs have an advantage in storage capacity and space economics but are costly in indexing and premastering processes. Concerning archival storage, there is a progressive relationship between the costs and time involved in the production of an indexing and retrieval system for a collection on one side and the size of the archived data on the other side. Whereas COM might be a better choice for such application, optical discs are the right choice for frequently searched databases that include information that needs less updating. This allows optical discs to compete directly with COM systems and other storage techniques, including magnetic media.

Both COM and optical disc technologies seem to complement each other. Nevertheless, an integrated system that allows data to be read on video display terminals with online, microfilm reading, and hard-copy printout capabilities is, however appealing for library applications, costly.

CD-ROM and Compact Disc Interactive

Although the technical capabilities of both CD-ROM and Compact Disc Interactive (CD-I) overlap in many areas, each format is designed for specific applications. CD-I is not a replacement for CD-ROM. It is a stand-alone system equipped with a microprocessor, a specified minimum amount of memory, and specified audio and video processing circuits. This multimedia system is an enhancement of CD-ROM and CD-digital audio.

CD-ROM can be considered a storage system in which data on the disc are to be matched to the target computer system. It is directed largely to professional markets, while the main markets for CD-I are expected to be consumer and institutional. This does not mean that CD-I is only for the home and entertainment markets. There are, for example, situations in the library, such as training and tutorials, where a dedicated CD-I station might be appealing. An audio feedback from the CD-I player to instruct and guide the user of an information referral service would be appropriate.

CD-I is expected to revive the traditional consumer electronic industry (audio/video entertainment), video games, and home computer (games, education).

CD-I is capable of storing text in a compressed or non-compressed bit-map process (an exact copy of the text or a picture of the text) or by character encoding as data in computers. The character in the bit-data process requires 5 bytes of storage memory compared to 1 byte on CD-ROM. This limits the maximum capacity of a CD-I disc to 120 megabytes, compared to the 543 megabytes of user data on a CD-ROM. In the bit-map process, the data cannot be manipulated, as opposed to character encoding, which can be manipulated by application software or the computer. The CD-I multichannel audio capabilities make it a natural choice for discs that require spoken material in foreign languages. Because of its storage strength in simulation and experiential learning, CD-I could improve productivity in the workplace. Although CD-I is not likely to pose a direct threat to the CD-ROM market, it may severely affect interactive videodiscs. Compared to interactive videodisc, CD-I has several advantages, including universal programming and playback standard; ability to mix graphics, audio, and motion on the same disc; and display capability on almost any television format.

CD-ROM, Erasable Optical Storage, and WORM

There are conflicts of opinion about whether or not erasable media will replace CD-ROM and WORM systems. The huge storage capacity (600 megabytes) and low price ($2 on average per disc) of CD-ROM make it an excellent medium for distributing large reference materials. Write-once devices, with their capability to store still-video images and with no mastering costs, are becoming accepted in today's business environment. In libraries, WORM systems could be used for storing archival collections and personnel records, because they are incorruptible and nearly indestructible. The fact that data on WORM discs cannot be altered makes WORM a perfect solution for archival storage compared with erasable media. Such systems can also be used in downloading and for limited distribution of reference data. These discs are not meant for mass replication and distribution of databases as is CD-ROM.

On the other hand, the enormous capacity of erasable optical media, 1 gigabyte and more, makes it an appealing medium for backup applications, such as end-user data storage, archival storage, and program storage. This will make the erasable optical media compete directly with the tape products used in backup systems. The market acceptance of the erasable optical media, however, depends on such factors as performance, reliability, standards, and price. Some manufacturers of erasable optical media claim 30-millisecond seek time and a sustained transfer rate of 10 megabits (8 bits = 1 byte) per second (the speed at which accessed data can be moved from one device to another). This high performance will undoubtedly compete with the existing Winchester drives in areas such as computer-aided design (CAD), computer-aided manufacturing (CAM), data collection, and network storage.

Since CD-ROM is considered a publishing as well as a distributing medium, it is unlikely to be threatened by the erasable optical media designed to store information. While the cost of producing a CD-ROM disc by pressing or stamping is very cheap—approximately $2 depending on quantity—the cost of erasable optical media by magneto-optic technology is more than $150. This will make erasable optical media very expensive to distribute information, which will leave this service to CD-ROM at least for the present. In general, as these technologies develop, each will find its own use and markets, and each will serve specific tasks.

Optical and Magnetic Media

Optical media have slow access speeds—in the case of CD-ROM, 500 milliseconds to access information on the innermost tracks and 1,000 milliseconds to reach the outer tracks—compared to magnetic drives (30 milliseconds on the average for a Winchester disk). This is likely to be a technical limitation of optical media for some time. Typically, the laser pickup head is heavy due to the weight of the focusing system and the lenses. The advantage of optical discs, however, are their huge storage capacity, ability to endure harsh environments without damage, and the ease with which they can be transferred. Floppy discs, on the

other hand, are still in use and have found new formats such as the
1.2-megabyte, 5.25-inch disc and the 800-kilobyte 3.25-inch format.
(The Bernoulli box and optical discs are alternative mass storage
devices. Winchester disks are approaching optical storage capacity with
5.25-inch discs boasting 150-megabyte capacity.)

When a limited amount of data is sent to one or more users, the
floppy diskettes are more effective as distributing media. The limited
capacity of floppy diskettes is the major disadvantage for the distribution of huge databases. As the number of users increases, the cost of
the 360-kilobyte data stays constant versus the number of diskettes
required for each user. On the other hand, the Bernoulli disk cartridge
is most effective when large amounts of data are sent to a limited
number of users. When 20 megabytes of data are distributed, the cost
per user is constant. When the size of the database exceeds 40 megabytes,
the Bernoulli disk cartridge has its disadvantage, since the user has to
swap or load the data to larger hard files.

However, when the number of users exceeds 150, the CD-ROM is
the most cost-effective medium. The cost per user starts to decrease
with additional users because the initial mastering cost of the CD-ROM
is shared by each user (Figure 5.3).

The disadvantage of publishing databases on CD-ROM is the slowness
of accessing and transferring data. This could be overcome by buffering
data from the CD-ROM onto hard disk or a disk cartridge for faster
access. But even with faster drives, the problem of currency of information still exists. Also, the initial mastering costs stay high unless the
product is shared with more than 150 users.

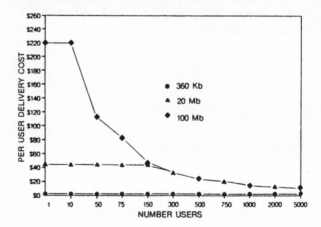

(Source: *Reference Services Review* 16, no.3:13 (1988).)

Figure 5.3 Minimum media cost per user.

In conclusion, it is believed by some that optical technology may overtake magnetic media both in popularity and price. In the future, if prices fall enough, erasable disc could emerge as the dominant medium for personal computer storage because of its capacity and capability to be used repeatedly. Optical discs are expected to back up hard disks and may become the standard for data storage for mainframe computer systems.

However, it is unlikely that optical discs will totally replace magnetic disk or tapes, though the technology will certainly augment and complement existing storage methods. In the area of optical publishing, CD-ROM will remain the method to publish data and information in formats that need to stay unchanged.

Selected Bibliography

Alberico, Ralph. "Expanding Memory and Storage." *Small Computers in Libraries* 6(8): 14–17 (Sept. 1986).

Ambrosio, Johanna. "The CD-ROM vs. Online Tradeoff: Rather Than Replacing Databases, Compact Disks Supplement Them." *Software News* 7(8): 69 (July 1987).

Anders, Vicki and Jackson, Kathy M. "Online vs. CD-ROM—The Impact of CD-ROM Databases upon a Large Online Searching Program." *Online* 12(6): 24–32 (Nov. 1988).

Banks, Richard L. "COM vs. Optical Disk: Where's the Beef?" *Journal of Information and Image Management* 19(2): 20–23, 30 (Feb. 1986).

Brewer, Bryan. "CD-ROM and CD-I." *CD-ROM Review* 2(2): 18–20, 25 (June 1987).

Calmes, Alan. "New Confidence in Microfilm." *Library Journal* 111(15): 38–42 (Sept. 15, 1986).

Carney, Richard D. "Infotrac: An Inhouse Computer-Access System." *Library Hi Tech* 3(2): 91–94 (1985).

"CD-ROM Assessed at Optical Publishing '86 Conference: CD-ROM and Online Should Operate in 'Close Harmony.'" *IDP Report* 7(17): 1–2 (Oct. 17, 1986).

Chadwick, David. "Optical or Magnetic?" *Systems International* 14(5): 23–24 (May 1986).

Churbuck, David. "CD-ROM Databases Attracting User Attention." *PC Week* 3(28): 103 (July 1986).

Danziger, Pamela N. "CD-ROM: Is the Future Now?" *Bulletin of the American Society for Information Science* 14(1): 19–20 (Oct./Nov. 1987).

"Discussion: The Videodisc, CD-ROM, Downloading, and the Future of Online." *Infotecture Europe* 67(2): 1–2 (Apr. 1985).

Downing, Jeff. "Planning for CD-ROM Technology; or, How to Stop Worrying and Embrace the CD-ROM." *Reference Services Review* 16(3): 21–26 (1988).

Epstein, Susan Baerg. "Will Optical Discs Be the End of Online Networks?" *American Libraries* 18(4): 253–54, 256 (Apr. 1987).

Green, Irving. "The New Face of C-O-M: Arkive IV/CRS." *Optical Information Systems* 8(2): 84–85 (Mar.-Apr. 1988).

Halperin, Michael and Pagell, Ruth A. "Compact Disclosure: Realizing CD-ROM's Potential." *Online* 10(6): 69–73 (Nov. 1986).

Halperin, Michael and Renfro, Patricia. "Online vs. CD-ROM vs. Onsite: High Volume Searching—Considering the Alternatives." *Online* 12(6): 36–42 (Nov. 1988).

Hecht, Jeff. "Optical Memories Vie for Data Storage." *High Technology* 7(8): 43–47 (Aug. 1987).

Hilditch, Bonny M. and Schroeder, Eileen E. "Pertinent Comparisons between CD-ROM and Online." *Bulletin of the American Society for Information Science* 14(1): 15–16 (Oct./Nov. 1987).

Holmstrom, Larry W. "Electronic and Media Delivery of Information Matching New Techniques to Products and Markets." *Reference Services Review* 16(3): 7–19 (1988).

Isbouts, Jean Pierre. "CD-I: An Analysis of Design and Application Strategies." *Optical Information Systems* 7(4): 253–57 (July/Aug. 1987).

Jack, Robert F. "Oh, Say Can You CD-ROM?" *Bulletin of the American Society for Information Science* 14(1): 17–18 (Oct./Nov. 1987).

Maglitta, Joseph E. "Optical Disk Drives Are Picking Up Speed as an Alternative to Tapes, Hard Disk Drives." *Digital Review* 3(16): 83–86 (Sept. 1986).

Melin, Nancy. "The Optical Alternative to Online." *Information Today* 3(5): 11ff. (May 1986).

Messmer, Ellen and Aaron, Diana. "On-line Databases Turn a PC into a Complete Library: But Which Services Should You Buy, and What About CD-ROM?" *Information Week* (128): 32–33 (Aug. 3, 1987).

Meyer, Rick. "Strategies For Libraries." *Bulletin of the American Society for Information Science* 14(1): 22–23 (Oct./Nov. 1987).

Miglore, Frances C. "CD-ROM: An Emerging Technology for Information Storage and Retrieval." *Journal of Accountancy* 162(4): 87–90 (Oct. 1986).

Moes, Robert J. "The CD-ROM Puzzle: Where Do the Pieces Fit?" *Optical Information Systems* 6(6): 509–11 (Nov./Dec. 1986).

Nihei, Wes and Brown, Eric. "On-Line Vendors Eye CD-ROM: Password: Communicate." *PC World* 4(7): 271–73 (July 1986).

O'Conner, Mary Ann. "Application Development and Optical Media." *Optical Information Systems* 6(1): 64–67 (Jan./Feb. 1986).

Oppenheim, Charles. "CD-ROM—Panacea or Hype?" *Aslib Information* 14(3): 50 (Mar. 1986).

Ramsay, Nancy C. "Using Optical Disk in Non-Image Applications." *Optical Information Systems* 8(4): 164–68 (July-Aug. 1988).

Reinke, Susan P. "An Online Searcher's Perspective." *Bulletin of the American Society for Information Science* 14(1): 21 (Oct./Nov. 1987).

Sabaroff, Lauryl. "Optical Disks Supplement Magnetic Media." *Computer Technology Review* 7(7): 16, 28 (June 1987).

Yerburgh, Mark R. "Studying All Those 'Tiny Little Tea Leaves': The Future of Microforms in a Complex Technological Environment." *Microform Review* 16(1): 14–20 (Winter 1987).

6 Hardware, Networks, and MSCDEX

Hardware

Essential hardware components of a CD-ROM workstation are:

Microcomputer (hard disk recommended)
Monitor (color or mono)
CD-ROM drive
Printer (optional but recommended)
Interface board and connection cable

A vendor may develop a database that will work only on IBM computers but not on some IBM clones. When a library owns hardware that could be used in a CD-ROM workstation, the library is advised to

(Courtesy of University Microfilms International.)

Figure 6.1 Workstation composed of NCR PC/286, 640K RAM, 20Mb hard disk, a floppy-disk drive, Toshiba XM-2100A CD-ROM drive with SCSI control card, and a Canon "bubble" jet printer.

inquire about compatibility between the hardware it owns and the CD-ROM product. In the meantime, some vendors offer their products to be used and inspected for sixty or ninety days at no risk to the buyer. The offer may include hardware and software.

CD-ROM Drives

There are many types of CD-ROM drives on the market produced by more than a dozen companies. The industry refers to CD-ROM drives by company, model, configuration, and interface (the connection between the CD-ROM drive and the microcomputer).

Example:

Company:	Hitachi
Model:	CDR-1503S
Configuration:	Stand-alone, front-loading
Interface:	Hitachi bus

A stand-alone drive can be front-loading (Figure 6.2) or top-loading (Figure 6.3), and half-height or full-height. It needs a controller interface (also called controller card, controller board, or bus) and a connection cable to connect to the host computer. The user has to install the interface board in an extension slot inside the computer. Controller interface documentation for a specific CD-ROM drive should be consulted.

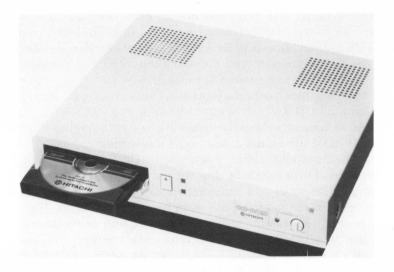

Figure 6.2   A Hitachi front-loading, full-size CD-ROM drive.

Figure 6.3   A Philips top-loading, full-size CD-ROM drive.

Once the controller interface is installed and the microcomputer is secured, the interface should be firmly connected to the CD-ROM drive with cable. It should be noted that front-loading drives are easy to stack because of their flat tops. They can also be placed between the computer disk drive and the monitor to save work space, provided that the ventilation slots are not blocked in any way.

An internal half-height or full-height drive, on the other hand, fits into the microcomputer and looks like an extra computer disk drive. However, an internal full-height drive will not fit in IBM/PS-2 computers and PS-2 clones. In case of internal drives, the interface is embedded inside the microcomputer, and the only thing needed is the cable for connecting the interface to the CD-ROM drive.

Not every company manufactures all of these configurations. However, almost all CD-ROM drives are sold in workstations accompanied by CD-ROM products. Manufacturers are not encouraging the retail sale of CD-ROM drives, not at least as of this writing.

An internally mounted drive might need a CD-ROM disc in a caddy in order to be able to access the disc. A caddy is also used to protect the disc from fingerprints and environmental contamination. There are many types of these caddies, such as those made by Philips, JVC, and Sony. These various caddies are not compatible with each other, which means that they cannot be used interchangeably between drives. The Sony caddy is used by Hitachi, Toshiba, and Apple (Figure 6.4).

Manufacturers of CD-ROM drives include Amdek, Apple, Denon, Digital, Hitachi, JVC, Laser Magnetic Storage, Lot, NEC Home Elec-

Figure 6.4 A Sony caddy.

tronics, Panasonic, Reference Technology, Sanyo, Sony, and Toshiba. For a list of CD-ROM drives see Appendix D.

CD-ROM drives are slow in accessing and transferring information due to the weight and movement of the laser head. The frequent movement of the head from inner tracks to outer tracks requires adjusting the disc speed to decode the timing on the track before any reading can be done, which causes slow data access and transfer. However, a sequential read on the same track or adjacent tracks requires minimum changes in speed, thus resulting in more speed. Another factor that attributes to the slowness of data transfer is the way data are formatted and arranged on the disc. This can be different from one product to another. Also, in contrast to a hard disk, which can be optimized once the user has data on it, CD-ROM does not have this capability (though an efficient file format will result in increased access and transfer of data).

Microcomputers

Most CD-ROM systems recommend use of a microcomputer with a hard disk and at least one floppy-disk drive with a minimum of 512K RAM (with 640K highly recommended). A floppy-disk drive can be used, but it can also make the search session cumbersome. For example, the search and retrieval software stored on floppy diskettes can be extensive; thus, little room remains for downloading data from the CD-ROM. Also, because of the amount of space MS-DOS CD-ROM Extensions require, installation on a floppy disk may not be possible since some CD-ROM systems software will not fit on the diskette. Using floppy diskettes requires swapping them during a search, which might result in the loss or damage of the diskettes in addition to the inconvenience and waste of time.

Systems generally require an IBM/PC, XT, AT, PS/2, or compatibles. There are some products that will run on Apple Macintosh SE and Macintosh Plus, using AppleCD SC CD-ROM drive. MacSPIRS is a SilverPlatter search and retrieval software for the Apple Macintosh that interfaces with CD-ROM databases in the SilverPlatter products. MacSPIRS works with the Macintosh Plus, Macintosh SE, or Macintosh II and requires an 800K floppy-disk drive, 1 megabyte of memory, and Macintosh system 6.0 or higher. A hard disk is recommended. The library has to inquire about the available hardware and the type of computer that will run a specific CD-ROM product.

A computer disk drive is usually equipped with expansion slots. These slots are basically needed to connect the computer to a printer, an external hard disk if necessary, a CD-ROM drive, a modem if the same workstation is going to be used for online searches, or more controller cards if many CD-ROM drives are to be connected to the same computer.

Printers

Most CD-ROM vendors consider printers as optional hardware. To provide fast search service, however, the library will have to provide a printer adequate to the task. In practice, the user should be given the choice to print citations as an option to downloading information on a floppy or hard disk.

Generally, any printer that works with the microcomputer will work with the CD-ROM system. However, the user might have to adjust certain switches on the printer. Before adjusting the switches, it is recommended that a diagram of the existing switch setting be drawn, just in case the original setting is to be restored. Sometimes the CD-ROM product includes instructions on how to set these switches; otherwise, the manual for a specific printer has to be consulted.

In a public service area, a quiet printer is recommended. In addition, a library has to increase its stock of printing paper, ribbons, or print cartridges in order to run a smooth operation without interruptions or complaints. This necessarily requires an increase in the allocations for materials in the budget.

Some CD-ROM products impose a limit on the number of printed citations, or the size of area to skip after a printing job is accomplished. This is usually done during installation of the CD-ROM product. A library can save on paper if it buys continuous printing paper that is 5.5

by 8.5 inches instead of 8.5 by 11 inches. Despite restrictions on the number of printed citations that are imposed by some CD-ROM products, the user can always override this limitation by escaping out of the print mode, then resuming the print mode and printing new records, and so on. (SilverPlatter products, for example, allow overriding this limitation by specifying the number of records in the specified record field at the time of printing.)

Controllers

Although CD-ROM drives contain functions such as data separation, error correction, and simple data buffering, a data connection still must exist between the CD-ROM drive and its host computer. The dialogue concerning commands and status between the CD-ROM drive and the computer is accomplished through a *controller.* The controller consists of an adapter card, device driver software (both are installed in the host computer), and a cable that connects the CD-ROM drive with the adapter. The bus signals of the computer are converted through the adapter to a series of signals understood by the CD-ROM drive. The cable acts as an electrical link between the computer and the CD-ROM drive, and the signals exchanged between the CD-ROM drive controller and the host computer are sent through a device interface. There are many device interfaces, such as IEEE 488, SCSI, Sony bus, and Hitachi bus. (It must be noted here that SCSI is becoming more common.)

Coin-Operated Systems

Providing a free CD-ROM service is a privilege that depends on the financial capabilities of each library. To overcome initial capital cost, paper cost, and continuous printing maintenance costs, library administrators may consider coin-operated machines hooked to CD-ROM workstations. Libraries can pass the cost of printing paper to the user by charging for keyboard time and/or pages printed.

A library may consider a VendaCard Debt Access System, which can be harnessed to printers and/or computers and accepts VendaCards encoded with value. If the library has this system already installed on its copying machines, it is wise to ask the same dealer to install the VendaCard system on CD-ROM workstations so users can use the same VendaCards on both the CD-ROM system and the copying machines. If the library decides to install VendaCard systems, it should also have a VendaCoder, which issues the encoded VendaCards. Because of the problems involved with the control interface, the library needs to make sure that the dealer is experienced enough to install VendaCard systems on CD-ROM workstations. VendaCard and coin-operated machines are sold by XCP Company of New York.

MS-DOS Extensions

While the High Sierra specifications describe a standard way of utilizing a CD-ROM, MS-DOS Extensions (Microsoft Disk Operating System Extensions) tell the computer disk operating system (MS-DOS) how to access the CD-ROM drive. MSCDEX, usually a free software available with every new CD-ROM drive, allows software applications to communicate with the drive. The MSCDEX, along with the controller card and the connection cable, form the link between the computer and the CD-ROM drive.[1]

A product of Microsoft Corporation, MSCDEX eliminates the need for each software application to be accompanied by special software to communicate with each type of CD-ROM drive.

Before MSCDEX, every publisher had to develop software for a specific CD-ROM product to access a specific CD-ROM drive. MSCDEX makes it easy for MS-DOS to consider the CD-ROM drive as a mass storage device, such as a sizable hard disk in a network. Because networking is supported by MS-DOS version 3.1, MSCDEX will not run under versions less than 3.1, as these versions do not support networking.

Using MSCDEX with High Sierra–compatible CD-ROM allows the use of MS-DOS commands to display the directory of the CD-ROM disc by typing DIR D: or copy files from the disc to a floppy or a hard disk [COPY D: filename C:], or display files from the disc on the screen [TYPE D: filename],· or [MORE < D: filename], where D: is the letter assigned to the CD-ROM drive. (Many files on the CD-ROM disc are in ASCII format.)

If the CD-ROM product is compatible with the High Sierra specifications, it will be easy to copy files, then edit them using a word processor. However, CD-ROM drives will not respond to Norton Utilities or MS-DOS utilities such as CHKDSK or FORMAT. Also, MSCDEX will not work with DOS 4.0 or OS/2 until these operating systems support CD-ROM drives. Until there is a real solution to the compatibility problem among systems and products, the user has to install the MSCDEX and set up the CD-ROM products on the computer. It is, of

1. For a good article on MSCDEX see Alan L. Zeichick, "Extending MS-DOS," *CD-ROM Review* 3(2): 42–44 (Mar./Apr. 1988).

course, beneficial to understand the relationship between the MSCDEX and the CONFIG.SYS file. The system configuration file CONFIG.SYS contains commands that are used by the disk operating system (DOS). Each time the system starts, DOS searches the root directory (the directory of the drive it was started from) for a file named CONFIG.SYS. If this file is not found, DOS assigns default values provided by the computer manufacturer. For example, the computer assigns the floppy disk drives letters A and B, and the hard disk drive is assigned letter C. The user can make the computer recognize the CD-ROM drive as D through the CONFIG.SYS file, which is explained here and in the next chapter.

CD-ROM Extensions comprise two components: MSCDEX.EXE file and another file, a device driver that will work with a specific CD-ROM drive. For example, the device driver HITACHI.SYS will work with a Hitachi drive, and a PHILIPS.SYS will access only a Philips drive. Such device drivers have to be placed by the user in the CONFIG.SYS file, which is placed in the root directory.[2] The CONFIG.SYS file, in conjunction with another file named AUTOEXEC.BAT, recognizes the presence of the CD-ROM drive. The format for the CONFIG.SYS file should include entries for the device driver as follows:

DEVICE = <driver.sys> /D:<device name> /N:<number> /P:<address>

The device driver (driver.sys) will be replaced by a full path name (a path name is composed of a drive letter (**A:, B:, C:,** . . . etc.), a directory or a subdirectory if applicable, and a file name of the device driver that is being installed on the system. HITACHI.SYS and PHILIPS.SYS are just names of device drivers provided in MSCDEX. The entry will read:

DEVICE =\C: HITACHI.SYS /D:CDROM1 /N:1

The C:\HITACHI.SYS is the path name that activates the device driver written for the Hitachi drive.

The switch /D:CDROM1 assigns the device a unique name, in this case, CDROM1. MSCDEX.EXE will use this name later in the AUTOEXEC.BAT to find this device driver. It is imperative to choose a

---

2. There are two boot files that any IBM microcomputer system searches for when it starts: first the CONFIG.SYS and then the AUTOEXEC.BAT file. The CONFIG.SYS file is used for configuring and altering the functions and features of DOS. The AUTOEXEC.BAT file can be used to set the prompt, the path, and other parameters, or it can be used to start an application. Both files must be in the root directory to be properly loaded by DOS. When booted, the system searches for a CONFIG.SYS file. If the file is not present in the root directory, the system searches for an AUTOEXEC.BAT file. Both files are written in ASCII code that contains command lines used by DOS to tailor the system.

device name that will not likely be chosen as a filename later.[3] The SETUP program included in the MSCDEX software usually assigns names to the device drivers it uses, such as MSCD000.

The /N: <number> refers to the number of the CD-ROM drives that are connected to the controller card in the host computer.

The device driver in this example, HITACHI.SYS, will control one CD-ROM drive. A device driver can support up to four CD-ROM drives connected to every controller card. The /P: parameter specifies the address of the controller card.[4] If there is more than one controller card, each should be specified by a different address. If the parameter is omitted, the default value is 300h. Addresses can take values such as: 200h, 220h, 240h, 260h, 300h, 320h, 340h, and 360h, where h means that the number is in hexadecimal notation.

On a hard-disk system that boots off drive C:—but where the HITACHI.SYS file is stored in a subdirectory named <DEV> and connects to six CD-ROM drives—the entry in the CONFIG.SYS will be:

```
DEVICE=\DEV\HITACHI.SYS /D:MSCD001 /N:4
DEVICE=\DEV\HITACHI.SYS /D:MSCD002 /N:2 /P:200
```

(MSCD001 and MSCD002 are device names.)

Device drivers support door lock/unlock, eject, audio, and controller cards.

Some switches are used by the AUTOEXEC.BAT such as:

/E to tell MSCDEX.EXE that the computer is using an expanded memory

/M to tell MSCDEX.EXE how much memory buffer to allocate for caching information on the CD-ROM.

Caching is the process of allocating blocks in the memory. This way ensures faster working area. The default value is 10, which is designated to reserve 10 blocks for sector caching for a single drive. It is recommended to use higher values for better performance, though there is less room on the CD-ROM for other applications. An AUTOEXEC.BAT may include the following:

```
C:\MSCDEX.EXE /D:MSCD001 /D:MSCD002 /M:20
```

---

3. Every installed device driver must have a unique name. Due to the way that MS-DOS handles file openings, if there is a device driver with the same name as a file in the directory, then a file-open call using that name will open the current device driver and not the file.

4. The *address* is a label, number, or name that designates a particular location in the computer memory, or any other data destination or source that allows the computer to find the location of a specific data item or instruction.

When the MSCDEX program is run, it searches for the device driver that was previously loaded in the CONFIG.SYS file under the name MSCD001. Once found, MSCDEX finds the device's MS-DOS handle and header address, assigns it a drive letter (D:), allocates twenty memory buffers, then tells MS-DOS that drive D: is a network drive and terminates.

The basic CONFIG.SYS file for a Hitachi drive includes the following statements:

```
FILES = 20
BUFFERS = 20
LASTDRIVE = Z
DEVICE = \DEV\HITACHI.SYS /D:MSCD000 /N:1
```

FILES specifies how many files can be opened at any time.

BUFFERS specifies how many disk buffers should be set up by MS-DOS. Buffers hold temporary blocks of data from the disk drives and may increase the speed of access to data on a disc. Any number of buffers can be specified, although it is usually not practical to exceed 20 buffers.

LASTDRIVE specifies the maximum number of drives that can be accessed.

DEVICE specifies other devices besides the standard keyboard, screen, and printer, such as a CD-ROM drive.

DEV is the subdirectory where the file HITACHI.SYS is located.

D:MSCD000 is the name assigned to the CD-ROM drive when MSCDEX was installed.

Daisy-Chaining

Daisy-chaining refers to the capability of multiple CD-ROM drives to be linked to a single workstation through a multiple controller interface installation or daisy-chain installation. A controller interface is able to support up to four CD-ROM drives from one port. However, each CD-ROM drive should be equipped with two ports (interface connectors), one for the ingoing cable, and one for the outgoing cable (Figure 6.5).

In order for a daisy-chain to function, all CD-ROM discs loaded in all CD-ROM drives should belong to the same database set. Mixing databases, such as *ERIC* and *Medline*, is not allowed. Also, the concept of daisy-chaining should be incorporated in the search and retrieval software. Some CD-ROM publishers, such as OCLC and SilverPlatter, are currently using software that has this capability. MacSPIRS, SilverPlatter's software, for instance, has the ability to function in a

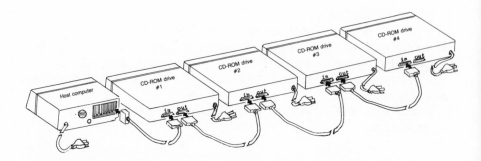

Figure 6.5   Daisy-chaining.

daisy-chained system with as many as six CD-ROM drives. Before acquiring any daisy-chained hardware, it is advisable to determine the required number of drives as well as drive type and model that support the daisy-chain installation. The number of controller interfaces should be determined depending on the number of open expansion slots in the microcomputer. Also, Microsoft MSCDEX should be determined for the type of drives used in the multiple-drive CD-ROM workstation. The CD-ROM vendor should be contacted to find out if the product supports daisy-chain configuration.

Multiaccess Systems and Local Area Networks

As CD-ROM applications grow in size and number, they become more network-intensive. Providing multiple copies of the same database for every CD-ROM workstation is by no means cost-effective. This might result in the reconfiguration of the present single-user workstation to a node (terminal) in a local area network (LAN).

A CD-ROM LAN allows multiusers to access multi-databases simultaneously. It allows users to work independently, thus reducing the reference staff overhead. It also provides more security for the databases.

CD-ROM LANs are becoming a new frontier of innovation in the field of optical technology. Because they are complex, CD-ROM LANs require technical expertise. However, there are some drawbacks. If the LAN goes down, every user suffers. Another drawback is the slow seek time of CD-ROM drives. This affects the data transfer rate and results in the minimization of the overall performance of the LAN. However, the success of a CD-ROM LAN is expected, judging from its acceptance by users and its cost-effectiveness.

LAN Hardware and Software

Basically, a CD-ROM LAN includes the following:

File Server

Usually a powerful microcomputer, 80286- or 80386-based CPU with a large hard disk drive (40+ Mb), is required. Servers usually cost from $6,000 to $10,000. The function of the file server is to permit data storage of the files that LAN users will access. It makes the attached printers, modems, CD-ROM drives, and other sources available to the workstations. The server's processor speed and cache memory compensate for the slowness of CD-ROM drivers. Servers are sold by companies such as CBIS, Meridian, Novell, 3Com, and Univation. Attached to the file server are the following:

Large-capacity memory board (10+ Mb RAM)
Printer adaptor
Monochrome or color monitor
LAN driver, which directs the operation of the file server
LAN software, which controls the flow of traffic on the LAN (such as Novell or MS-Net)
Disc operating system
Network printer with a print-sharing device
Uninterrupted power supply

LAN Interface Cards

Interface cards allow the stream of communications. They cost about $230 each. They are installed in each file server and workstation.

Cables

The network interface cards usually determine the type of cabling to connect the file server and workstations. There are different types of cables, including: twisted-pair telephone wire, shielded twisted-pair data-grade wire, coaxial cable, and fiber-optic cable. The selected type of wire ought to match the installed wire in the building.

Workstations

Each workstation will be composed of an 80286- or 80386-based CPU with 640K RAM, one floppy-disk drive, a hard-disk drive (20+ Mb), a LAN interface card that connects the workstation to the LAN via a cable, and MS-DOS Extensions. The number of workstations depends on the capacity of the LAN.

CD-ROM Drives

The number of CD-ROM drives depends on the capacity of the LAN.

Communication Server

If remote sites are to be served through the LAN, a communication server is required. The server may also be used for online searching. It can be an 80286- or 80386-based CPU with one floppy-disk drive, large capacity memory board, monochrome or color monitor, large hard-disk drive, internal or external modem, and communications software.

Network Topologies

There are different topologies in connection to a LAN. In LAN jargon, topology means the map of the network. The *physical topology* describes how the wires and cables are laid out, and the *logical topology* describes how the messages flow. A CD-ROM LAN can be designed to include many CD-ROM products running on many CD-ROM drives, which can be accessed by several users through remote terminals.

The simplest computer LAN is composed of two computers connected by a wire. If a third computer is connected to the same wire, the result is a *bus topology*, also known as a *straight line topology* (Figure 6.6). Ethernet (a network cable and access protocol scheme originally developed by Xerox, now marketed mainly by Digital Equipment Corp. and 3Com) is one of the popular LANs that uses a bus topology. The problem with Ethernet is that the bus becomes saturated when many computers are trying to access a specific CD-ROM drive at the same time. However, Ethernet allows the user to add or disconnect any microcomputer very easily at any time.

The *star topology* is another system configuration in which each computer is connected to a central hub. A hub is a central point in the star topology into which cabling for the workstations and file servers is connected. It directs data between the various components of the network. AT&T's Starlan is a popular computer area network that uses a star topology. The advantage of the star topology is that services, troubleshooting, and wiring changes all take place at the hub. The disadvantage of the star topology is that if the hub goes down, so does the network.

Another topology is the *ring topology*, where each computer is connected in a series to form a closed loop. IBM Token Ring is a popular LAN. In the star-wired ring topology, star subnetworks are formed, then the hubs are connected to each other. The disadvantage of the ring

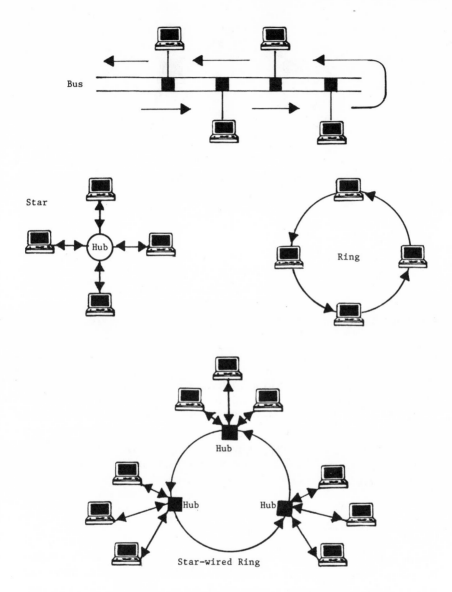

Figure 6.6 Network topologies. Arrows represent the flow of messages.

topology is that a break in the ring, either through the cable or any other device, brings down the entire network.

Several LANs can be linked together via bridges using more CD-ROM servers forming a wide area network (WAN). A bridge is a hardware/software combination that enables one LAN to communicate with another LAN. It can be internal or external. It can connect LANs

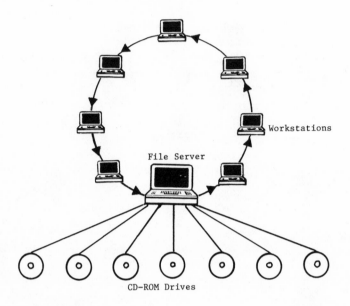

Figure 6.7 A ring CD-ROM LAN.

of different topologies, such as an Ethernet LAN and a Token LAN.
Figure 6.7 illustrates a ring CD-ROM LAN. Basic components of each PC-compatible workstation include a LAN card, driver software, and MS-DOS Extensions. The file server includes LAN cards, LAN software, driver software, and MS-DOS Extensions. In an integrated system, workstations can access CD-ROM drives using a mainframe or a minicomputer through a PC-compatible equipped with LAN cards and MS-DOS Extensions. In this configuration, communications software is needed to connect remote sites into the network.

LAN Vendors

Among CD-ROM LAN vendors are Meridian Data, Inc., Online Computer Systems, Compact Cambridge, Artisoft Inc., and Micromedex.

Meridian produces CD Net, a stand-alone CD-ROM read-only network server that supports up to 75 workstations (microcomputers). The system provides its own software and hardware. It runs under Novell network software and MS NET software using ARCnet (Attached Resources Computing, a network architecture marketed by Datapoint and other vendors), Ethernet, or Token Ring network interface cards. CD Net is compatible with ISO/9660 format. It accepts multiple copies of the same database to increase the overall performance. The system uses caching software to temporarily transfer information from the

CD-ROM disc into the computer RAM cache to ensure high access speed. Up to seven CD Nets can be daisy-chained together, offering a total of 21 CD-ROM drives to network users. The cost for CD Net is $2,995 for a base system with one CD-ROM drive. (Another product from Meridian is the CD Server, which integrates all the features of CD Net with increased RAM and expanding hard disk up to 2.4 gigabytes.)

Artisoft developed LANtastic, a low-priced LAN system that supports CD-ROM drives. According to the manufacturer, LANtastic seems to work with almost any number of CD-ROM drives from different manufacturers and any number of workstations. The full-function system requires 12K of RAM per workstation and about 40K of RAM for the server. MSCDEX is required only on the nodes that are connected to CD-ROM drives. A $399 LANtastic starter kit comes with two adapter cards, a LAN-adapter user manual, a two-user version of the LANtastic NOS (network operating system) software, one 15-foot cable, and terminators. An additional LANtastic adapter with 15-foot cable costs $199; a LANtastic NOS license costs $295. The software fits on one 360K disk and comes with a 112-page manual. The system transmits data at the rate of 2 megabits per second and will support total network cable length of over 1,500 feet. Installation of the LAN is easy, and it is well explained in the LAN adapter user manual. The adapter is a half-size card with an on-board 10-MHz (megahertz) coprocessor, 32K of buffer RAM, and a 2-megabit-per-second link to other adapters. To reduce the size of the required computer RAM, LANtastic stores a significant portion of the network software on the interface card. The software allows for either menu-driven or command-line access. The set-up process can be accomplished through a menu that allows the information manager to make CD-ROM drives available to the whole network. The system also can be used for electronic mail to send messages to the CD-ROM users. Sharing printers is supported by LANtastic.

SilverPlatter uses CD Net with IBM PCs, Novell LAN software, and MultiPlatter software to form its MultiPlatter system. With MultiPlatter, each computer can access any of the CD-ROM discs in the network, and multiple users can perform searches on the same CD-ROM disc. MultiPlatter includes up to 21 CD-ROM disc drives with network interface cards, MS-DOS Extensions, and two network servers. It supports up to ten microcomputers; however, the response time will increase as more users access the same CD-ROM disc. Other CD-ROM products can run on MultiPlatter provided they conform with ISO/9660 standards and support MS-DOS Extensions. It should be noted that SilverPlatter does not provide support for non-SilverPlatter products.

Online Computer Systems produces OPTI-NET, which supports both CD-ROM and WORM systems. It provides caching and uses

(Courtesy of Compact Cambridge, Bethesda, Md.)

Figure 6.8 The MultiDisc eliminates changing of discs of a multivolume database.

IBM/PC and Ethernet networks, and 3Com or Novell software. The PC network supports up to 32 users simultaneously, and through the Ethernet system it supports up to 128 users.

Compact Cambridge produces MultiDisc, a CD-ROM multidrive that can be used with multivolume databases, such as *Medline* (Figure 6.8).

On a network, mounting CD-ROM databases in a minicomputer or a mainframe environment and accessing the databases through computer terminals have been explored by Micromedex, Inc. Micromedex is marketing a multiaccess CD-ROM system. In this system, a particular software application runs on a host computer, which in turn serves multiple users. Included in the turnkey system are Micromedex's CD-ROM file system administrator, Quantum Software's QNX operating system, a SCSI host adapter, a Philips 110/210 or Toshiba XM 2100/3100 drive, a four- or eight-serial-port card, and a Compaq Deskpro PC.

The cost of a LAN is high. For instance, a MultiPlatter system that supports five CD-ROM drives costs $17,440 using Ethernet Network Interface cards, and $20,640 using Token Ring Network hardware. These prices do not include either cables or interface cards. Prices for

Table 6.1 Comparison of Charges

Database	Single user	Multiuser
CANCER-CD	$1,750	$2,500
PsycLIT	$3,995	$5,995
Sociofile	$1,950	$2,995
Petersons College Guide	$595	$995

systems that support 21 CD-ROM drives are $47,335 for Ethernet systems, and $52,935 for Token Ring systems (prices are quoted from the MultiPlatter Winter 1989 price list).

Price policies of CD-ROM publishers differ from one publisher to another. Some publishers impose higher prices if their products are to be used in a LAN configuration. For example, Microsoft charges $65 per node to run Bookshelf in a LAN. Wilson Company does not issue license agreements for the use of its CD-ROM databases on LANs, while SilverPlatter issues a network site license and charges more to run some of its CD-ROM databases in a LAN configuration. SilverPlatter charges are shown in Table 6.1.

CD-ROM LAN Vendors and Developers

Artisoft Inc.
3550 N. First Ave., No. 330
Tucson, AZ 85719
(602) 293-6363

Compact Cambridge
7200 Wisconsin Ave.
Bethesda, MD 20814
(800) 227-3052
(301) 951-6757

Meridian Data Inc.
4450 Capitola Rd., Suite 101
Capitola, CA 95010
(408) 476-5858

Micromedex Inc.
6600 Bannock St., Suite 300
Denver, CO 80204-4506
(800) 525-9083
(303) 623-8600

Online Computer Systems
20251 Century Blvd.
Germantown, MD 20874
(800) 922-9204

SilverPlatter
37 Walnut St.
Wellesley Hills, MA 02181
(800) 343-0064
(617) 239-3036

Jukeboxes

Jukeboxes are massive storage devices that are capable of holding hundreds of compact discs and accessing any disc by means of mechanical arms. A jukebox includes a computer to direct the traffic of discs between the storing shelves and CD-ROM drives.

Jukeboxes are not yet available on the market. However, some are under development. Voyager, a prototype jukebox developed by Next

Technology Corp. (St. Johns Innovation Centre, Cambridge, CB4 4WS, England), has the capability of holding 270 CD-ROM discs. Voyager is being tested at the British Library as part of the ADONIS Project, which provides information from more than 200 biomedical journals.[5] In the United States, Voyager is being tested at Disclosure Inc. and UMI. Jukeboxes can be connected to local area networks.

References

For more information on LANs consult the following publications:

PC Magazine, June 14, 1988, p.92+, and Mar. 28, 1989, p.94–131.
BYTE, July 1987, p.145+.
Rowland Archer, *The Practical Guide to Local Area Networks* (Berkeley, Calif.: Osborne/McGraw-Hill, 1986).
"Building Workgroup Solutions: Low LAN's," *PC Magazine*, Mar. 28, 1989, p.94–131.
"Bus, Star, Ring Topologies Increase Network Options," *Info World*, Jan. 9, 1989, p.12.
Frank J. Derfler, "Networking Acronyms and Buzz Words," *PC Magazine*, June 14, 1988, p.102–6.
Dick Lefkon, "A LAN Primer," *BYTE*, July 1987, p.147–54.
Michael Goodwin, "LAN Servers for Less," *PC World*, June 1988, p.126–33.
Linda Helgerson, "For CD-ROM in a LAN, Artisoft's LANtastic Is the Answer for Now," *CD Data Report* 5: 1–5 (Nov. 1988).
Linda Helgerson, "Two-Disc Databases, Multiple CD-ROM Drives & LANs— What's Up," *CD Data Report* 4: 1–10 (July 1988).
Lou Hoffman, "Networked: CD-ROM Drives: A Natural for the Library Environment," *CD Publisher News*, July 1988, p.1–4.
Christine Strehlo, "The Promised LAN," *Personal Computing*, Jan. 1989, p.93–98.
David C. Traub, "The CD-ROM Markets Emerge: Microsoft's 3rd Annual CD-ROM Conference," *Optical Information Systems*, Sept./Oct. 1988, p.242–45.

5. Barrie T. Stern and Robert M. Campbell, "ADONIS: Delivering Journal Articles on CD-ROM, Part I," *CD-ROM Librarian* 4(2): 9–13 (Feb. 1989). Part II was published in same journal 4(3): 15–22 (Mar. 1989). See also Nancy Melin Nelson, "On the Cutting Edge: Next Technology's CD-ROM Jukebox," *CD-ROM Librarian* 4(9): 22–24 (Oct. 1989).

7 Automating the CD-ROM Workstation

Batch Files

Automating a CD-ROM workstation means turning it into a menu-driven workstation where databases can be accessed through a menu. On a workstation that has many databases installed, it is easy to select a specific database from a menu by just typing the number or the letter assigned to the database. The menu will eliminate the need to memorize names of subdirectories and structure or syntax of commands required to operate different databases. It will also eliminate listing them in manuals or fact sheets. This can be done easily using the power inherent in very short files known as batch files or just "bat files." These files, which have the extension ".BAT" in their names, contain DOS commands and are understood only by IBM-Disk Operating System (DOS) or MS-DOS. These commands are usually executed one by one in the order they are listed in the file, hence, each file will contain a sequence of commands that will lead to the loading of a CD-ROM application software and eventually its execution. When saving a batch file, assign a filename with the extension .BAT, such as 1.BAT, where 1 is the filename and .BAT is the filename extension.

Batch files can be created or edited by many available word processors that have the capability to save files in ASCII format (known also as DOS format). Files saved in this format can be displayed or printed in plain English using DOS commands such as:

C>TYPE filename
C>MORE < filename

The other way to create batch files is to use DOS itself if a word processor is not available. The DOS command "COPY CON" will be used here to create two text files: MENU.TXT and CONFIG.SYS, in addition to the batch files that will be used to program the menu. No software is used, as the command "COPY CON" instructs the computer to accept text directly from the keyboard console. No knowledge of programming is required, since no higher programming language of any sort is used.

(For librarians who know how to apply simple DOS commands, this section will look familiar. All the commands mentioned in this section are DOS commands. They can be found in the DOS manual that accompanies the PC.)

Files created by COPY CON are saved on the disk by pressing the "F6" key (or Ctrl-Z) and the "Return" key <Ret> at the end of the text. DOS does not allow text editing once the "Return" key is pressed at the end of a command or a line. Editing, however, is done after saving the file, through another DOS feature known as "EDLIN." The line-editing DOS file, EDLIN.COM, should exist on the system. Reference is made to DOS or MS-DOS user's guide on how to use this command and the function keys associated with it. The user will not need the advanced features of EDLIN since the files are simple and very short. The most editing features and function keys that might be used are shown in Figure 7.1.

(On IBM PCs and compatibles, when you type in a command and press the "Return" key, a copy of the command is sent to a temporary storage location called the *template*. When you press F3, this template is copied in full to the command line, but the command is not executed until you press the "Return" key.)

In the following example we assume we have an IBM or a PC/clone with 20-megabyte hard disk, one floppy-disk drive, color monitor, and a Hitachi CD-ROM drive. The MSCDEX has been installed and the workstation has been declared nondedicated, which means that when the user terminates a search session, the DOS prompt should be displayed. This is in contrast to a dedicated workstation, where the user

Key	Example	Function
L	L <Ret>	Lists the text
D	3D <Ret>	Deletes line number 3
I	4I <Ret>	Inserts lines after line number 3
Q	Q <Ret>	Quits editing without changing the text
E	E <Ret>	Ends editing and saves the text on disk
F1		Copies one character at a time from the template.
F3		Copies the entire template to the screen.
ESC		Lets you start typing the command all over because it leaves the template unchanged.
INS		Insert key will open a gap in the template and accept text in the gap by moving existing characters to the right.
DEL		Delete key deletes characters to the right.

Figure 7.1. EDLIN keys and functions.

Table 7.1 Names of Subdirectories and Files to Be Changed.

Product	Subdirectory	Files to Change
SILVERPLATTER	SPIRS	——
UMI	UMI	SEARCH.BAT
Wilsondisc	WILSONPC	WDISC.BAT
DIALOG	DLINK	——

has to reboot the system to display the DOS prompt. It should be noted that most products have different set-up procedures, and the user has the choice between declaring the database as dedicated or nondedicated during the set-up of the database on the workstation. We also assume that the CD-ROM databases are running on the system, but the user has to type in the commands at the DOS prompt every time a new database is to be used. We assume that the following databases have been installed on the workstation:

SilverPlatter: *ERIC, PsycLIT,* and *Sociofile*
UMI: *Dissertation Abstracts, ABI/Inform,* and *Newspaper Abstracts*
Wilsondisc: *Art Index*
Dialog: *Medline*

These are diverse products from different producers. Our main objective is to make them run in harmony by using a main menu. At the time of installation, each of these products usually creates its own subdirectory on the hard disk, then copies the programs from the software floppy disk onto the subdirectory. Some of the files that are created during the set-up process might need minimum changes in order to display the menu at the end of each search session. Table 7.1 presents the subdirectories created by these products and the files that need modification.

Creating the Main Menu

Let us proceed first to create the main menu, which will be saved in a file named MENU.TXT. Do not forget to press "Return" or "Enter" after each line, statement, or command in order for the DOS processor to accept it. At the DOS prompt [C>] type:

C>COPY CON:MENU.TXT

[Press F6 then Return to save MENU.TXT]

At the DOS prompt, if you type:

C>TYPE MENU.TXT <Ret>

the menu will be displayed on the screen (Figure 7.2). However, we can make this process easier by creating the following batch file.

LIBRARY NAME

CD-ROM WORKSTATION

1 SilverPlatter : ERIC, Psyclit, Sociofile

2 UMI : Dissertation Abs., ABI, Newspaper Abs.

3 Wilsondisc : Art Index

4 Dialog : Medline

Select a number, then press ENTER or RETURN

Figure 7.2. Main menu.

Creating MENU.BAT

```
C>COPY CON:MENU.BAT
ECHO OFF
CLS
TYPE MENU.TXT
```

[Press F6 then Return to save MENU.BAT file]

This file will clear the screen then display the menu when you just type "MENU" at the prompt:

C>MENU<Ret>

The command "ECHO OFF" will inhibit the display of batch commands throughout the rest of the file. "CLS" will clear the screen, and "TYPE MENU.TXT" will display the main menu.

Creating the CONFIG.SYS File

```
C>COPY CON:CONFIG.SYS
FILES = 20
BUFFERS = 20
LASTDRIVE = Z
DEVICE = \DEV\HITACHI.SYS /D:MSCD000 /N:1
DEVICE = ANSI.SYS
```

[Press F6 then Return to save CONFIG.SYS file]

If this file already exists on the disk, you can use EDLIN to alter the existing version.

The commands in the CONFIG.SYS file have been discussed in Chapter 6. We should note here that you may add as many DEVICE lines as you want. In our example we added DEVICE = ANSI.SYS, where ANSI.SYS is a device driver that is included with MS-DOS and can be used to replace the standard keyboard and screen drivers. Check the directory to see if ANSI.SYS is one of the DOS files. Using this driver will allow you to control the screen by setting its background and foreground colors when booting the system. The command for color will be included in the following batch file, the AUTOEXEC.BAT. In case of mono display, this command should not be used in the CONFIG.SYS file.

Creating the AUTOEXEC.BAT File

The AUTOEXEC.BAT file is an important file. Every time the system is booted, and once the CONFIG.SYS file is executed, the computer usually searches for another file called AUTOEXEC.BAT. This file will be used to change the color of the screen and then display the menu.

```
C>COPY CON:AUTOEXEC.BAT
PATH = C:\BIN
PROMPT $e[40;35m
ECHO OFF
CLS
MENU
```

[Press F6 then Return to save AUTOEXEC.BAT file]

The command "PATH = C:\BIN" instructs the operating system (DOS) to execute files in the BIN subdirectory. On many systems when you copy MS-DOS files to the hard disk, DOS creates a subdirectory named "BIN"; this is where all DOS files are stored. If you have saved MS-DOS files under any other name, include the name here.

"PROMPT $e[40;35m" will change the color of the screen to black background and magenta foreground. Table 7.2 is a list of colors used by the device driver ANSI.SYS, which was included in the CONFIG.SYS file. You may select any other color combination that is easy on the eyes. The format for this command is

PROMPT $e[#;#;#m

where the first number is the background and the second number is the foreground. If the computer can handle high-intensity display, the

Table 7.2 A Partial List of Color Rendition Codes

Code	Explanation
1	High intensity (boldface) on
30	Foreground black
31	Foreground red
32	Foreground green
33	Foreground yellow
34	Foreground blue
35	Foreground magenta
37	Foreground white
40	Background black
41	Background red
42	Background green
43	Background yellow
44	Background blue
45	Background magenta
46	Background cyan
47	Background white

WARNING: Do not select two codes of the same color. Now reboot the system for testing by pressing "Ctrl-Alt-Del" keys simultaneously. The menu will be displayed on the screen with black background and magenta foreground.

command will be: "PROMPT $e[40;35;1m." In case of mono display, this command should not be used in the AUTOEXEC.BAT file.

"MENU" is a call to invoke the MENU.BAT file, which in turn displays the menu on the screen.

Creating Other Batch Files

1.BAT

To activate SilverPlatter databases we create a batch file with the name: 1.BAT.

```
C>COPY CON:1.BAT
ECHO OFF
CLS
\BIN\MSCDEX.EXE /D:MSCD000 /M:8
CD\SPIRS
SPIRS MSCD000
CD\
MENU
```

[Press F6 then Return to save 1.BAT file]

This file will activate SilverPlatter databases when you type *1* then press "RETURN."

\BIN\MSCDEX.EXE /D:MSCD000 /M:8 allows MSCDEX.EXE to recognize the CD-ROM drive.

CD\SPIRS changes the directory to SPIRS subdirectory where the SilverPlatter files are stored on the hard disk.

SPIRS MSCD000 activates a file called SPIRS.EXE to access the CD-ROM disc drive by using the device driver MSCD000.

CD\ changes the current subdirectory (SPIRS) back to the root directory, C, when the search session is over.

MENU command activates the MENU.BAT file, which in turn clears the screen then displays the main menu for the next user.

Load the CD-ROM drive with any SilverPlatter disc. At the C> prompt, type *1*, then press "RETURN":

C>1 <Ret>

The computer should start accessing the CD-ROM drive searching for any SilverPlatter database. After using the SilverPlatter database, if you quit normally by pressing the correct key sequence (Esc-Q), the main menu should be displayed again.

Proceed to automate the command for the UMI databases.

2.BAT

```
C>COPY CON:2.BAT
ECHO OFF
CLS
\BIN\MSCDEX.EXE /D:MSCD000 /M:8
CD\UMI
SEARCH MSCD000
```

[Press F6 then Return to save 2.BAT file]

This file activates UMI databases when you type *2* then press "RETURN."

CD\UMI changes the current directory to the UMI subdirectory, which the UMI software created at the time of installation. By the way, UMI files are stored on the hard disk on that subdirectory.

SEARCH MSCD000 starts the SEARCH.BAT file, which in turn calls another UMI file, RESEARCH.EXE, to access the CD-ROM drive.

The SEARCH.BAT is a file created by UMI software at the time of installation. If we use 2.BAT as is, it will initiate UMI databases. However, at the end of the search session, it will not display the main menu unless we modify the file "SEARCH.BAT" of the UMI. This file is located in the UMI subdirectory. Change directory:

C>CD\UMI <Ret>

Use EDLIN or a word processor to modify SEARCH.BAT by adding:

CD\
MENU

right after the following line:

C:\UMI\RESEARCH -C C:\UMI\DBCTRL.DAT -D D: -B 50

This ensures that the SEARCH.BAT file will change the subdirectory back to the root directory and display the menu for the next user. Enter the following command:

C>EDLIN SEARCH.BAT
End of input file
*_

At the EDLIN prompt * type L <Ret> to list the text, then find the exact location to insert the two new commands. If the line (C:\UMI \RESEARCH -C C:\UMI\DBCTRL.DAT -D D: -B 50) is number 9, for instance, type:

*10I <Ret>
10:*CD\
11:*MENU
12:*_   [Press Ctrl-Break to end the Insert mode]
*_   [type L <Ret> to display modified text]

If the text is correct, type *E*, then press "RETURN" to save the file. The SEARCH.BAT file will look something like the following:

```
ECHO OFF
:CHKFILES
CLS
IF NOT EXIST C:\UMI\RESEARCH.EXE GOTO RESEARCH
IF NOT EXIST C:\UMI\DBCTRL.DAT GOTO CTRL
ECHO ^@
ECHO ^@
ECHO        LOADING RESEARCH, PLEASE WAIT...
C:\UMI\RESEARCH -C C:\UMI\DBCTRL.DAT -D D: -B 50
CD\
MENU
GOTO END
"              {MORE COMMANDS}
"
"
"
:END
```

Now type MENU at the DOS prompt:

C>MENU <Ret>

The menu should be displayed. You may now access UMI databases by selecting *2* from the main menu, then press "RETURN." If you exit UMI normally, the main menu should be displayed again. Proceed to automate the command for the Wilsondisc databases.

3.BAT

```
C>COPY CON:3.BAT
ECHO OFF
CLS
\BIN\MSCDEX.EXE /D:MSCD000 /M:8
CD\WILSONPC
WDISC MSCD000
```

[Press F6 then Return to save 3.BAT file]

This file will activate Wilsondisc databases when you type *3* then press "RETURN."

CD\WILSONPC changes the directory to the WILSONPC subdirectory.

WDISC initiates the Wilsondisc WDISC.BAT file, which in turn activates another file, WDISC.EXE, to access the CD-ROM drive.

As is, the file 3.BAT will not display the menu at the end of the search session. This is done through WDISC.BAT, which is located in the WILSONPC subdirectory. Change the root directory to WILSONPC subdirectory

C>CD\WILSONPC <Ret>

then use EDLIN to modify WDISC.BAT by adding the following commands at the end of the file:

```
CD\
MENU
```

The WDISC.BAT file will look as follows:

```
ECHO OFF
WILSON %1 %2 %3 %4 %5
CD\
MENU
```

At the DOS prompt if you type MENU:

C>MENU <Ret>

the main menu should be displayed. Now you may access Wilsondisc databases by selecting *3* from the main menu, then press "RETURN."

If you exit Wilsondisc normally, the main menu should be displayed again. Now proceed to automate the command for Dialog databases.

4.BAT

```
C>COPY CON:4.BAT
ECHO OFF
CLS
\BIN\MSCDEX.EXE /D:MSCD000 /M:8
CD\DLINK
CLS
ONDISC
CD\
MENU
```

[Press F6 then Return to save 4.BAT file]

This file will activate the Dialog *Medline* database when you type *4* then press "RETURN."

Now all products have been automated and the menu should be ready, provided that you have tested each product after creating its batch file. The logic of the menu is obvious, and the reader can proceed to include different databases or modify the batch files in order to use them with other CD-ROM drives and device drivers. Also, when a publisher upgrades the software, there is a possibility that the accompanying batch files might have been altered. The user has to be aware of any changes to include them in the appropriate batch file.

Security

In libraries, CD-ROM workstations are usually placed in public reference areas where they are vulnerable to theft, vandalism, and misuse. Although librarians have voiced concern over security of the workstation equipment, vendors have done little in this area.

Anyone can wipe out all the information on the hard disk by issuing commands such as "FORMAT," "PART," or "PREP." Or, deleting the COMMAND.COM file will cripple the workstation. Altering filenames or erasing subdirectories is very hard to track, and the situation can require the reinstallation of the software on the workstation. Replacing lost CD-ROM discs is costly. Using an online service without searching the CD-ROM database might go undetected. Placing a CD-ROM disc in the computer disk drive will knock the drive reading mechanism out of place.

Correcting any of these problems can be costly and time-consuming. Point in fact, the totally burglar-proof workstation does not exist. Nevertheless, many libraries have developed procedures and measures to minimize security problems. Some of these might include: closely monitored sign-in procedures and checking of identification cards; staff assistance in operating the workstation (placing the disc in the CD-ROM drive); use of locking mechanisms that cannot be opened without a key; purchase of special cabinets that will hold all of the workstation hardware; bolting or chaining the equipment with security cables. Finally, the library might consider using metal or wood workstations with locking doors.

Libraries are also encouraged to use software utilities to "HIDE" all files and subdirectories and turn all files to READ-ONLY mode. It is advisable not to run any memory-resident programs on the workstation, as this type of program interferes with the performance of MSCDEX (which itself is a memory-resident program).

8 CD-ROM Product Considerations

A high percentage (about 80 percent) of all CD-ROM products are geared to libraries (see Appendixes A and B). These products can be roughly divided into three categories:

1. *Bibliographic references.* Most of the products in this category are versions of databases already in libraries in one form or another, such as paper, microforms, and magnetic media. Many of these products are also available online. This category is mostly indexes, abstracts, and bibliographies.

2. *General references.* This category consists mostly of ready-reference materials, such as dictionaries, encyclopedias, directories, statistical data, biographies, book reviews, and computer applications and public domain software.

3. *Library operations.* There are more than fifty CD-ROM products (see titles in Appendix B under "Libraries") used to support library operations in acquisitions and collection development, cataloging (current and retrospective) and bibliographic control, public access catalogs (PACs), circulation, and interlibrary loan.

Among the factors limiting CD-ROM's use in libraries since its introduction in 1985 are the following:

The expensive hardware and databases.

The instability of the optical market, as new products such as CD-I, DVI, CD-ROM XA, WORM, and erasable discs were or are about to be introduced to the consumer before CD-ROM could establish itself in the market.

The lack of juke-boxes and reasonably priced LANs for CD-ROM, which caused the single-user concept to prevail (one workstation per one user). Furthermore, many products such as BiblioFile are sold with the intent of turning a PC into a dedicated, single-application workstation, thus limiting the use of the microcomputer.

The lack of standards from 1985 to 1988 prevented many developers from entering the market with innovative ideas.

The small amount of information on the disc and the lack of up-to-date information compared to online databases. The

600-megabyte capacity of CD-ROM sounds impressive, until compared with multiple gigabytes in online systems. While online databases are dynamic, CD-ROM products are typically updated quarterly or monthly.[1]

Other important factors include the lack of SCSI penetration, CD-ROM Extensions, standard ports, and software incompatibility.

Criteria for Assessing CD-ROM Products

As the number of CD-ROM products and services increases, product assessment will be greatly needed. No matter what type of information is stored on the disc, be it bibliographic, data, archival, or full text, such information has no value unless it can be easily and quickly accessed, retrieved, and utilized. CD-ROM products can be evaluated according to many criteria, such as:

1. User interface
   a) Software friendliness, ease of use, and overall user impression.
   b) Levels of interface, whether the system includes novice level, expert level, or both.
   c) Context-sensitive help that responds appropriately from any point in the search.
   d) The quality of the help offered.
   e) Use of a search break.
   f) Error handling and clarity of error messages.
   g) Whether the system is menu-driven, command-driven, or both. The use of mice, guided tours and online tutorials, and error handling.

---

1. The impressive capacity of CD-ROM by microcomputer standards is much less impressive when dealing with very large bibliographic or full-text databases. Realizing this problem, scientists are trying to find other innovative technologies to increase the capacity of compact discs to limits far beyond what is available today (600 Mb). In his "Experiments Increase Optical Storage Densities," Norman Desmarais reports that IBM's Almaden Research Center in San Jose, California, and Harvard University's Department of Physics are among those engaged in experiments to write the data on optical discs as color-coded data bits. This will increase the capacity of the optical disc by almost a thousandfold. Reading or writing data will be done by using different lasers with different wavelengths (colors), allowing as many as 10,000 bits to be recorded on one spot compared to the present one bit per spot. See Norman Desmarais, "Experiments Increase Optical Storage Densities," *Optical Information Systems* 8(3): 120–22 (May-June 1988).

2. Searching capabilities
   a) Boolean search: full Boolean, simple Boolean, or both.
   b) Query by example and interactive query-building.
   c) Search by range or value.
   d) Wildcard. (Wildcard characters are characters that substitute for letters or numbers in a search query. For example, a single wildcard such as the asterisk in *wom*n* could retrieve *woman* or *women*. A multiple wildcard at the end of a word, such as *child**, could retrieve *child, childbirth, childhood, childless, children*, etc.)
   e) Different types of text, graphics, and data fields that can be freely mixed within the same database, while each field is either fixed or variable.
   f) Graphics support, i.e., the capability of the system to link images to text, where any image is treated as a field type and can be included in the database along with other types of information.
   g) Proximity searches in full text, mixed text, and data text. Search capability by a combination of words or phrases within the same document, paragraph, record, or field, or within a specified number of words.
   h) Synonym searches performed by the system.
   i) Field search: searching one specified field or more.
   j) Number of hits displayed so the user can immediately edit and re-execute the query if too many or too few hits are generated.
   k) Saving search strategies on hard disk or floppy diskette for re-execution.
   l) Availability and direct selection of terms from a thesaurus or a word list for controlled vocabulary search.

3. Response time
   a) Search time of a single word, complex multiple searches, and truncated words.

4. Output and post processing
   a) The ability to browse within data sets (search results).
   b) Changing of display formats.
   c) Printing complete or partial lists. Printing the most significant fields in the default format. Possible alteration of the default format. Capability of printing selected fields from specific records.
   d) Saving selected data. The user can save all or any portion of the search results to either floppy or hard disk. Are data

compatible with other programs, such as spreadsheets, word processors, or database managers? Can graphics be saved for later use with any paint program?

e) Sorting capability on significant fields.

f) Appending data to files. Data can be saved to a new file or appended to any existing file.

g) Are common printers supported?

h) Is it possible to override the original set-up of the system?

5. Display capabilities
  a) Effective use of colors, graphics, windowing, sound, and warning features.
  b) Clear screens and attractive display.
  c) Special requirements such as EGA (Enhanced Graphics Adapter) and VGA (Video Graphics Array).

6. System requirements and compatibility
  a) Hardware needed and compatibility with the High Sierra and the Microsoft Extensions.

7. Documentation and ease of learning
  a) Availability of well-illustrated installation manuals, user manuals, reference cards, templates, and posters.

8. Technical support
  a) Type and quality of assistance provided by the vendor such as a toll-free number or a local service station.

Criteria for Full-Text Applications

In addition to the criteria for assessing CD-ROM products mentioned above, a full-text application should:

1. Support browsing and full Boolean searches.
2. Use proximity relationships, truncation, stemming, and inverted files.
3. Preserve the intellectual content of the original product such as type fonts, key notes, paragraph numbers, tables of contents, and graphics.
4. Include electronic note pad or word-processing capability and electronic bookmarks to save a place so that the user can refer back to the same article of interest.

Systems with Multiple Path Access

More advanced systems seem to be under development. Such systems have capabilities to permit the user to move from one topic to other related topics with great ease without losing track of his or her path. These systems that have multiple path access to information are Hypertext, Hypermedia, or Hypermultimedia.

Hypertext

Hypertext is a concept that allows the user to link related words, sentences, paragraphs, attributes, or concepts both within and between files or documents. A linking capability that allows the nonsequential, or the nonlinear, access and retrieval of text is an essential feature of any hypertext system. Hypertext also features a windowing system that has a one-to-one correspondence with files in the database. Windows usually use icons or other smaller windows to open files and access texts.[2] This activity of accessing and linking is mapped on the screen in a browser window (Figure 8.1), which is vital since it is easy for a user to become disoriented in a maze of links and opened files. In hypertext, the user can link information about the history of embalming in ancient Egypt in file A, for example, and the architecture of the pyramids in file B.

Users who become interested in the religious beliefs of ancient Egyptians can access, via a command, a third file on religion, and connect the information on embalming and the pyramids with the information on the religious beliefs in ancient Egypt. They can also access a fourth bibliographical file D, and retrieve specific citations on the whole topic. Users might become interested in the topic and try to search a guide file on local museums to find which museum displays mummies and other Egyptian artifacts. In addition, personal notes and comments may be inserted in the text.

Thus, hypertext facilitates online authoring and note taking. The hypertext concept is necessarily based on the way the human brain functions. For CD-ROM users, hypertext will allow hierarchical movements or associations through a large database, where each chunk of information resides anywhere in the database. In our example, "embalming" can be organized under a hierarchy of medical data,

2. For reviews and a thorough outline and survey of hypertext systems, refer to Jeff Conklin, "Hypertext: An Introduction and Survey," *Computer* 20(9): 17–41 (Sept. 1987). See also: Karen E. Smith, "Hypertext Linking to the Future," *Online* (Mar. 1988), p.32–40; and Carl Franklin, "An Annotated Hypertext Bibliography," *Online* (Mar. 1988), p.42–46.

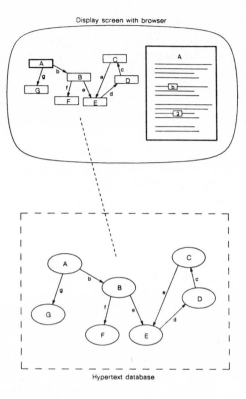

Display screen with browser

Hypertext database

(Reprinted by permission from *Computer* 20(9) Sept. 1987 ©1987 IEEE.)

Figure 8.1 Display screen with browsers linked to a hypertext database. The screen at the top illustrates how the hypertext browser provides a direct two-dimensional graphic view of the underlying database. In this illustration, the node *A* has been selected for full display of its contents. Notice that in the browser view you can tell not only which nodes are linked to *A* but also how the subnetwork fits into the larger hyperdocument. (Of course, hyperdocuments of any size cannot be shown all at once in a browser—only portions can be displayed.)

while the "building of the pyramids" is organized under architecture, religion, or civilization. This link—which connects words, sentences, and concepts, opens gaps into the text, then incorporates other texts—is done electronically in a hypertext environment.

Hypertext is not a new concept; however, the large capacity of optical discs and high-resolution displays are about to move this concept from the labs into the real marketplace. Navigation through a web of materials has been under development for more than two decades. Three of the pioneers in the hypertext concept are Vannevar Bush, who is the first to describe hypertext in his 1945 article "As We May Think."[3] Bush called for building a mechanized scientific literature system that would contain an extensive library, personal notes, photographs, and sketches. He talked about a machine, the Memex, which could be built for browsing and making notes in an extensive online text and graphics system. Although the Memex did not use a computer, it had screens and could link or tie two items in the library using microfilms and photocells.

Influenced by Bush's imaginary Memex, Douglas Engelbart, the inventor of the "mouse," of the Stanford Research Institute (SRI) wrote "A Conceptual Framework for the Augmentation of Man's Intellect" in 1963.[4] Engelbart predicted a human evolution as a result of using computers. His system NLS (oN Line System) was built in 1968 at the Augmented Human Intellect Research Center at SRI. NLS featured a database of nonlinear text, view filters to select information from the database, and views to structure the display of information. The system has evolved over the years and is now marketed commercially by McDonnell Douglas under the name Augment or NSL/Augment.

By 1968 Ted Nelson, Andries van Dam, and a group of Brown University students began building hypertext systems such as Intermedia, and Nelson's Xanadu.[5] It was, in fact, Nelson who coined the term *hypertext*. Nelson envisioned a world of linked documents accessible by reasoning, a process that simulated human thought. Nelson's experimental hypertext system Xanadu is a computer-based system that links large bodies of online literature. (Nelson worked on Xanadu during the 1960s while Engelbart was developing NSL.) In Xanadu, storage space is saved by the heavy use of links. The document in Xanadu is viewed as the fundamental unit that has windows to any other documents in the system, while the evolving text is continually expandable.[6] Nelson defines *hyper* as "extended, generalized, and multidimensional."[7]

In the 1980s, other systems emerged such as Xerox PARC's NoteCards, the University of Maryland Hyperties, and Apple computer's HyperCard.

In his "Hypertext: An Introduction and Survey," Jeff Conklin described the essence of a hypertext system from a computer science viewpoint:

3. Vannevar Bush, "As We May Think," *Atlantic Monthly* 176(1): 101–8 (July 1945).

4. Douglas Engelbart, "A Conceptual Framework for the Augmentation of Man's Intellect," in *Vistas in Information Handling*, Vol. 1 (London: Spartan Books, 1963).

5. Xanadu is the name of the magic place of literary memory in Samuel Taylor Coleridge's poem "Kubla Khan."

6. Theodore H. Nelson, "Replacing the Printed Word: A Complete Literary System," *IFIP Proceedings*, Oct. 1980, p.1013–23).

7. Theodore H. Nelson, "A Conceptual Framework for Man-Machine Everything," at 1973 National Computer Conference and Exposition, June 4–8, 1973, New York, N.Y., in *AFIPS Conference Proceedings, Volume 42* (Montvale, N.J.: AFIPS Press, 1973), p.M22–M23.

The essence of hypertext is precisely that it is a hybrid that cuts across traditional boundaries. Hypertext is a database method, providing a novel way of directly accessing data. This method is quite different from the traditional use of queries. At the same time, hypertext is a representation scheme, a kind of semantic network which mixes information textual material with more formal and mechanized operations and processes. Finally, hypertext is an interface modality that features "control buttons" (link icons) which can be arbitrarily embedded within the content material by the user. These are not separate applications of hypertext: They are metaphors for a functionality that is an essential union of all three.[8]

Two types of hypertext may be set by a hypertext designer: static hypertext and dynamic hypertext. In the static hypertext, the links are set by the producer and cannot be changed or altered by the end user, such as the *Knowledge Set*, the CD-ROM version of Grolier's *Electronic Encyclopedia*. Dynamic hypertext allows users to create their own links. It has the ability to maintain multiple versions of any document.[9]

The Search Express is a hypertext retriever produced by Technologies, Inc. It allows users to intermix text, spreadsheets, audio, CAD/CAM drawings, and images within a single database. This software is compatible with CD-ROM and WORM drives. It has a hypertext feature that lets users creatively link text, images, and other objects. It supports full-text searching and retrieving, and it has the capability of searching one million objects. The CD-ROM version includes a bundled image display capability, note pad, enhanced hypertext capability, and concordance. The CD-ROM version is listed at $5,000.

Window Book, created by the Box Company, Inc., of Cambridge, Massachusetts, has hypertext features. This software is used by Virginia Polytechnic Institute with its Virginia Disc CD-ROM demonstration.

Hypermedia

While hypertext limits linking to textual information, hypermedia extends linking from text to other media, such as audio recordings, video, graphics, spreadsheets, animation, digital speech, pictures, film clips, and others. To simplify this, we may look at the library as a crude hypermedia system where the user can obtain diverse media (books, articles, films, slides, film strips, audio recordings, videotapes, videodiscs, etc.) from different locations to cover a specific topic.

8. Jeff Conklin, p.33.
9. T. J. Byers, "Built by Association," *PC World* 5(4): 244–51 (Apr. 1987).

Because of the large storage and speed needed for hypertext and hypermedia systems, all experiments done so far have used mainframes or minicomputers. However, with the advances in personal computers and the advent of optical technology, hypermedia developers have begun to explore the utilization of microcomputers. The capability of microcomputers to display windows and more graphic objects such as icons on the screen makes the microcomputer an interesting machine with which to implement hypermedia applications.

Some look at the HyperCard program for the Apple Macintosh as the perfect use of a hypermedia system, since it is capable of accessing CD-ROM drives and videodiscs and possesses the power of browsing, editing, and creating. HyperCard was developed at Apple by a team led by Bill Atkinson. A hypermedia product called *The Whole Earth Learning*, a version of *The Whole Earth Catalog*, currently under development by Broderbund Software, is an equivalent to a pictorial encyclopedia. A recent competitor to HyperCard is called SuperCard. Developed by Silicon Beach Software, it provides full color and a number of options not found on HyperCard.

Hypermultimedia

Hypermultimedia is the logical conclusion of an evolutionary process. It encompasses voice, sound, video, graphics, animation, and others. It is not so much a feature of a system or a marketing product as it is a concept.

Hypermultimedia can help create multimedia environments through authoring tools and interactive programs without the use of traditional video and graphics equipment. It will help users to record information easily, integrate other media into text, and control attached devices such as videodisc players and CD-ROM drives. Tools that are used in experiments on multimedia include the HyperCard of Apple and Infowindow of IBM. HyperCard is used in Apple's planned project, Knowledge Navigator, which is a system with an extensive data network linked to videodisc players and CD-ROM drives. IBM's Infowindow is a multimedia product that combines laser disc technology with a touch screen on a monitor. Infowindow is used in education and training.

DVI, developed by GE/RCA and now owned by Intel Corporation, is considered a multimedia technology, combining audio and full-motion video with data access and processing within interactive applications. In the meantime, Philips, Sony, and Microsoft are planning to develop an extended CD-ROM format that will incorporate the audio and video capabilities of CD-I and also allow CD-ROM discs to be used on both players: CD-I and CD-ROM. The new format will be called *CD-ROM Extended Architecture* (CD-ROM XA).

No products have been announced for DVI or CD-I at present, although both have prototype applications. Optical Media International of Los Gatos, California, has produced a multimedia CD-ROM containing "The Constitution Papers," a collection of related papers and works from early U.S. history. The disc also contains a digital audio recording of music called "Heartland/An American Anthem" and sound effects from the company's "Universe of Sounds."

CD Assist from Philips and DuPont Optical, Wilmington, Delaware, is a software application for interactive use of CD-ROM media. It includes a production guide for interactive, multimedia CD-ROM, a software tool kit to access CD-ROM as if it were a videodisc, and a promotional offer to master a multimedia CD-ROM. CD Assist is supposed to provide standard guidelines to exploit the capability of CD-ROM as a multimedia (or "mixed mode") medium in an interactive environment.

9 Library Applications: Cataloging Support

CD-ROM systems in this category are used in both retrospective as well as current cataloging processes: they have the capability to produce cards and book labels, and they are mostly used by small libraries to convert cataloging records to machine MARC format. Usually, in the case of retrospective conversion, the search results are saved on floppy diskettes, then sent to the vendor to be searched in a central database. Then the records are added by the vendor to the library's master file.

This approach seems to be more economical than using telecommunications. Hit rates of over 90 percent reported by vendors seem to be very high, while research and large libraries might find the hit rate considerably low compared to large national bibliographic utilities such as OCLC, RLIN, or UTLAS. However, hit rates for CD-ROM searches will vary with the type and size of the library. If the CD-ROM product allows for online searches for the unfound records, the rate might increase considerably.

The following is a list of some of the available cataloging systems on the market:

1. *BIB-BASE/CD-ROM* from Small Library Computing is an add-on module that permits libraries to search the complete Library of Congress MARC database and to transfer records to the library's *Bib-Base* database. The module is fully integrated with *Bib-Base*'s acquisitions and cataloging modules. Small Library sells the English-language MARC on three BiblioFile CD-ROM discs for $1,500. The LC MARC database contains nearly three million records for books, serials, government documents, maps, films, and music. It is indexed by title, author/title, LCCN, ISBN, ISSN, and SuDoc number. Title and author/title searches can be qualified by date and other criteria. The subscription for the quarterly updated BiblioFile discs is $870/year and $500/year for foreign MARC. In order to use Bib-Base/CD-ROM the library has to purchase the core module ($495) and one or more of the major modules: /Acq (acquisitions), /Cat (cataloging), or /Subject ($495 each; a demo is available for $20). The cost for the /CDROM is $995 (no demo is available).

2. *BiblioFile Catalog Maintenance* from Library Corporation stores

up to 32,000 full MARC records in the PC. These records can be produced by the company on a CD-ROM. For MARC files that contain more than 32,000 records, the company offers Enhanced BiblioFile. This $975 system includes multiple online CD-ROM databases, LC-MARC English language, and LC-MARC foreign language. It prints catalog cards and labels. The system provides up to 99 different blank templates for original cataloging for typical MARC records for different types of material. When a search request is made, Catalog Maintenance searches MARC files on the hard disk. If the record is found, it will be displayed on the screen. If the record is not found, Catalog Maintenance searches LC-MARC database on CD-ROM. The record is displayed on the screen ready for editing. If a record is not available, an original cataloging template is provided upon request.

3. *BiblioFile Catalog Production* from Library Corporation is a retrospective conversion system. It contains one million shared plus three million LC MARC records in English and foreign languages, including monographs, serials, maps, films, music, and visual materials. Published since 1985, BiblioFile is considered one of the earliest CD-ROM products. Search arguments can be entered for author, title, ISSN, ISBN, or LCCN. Search can be narrowed by publication year, type of material, number of pages, or author's name. Through the text editor, the user can add, delete, or change the data. Cards as well as book labels can be printed. Records are saved for loading into the Intelligent Catalog and BiblioFile Circulation. Both are Library Corporation products. Records can also be sent to the library's online system. Annual subscription for LC MARC English-language discs is $870 with quarterly updates and $1,470 with monthly updates. Annual subscription for LC MARC foreign-language discs is $500 with quarterly updates.

4. *CAT CD450* from OCLC is a cataloging system that enables users to search, create, edit, and print catalog records and spine labels offline and access the 19 million bibliographic records on the OCLC Online Union Catalog (OCLC/OLUC) through telecommunications. The system produces standard card sets locally or centrally at OCLC. CAT CD450 uses subsets from the OCLC/OLUC. The user can validate MARC tags, indicators, and subfield codes. Files are arranged alphabetically with indexes and records residing on each compact disc.

Search is done by name, title, OCLC number, ISBN, ISSN, LCCN, SuDoc number, publication date, reproduction, language, subject headings, and cataloging source field, individually or in combination using Boolean logic on compact disc subsets. CAT CD450 allows the user to log-on to perform immediate online searches or save unsuccessful compact disc searches for batch searching in the OLUC. The batch processing takes advantage of OCLC's non-prime-time price structure.

Records retrieved from the CD-ROM disc are stored, searched, and edited from a local "save" file on hard disk. New records are also created and edited on hard disk and can be uploaded to the OLUC. The system is also capable of transferring data from authority records to bibliographic records without rekeying. Exporting bibliographic records in OCLC-MARC format to any local system is feasible. Hit rates during the product field test (July–Sept. 1988) had a 90 percent average. This rate can be raised by searching OLUC online.

CAT CD450 system consists of seven discs:
a) The Recent Books Cataloging Collection (two discs) includes the most recently used LC and member-input records in the Books Format restricted by imprint date to the most recent six years; approximately 1.2 million records, issued quarterly.
b) The Older Books and Most-Used Nonbook Cataloging Collection (two discs) includes the most-used records for nonbooks and books with imprints predating those in (a), above; approximately 1.2 million records, issued quarterly.
c) LC Authority Collection (three discs) includes the complete file of Library of Congress Name and Subject Authority Records. The Authority Collection may be purchased separately or as part of the CAT CD450. It is issued semiannually.

Law and medical cataloging subsets are sold for about $500 each. The music subset is planned for February 1990.

The system runs on OCLC M300 (should be upgraded to 640K RAM), M300XT, M310, with at least 20 megabytes hard disk. A daisy-chain configuration and a dial-access modem or OCLC communications controller are supported. Documentation provided with the system includes a user guide with set-up instructions, reference guides, keyboard templates, and computer-based training courseware.

OCLC membership is required for the purchase of the complete set of the CAT CD450. However, the LC Authorities Collection is available to nonmembers for about $400.

5. *Cataloger's Tool Kit* from EBSCO Electronic Information includes MARC English; the full English-language titles cataloged by LC in all formats and distributed by LC's MARC Distribution Service; MARC-STM, intended for scientific, technical, and medical libraries; and MARC-LAW, English-language legal materials cataloged and distributed by LC. The system produces catalog cards and labels. It can be linked to other local online and circulation systems.

CD-CATSS from Utlas International offers a multilingual cataloging system on a stand-alone or online basis. It comprises four different databases on CD-ROM for a total of over eight million records on nine separate discs, as follows:

6. *Current Cataloging Database* is a subset of CD-CATSS on three discs holding 1.5 million MARC records from national sources and Utlas users. It contains records in all languages for material in different formats published since 1983 and is updated quarterly. In addition to 100,000 original Utlas user records, it includes the following source files: LC-Books All, LC-Serials, LC-Visual Materials, LC-Maps, LC-Music, LC-Minimal Level, LC-COBRA, National Library of Canada, The British Library, Government Printing Office, and the National Library of Medicine.
7. *DisCON* is a four–CD-ROM disc database holding six million abbreviated LC MARC and REMARC monograph records. Records found in DisCon are sent to Utlas, where the full MARC record is extracted from the Utlas full-record database. DisCon is available for $800 per month, while records retrieved cost extra ($0.020 per record).
8. *LawMARC* is a subset of the Utlas database CD-CATSS, on a single disc holding 485,000 pre-1985 monograph records in full MARC format. The records are Library of Congress and REMARC records from the *K* classification, the LAW class, and selected subject terms. LawMARC will help in retrospective conversion of law collections.
9. *Serials*, a subset of the Utlas database *CD-CATSS*, is on a single CD-ROM disc containing 460,000 full MARC, pre-1987 serial records. The records are a mix of Utlas user records and authenticated CONSER records from the Library of Congress and the National Library of Canada. The Serials disc can be used in conjunction with the *Current Cataloging* database or by itself as part of the retrospective conversion of a serials collection.
   The standard LCCN, ISBN, and ISSN access points are

supplemented in CD-CATSS by SuDoc number, publisher's number for music, CODEN, standard film number, standard technical report number, standard recording number, and report number. Searching is also done by author, title (main title and alternate title), and series title. Title and author searches can be qualified by any or all of the following: author/title, date, material type, level, edition, place of publication, publisher, and language. Truncation is automatic unless specified otherwise. Title and author keyword searches are allowed. Boolean operators (AND, OR, NOT) are used in search arguments. It has a browsing feature. The workstation has online access to Utlas's central database of more than 5 million MARC records. Records can be imported from the central database to the CD-CATSS workstation, where they can be edited. The user can establish profiles for required bibliographic fields, standard entry formats, and other elements.

MARC records can be sent electronically or on diskettes to Utlas where they are processed using authority files. Insert, delete, duplicate, and change data in fields are done on screen. CD-CATSS supports the input and display of full ALA characters. Character sets that are standard on the workstation include Hebrew, Greek, and Cyrillic. CD-CATSS displays a keyboard guide on the screen to assist the user with the correct key to use for special characters and diacritics. The system includes original record entry, multiple work files, administrative functions, and card printing.

Cost: CD-CATSS costs $2,675 initially. Software licensing and maintenance go for $550 per year. The database itself sells for $1,800 per year after the first year.

10. *CDMARC Bibliographic* is the bibliographic file of the Library of Congress. Still under testing, it will include four million records that have been in the LC MARC system since 1968. CDMARC Bibliographic is planned for the winter of 1990. It uses Boolean logic with indexes arranged by record number, LC classification number, ISBN, ISSN, keywords, name headings, and subject headings. The user can narrow search criteria by record format (books, maps, serials, etc.), languages, personal name, corporate name, or date. In the BROWSE mode the system provides five separate indexes: authors, titles, subjects (including names as subjects), keywords, and LC classification numbers. The user will be able to save records to a disk file. Display options include MARC tags that appear with an English-language label; a MARC tagged-record display; a catalog-card display; and even any display

defined by the user. It is expected to be a useful tool in cataloging retrospective conversion.

11. *CDMARC NAMES*, a name authority file of the Library of Congress, includes approximately 2.1 million personal, corporate, series, and title authority records on compact disc. CDMARC NAMES, available for $375, includes SEARCH and BROWSE capabilities. SEARCH enables the user to search the following six indexes along with their respective indexed fields and subfields:

Name: Matches headings beginning with search string in fields 1XX and 4XX.

Title: Matches headings beginning with the search string. All fields and subfields of 130 and 430 are indexed as well as subfield $t and subsequent subfields of 100, 110, 111, 400, 410, and 411.

Keyword: Matches headings or cross references anywhere in the record the search string appears, i.e., fields 1XX, 4XX, and 5XX.

LC Class number: Matches headings with the assigned Library of Congress classification number from fields 050 and 053.

Authority control number: Matches the Library of Congress unique authority control number.

Search can be limited through the following seven qualifiers:

ALSO: *See also* references that link headings; usually reciprocal but not necessarily so. Only 5XX fields for which there is no corresponding 1XX are indexed.

CORP: Corporate name headings. Fields 110, 410, and those 510s that are indexed.

MAIN: All main entries. Fields 1XX.

MEET: Named meetings. Fields 111, 411, and those 511s that are indexed.

PEERS: Personal name headings. Fields 100, 400, and those 500s that are indexed.

PEFR: *See* from references that are variants of headings. Fields 4XX.

TITL: Titles appearing as main entries and in subfield $t of selected fields. Fields 130, 430, and those 530s that are indexed, as well as subfield $t and subsequent subfields from 1XX, 4XX, and 5XX fields that are indexed.

A demonstration is available on a floppy disk from the Library of Congress, Cataloging Distribution Service, Washington, DC 20541 (202-707-6100).

12. *CDMARC SUBJECTS,* a compilation of the Library of Congress subject authority file, allows the user to maneuver through layers of interrelated subject terms, to select broader, narrower, and related-term references. Relationships between subject headings can be identified by using Boolean operators (OR, AND, NOT). The user can browse through the file and download records to the PC or local system. The downloading feature might be helpful in building a link between the local applications and LC Subject Authority File. The full ALA extended character set can be displayed through a Hercules Plus or Hercules Incolor graphics card. Printing the full ALA extended character set requires a Hewlett Packard LaserJet Plus. The quarterly updated CDMARC Subjects is available by subscription only for $300 (U.S.) and $370 (international).

13. *Enhanced BiblioFile* from the Library Corporation is used for high-volume processing (if the size of the file is larger than 32,000 records). The system allows for up to eight workstations to be linked to one LC-MARC database in a LAN, a bar-code reader, and hard-disk drives for storing and editing added records.

14. *LaserQuest* from General Research Corporation (GRC) is a four-CD-ROM disc database holding five million USMARC and CANMARC records, of which two million records were contributed by GRC's customers in public libraries, universities, community colleges, schools, and special libraries, including English and foreign titles for books, serials, visual materials, maps, and manuscripts. Hit rates reported have an average of approximately 90 percent. LC MARC records are available, and over 1.8 million book records have a pre-1968 publication date.

    The database access is primarily by title. The non-book materials are found only on the fourth disc. For ongoing input, bimonthly supplement discs add approximately 150,000 new titles with each edition. Serials can be searched by title, ISSN, or any cataloged variant title. Extraction and editing of records are provided from the database as they are converted. For serials retrospective, holdings can be keyed into the system and saved on diskettes, then sent to GRC online or sent by mail to be loaded into a national bibliographic database. Records are edited as they are converted.

    To allow simultaneous access to the entire database, in order to save time and effort, a daisy-chained configuration is recommended. The company claims productivity ranging from 40 to 80 records per hour for searching, verifying matches, saving records, and adding fields. In addition, 100 unedited records per hour can be searched and saved by experienced catalogers. Catalog cards and spine and pocket labels may be printed using LaserQuest. MARC records can be printed directly from the screen.

LaserQuest records can be transferred to nine-track magnetic tapes for loading into any system that accepts MARC tapes. Records cataloged on LaserQuest can be transferred instantly to LaserGuide, a public access catalog produced by GRC and using LaserMerge software and a hard disk in order to make all records available to the user.

15. *SuperCAT* from Gaylord Information Systems is composed of three compact discs. Two discs contain over two million LCMARC English-language records with all formats, while the third disc, which is optional, includes one million foreign-language records. Using proprietary software, the system supports a network configuration that allows several workstations to share the CD-ROM database. It has edit capability and full print control through print production tables. It can print catalog cards and book labels. SuperCAT can transmit records to other systems and produce standard purchase orders. It stores local records on a hard disk. The system supports ALA extended character sets of diacritics and special figures, both on-screen and in all printed output. It displays MARC tag labels while editing and provides session statistics at log-off. The user can create macros to store often repeated keystrokes, such as consecutive commands and texts such as library name, cataloger name, and automatic tag entry.

SuperCAT has the capability to search LC MARC records and processed MARC records by LCCN, ISBN/ISSN, author, or title. Search can be limited by date or format of material. The system can create original records in many formats on templates such as book, serial, sound recording, map, archive, manuscript, and computer format. It stores new and edited records on the hard disk (40,000 records can be stored on a 30-megabyte hard disk). SuperCAT can prepare sorted bibliographies and new book lists with call numbers, main entry, title, and date information taken directly from the MARC records. It performs print batch functions and data disk utilities. Sorting can be done by author, title, or control number for rapid retrieval. (It displays the number of hits.) SuperCAT utilizes split screen for a visual comparison between two records while the differences are highlighted. Context-sensitive "help" screens are accessible at all times. Session statistics provide user name, date, time of log-on and log-off, total of MARC records read, new records added, original records, records updated, records deleted, card sets printed, label set, and book orders.

Costs and hardware: Gaylord provides free tutorial and demo disks. Basic processor and keyboard include 8088 processor with 640K, single and parallel interface, single floppy-disk drive, PC AT–type keyboard, and DOS. Gaylord strongly recommends the use of a configuration with a hard disk or hard card, both to support the ALA character set and also to eliminate swapping of disks during operation. The system can run on monochrome or color monitors. License for a single workstation/site is $1,500; any additional workstation is $250. Subscriptions for CD-ROM LC MARC-English: first copy, $850; monthly updates, $1,400; semi-monthly updates, $2,400; LC MARC-Foreign quarterly updates, $500.

10 Library Applications: Public Access Catalogs

Most public access catalogs on CD-ROM have the capability to interface with circulation systems as well as read MARC (machine-readable cataloging) format. Audio capability represented in verbal interface is added to at least one public access catalog, BiblioFile Intelligent Catalog from Library Corporation. Capacities of such catalogs exceed one million titles, with quarterly updates. The actual number of titles on a disc depends on the size of the records and the amount of indexing.

Public access catalogs (PACs) use Boolean and keyword searching. They are capable of printing bibliographies, cards, and labels. Unlike online catalogs, PACs do not impose any telecommunications costs. To overcome the problem of updating PACs, many companies recommend the use of a hard disk, so that new records can be saved on it.

The search software will search both the CD-ROM and the hard disk. Thus, old and new records can be searched and retrieved until the time comes to incorporate both new and old records on a new CD-ROM disc. The following provides information on some available PAC systems.

CD/2000

CD/2000 from OCLC stores a library's bibliographic and holdings information on a compact disc. The system features a user interface employing Boolean operators (AND, OR, NOT) and positional operators (WITH, ADJacency). OCLC will transfer all of a library's holdings on CD-ROM discs. Premastering is done by OCLC, including indexing and formatting of a library's tapes and transmittal of tapes to a CD-ROM manufacturer for mastering the disc.

OCLC CD/2000 is designed as a backup for the LS/2000 online catalog. It allows LS/2000 users to access a CD-ROM copy of the library's bibliographic database. It is used as a backup when the online system is down. It accepts both controlled and free-text phrase searches. The LS/2000 library system is a fully integrated local system that provides circulation control, bibliographic control and authority maintenance, online public access catalog, administrative reports, and acquisitions and serial control.

IMPACT

With IMPACT, from Auto-Graphics, Inc., the system architecture allows for different modules to be used, such as:

1. *Browsing access on patron level.* This includes access capability for authors, titles, subjects, or all three combined; call number browsing in shelflist sequence; the library news and help screen display functions; search redirection via cross-references generated from the LC name and subject authority files.
2. *Keyword access on expert level.* This provides keyword indexing and associated techniques for refining searches. The system can search using combinations such as author/title, author/author, author/subject, series/subject, and subject/subject.
3. *Location access.* This allows the CD-ROM disc to be used as a branch, library, or library system catalog, allowing the searching of specific locations.
4. *Research level.* This allows for the assembly of bibliographies.

Because IMPACT is essentially a union catalog, it has interlibrary loan capability. It uses Boolean operators (OR, AND, NOT). The system displays the library's local news.

Updating. New records are added to the hard disk where they can be searched simultaneously with records from the main CD-ROM catalog using software designed for patrons. Records from both sources will be interfiled for the purpose of display. The capacity of the CD-ROM disc is about 500,000 full records, in addition to indexes, pointers, and authority records.

Maintenance. Catalog maintenance can be done online, via the AGILEII database maintenance system, offline, via floppy diskettes or magnetic tape, or upgraded from pre-MARC records.

Hardware and Cost. The standard IMPACT public access station includes a compatible IBM/PC model PC-II-AG using MS-DOS with internal Sony CDU-510 CD-ROM drive, a single 5¼-inch 360K floppy disk, 150-watt power supply, 8MHz clock, parallel printer interface, Hercules graphics card, front security panel, all cabling and connectors, and swivel and tilt-base Samsung MA-2565 amber monitor. The general cost—$1,825—includes the purchase price plus $180 annual maintenance. The hard-disk drive and the printer are optional components and will cost extra. Software for the search levels is provided under an annual agreement ($50 each), except the system administrations software, which is provided at no charge. Premaster processing per record is $0.03. CD mastering is $1,500. CD replicates are $20 per disc. Training per day is $400. Building of database and catalog processing will cost $0.02 per record for a MARC record match by number match and $0.035 per record for MARC record match by author/title match. Running a machine authority control costs $0.035 per master file record. The largest number of records on CD-ROM belongs to Enoch Pratt Free Library, Baltimore, Maryland—almost one million records.

Intelligent Catalog

Intelligent Catalog, from the Library Corporation, combines artificial intelligence, graphics, CD-ROM-based data, and sound. Verbal instructions and on-screen tutorials are provided. It searches the note and other text fields, provides help and error messages, and allows subject area and shelflist browsing. The system displays maps of library stacks and a bulletin board of events. Maps of the library can be zoomed out to the city and world, or zoomed in to molecules and atoms. Intelligent Catalog performs dictionary, keyword-in-context, or Boolean searches. It responds to natural language requests. Proximity search and full Boolean operators are built in. Cross-references for authors and subjects are provided. It prints notes, sorted bibliographies, and saves a log of search paths. It also recommends works of fiction in the library collection.

Updating. The computer hard disk incorporates new and changed data. Catalogs can be updated as frequently as once a month. Search requests are searched on both CD-ROM disc and hard disk since dynamic interfiling integrates updated records with existing records. The library sends new and updated MARC records to Library Corporation on a standard MARC tape. Cassette tapes are then prepared by Library Corporation. Library staff members transfer the contents of the cassette tape to the hard disk of each workstation. Library Corporation accepts local MARC files from sources such as BiblioFile, Brodart, GRC, OCLC, RLIN, Utlas, and WLN.

Hardware and Cost. A one-time purchase price of each Intelligent Catalog workstation is $2,770. The station is equipped with a 10MHz PC-XT-compatible computer with 42-megabyte hard disk and one floppy disk, built-in CD-ROM drive with sound graphics, clock/calender, an RS232 port (for connection to circulation), and MS-DOS. The computer is contained in a locking desk with power conditioner, tilt-base amber monitor, silent printer, speed keyboard with special colors and labels, plus a speaker, earphones, and a telephone hand-set. A $450 per year charge is made for loading and updating the Intelligent Catalog each month, remastering, and software enhancements. (Daily updates cost extra.) Toll-free customer support and replacement of components via courier are available. A one-time charge of $0.035 per record is required for initial de-dupe and match-merge of local MARC file.

LaserGuide

LaserGuide, from General Research Corporation (GRC), provides different search modes. In the Basic mode, the user can search by authors, titles, and subjects. Search words are placed in the appropriate window for author, title, or subject. Boolean search is provided in the Expert search mode.

Search results are displayed in a list that can be scanned by the user, who in turn can request a display of the full bibliographic record. LaserGuide suggests additional related topics to be searched to expand and/or narrow the search. It provides a floor plan of the library to help patrons to locate materials according to call number and location codes. It also provides a shelflist scanning.

Updating. Instant access to newly cataloged titles is available through the optional hard disk update feature. The new records are added first to a floppy diskette, then a LaserMerge program is used periodically to transfer new titles to the hard disk. LaserGuide usually searches the CD-ROM disc and the hard disk simultaneously, then displays the new records from the hard disk first.

Hardware. GRC recommends that the user purchase and maintain the hardware locally. LaserGuide requires an IBM/XT/AT or compatibles; 640K RAM; one floppy-diskette drive, monochrome or color monitor—CGA (Color Graphics Adapter), EGA (Enhanced Graphics Adapter), or MCGA (MultiColor Graphics Array) used in PS/2 model 30 computers. LaserGuide uses internal or external Hitachi CD-ROM drives. However, the internal model does not fit into PS/2 systems. A hard disk is required only for the updating option and search statistics. LaserGuide supports any printer that runs on IBM computers.

Le Pac

Le Pac, from Brodart Automation, provides two types of access. First, Browse Access is done through author, title, or subject. Truncation is allowed. It displays a list of related items, and the chosen item is highlighted for display. Second, Express Access is used to locate items by location or combined access points (author, title, subject, any word from author, title, or subject). Boolean operators (AND, OR, NOT) are used. Includes help screens and *see* and *see also* references. New entries are added on a hard disk. Optional access points include location, call number, or publication date. Brodart will process the library's database (MARC formatted) on its central computer system or create a database if the library is not already using Brodart's services. The database will be transferred to CD-ROM for library use. The system provides for the storage capacity of over one million MARC-formatted records. A demo floppy diskette is available from the company.

Hardware and Cost. The self-contained individual workstation is priced between $2,000 and $3,000 depending upon configurations. Hardware includes IBM or compatible computers; MS-DOS, PC-DOS 2.0 or higher, or Brodart's own operating system, PRO-DOS; Le Pac keyboard with ten specially engraved keys. Cost per title is about $0.029.

Marcive/PAC

Marcive/PAC, from Marcive, Inc., provides keyword searching of authors, titles, and subjects; Boolean operators (AND, OR, NOT) are used; and help screens can be modified by the library. Marcive/PAC can create indexes such as author, title, subject, call number, LCCN, ISBN, and contents notes. Cross-references, *see* and *see also*, are automatically generated. Bibliographies can be compiled, alphabetized by main entry, and printed on paper or written to diskettes. The company sells a demo kit on four diskettes and the user manual with installation instructions for $49.95, which is later deducted from the purchase price of the Marcive/PAC.

Updating. New and revised titles are added to the microcomputer's hard disk and interleaved with titles on the CD-ROM disc. The system will search both the CD-ROM disc and the hard disk at the same time. When the library decides to update its CD-ROM database (monthly, quarterly, or semiannually), it sends the new records to Marcive for incorporation into the library's PAC database. If the library uses a bibliographic utility such as OCLC or RLIN, it sends its monthly subscription tapes to Marcive for merging with its PAC database. Withdrawn records can be deleted from the PAC database either by a cancel or delete command. Also, the library may write lists of database control numbers and send them to Marcive for deletion from the PAC database. The new, revised, and deleted records are processed at Marcive, and a permanent file is created as a backup to the library's master database. Marcive creates an update tape on a tape cartridge that is mailed to the library, where it is loaded onto each workstation's hard disk.

Hardware. The PAC works on PC/XT or compatibles, 640K RAM, 20-megabyte hard-disk drive, one floppy-disk drive, Hitachi CD-ROM drive, and color or mono monitor.

Spectrum 200

Spectrum 200, from Gaylord Information Systems, is a public access catalog which performs Boolean combinations (AND, OR, NOT) within one index or multiple indexes. It can create complex search strings, including nested parenthetical statements. Searches can be limited by location, date, or range of dates. Display formats can be changed and records can be saved on floppy diskette or hard disk. Bibliographic records can be combined with a word-processing package to create lists. In-context HELP and a quick reference card are provided to help the user. Brief citations are displayed in reverse chronological order, new books first. It displays complete citations in standard catalog card form or in the customer-specified labeled format. The user can see library holdings, including location-level call number and in-library location. The system prints brief or full citations.

11 Other Library Applications

Acquisitions and Bibliographic Tools

The available acquisitions systems on the market enable the user to search a database such as *Anybook* of Library Corporation or *Books in Print Plus* of R. R. Bowker, then create a file of selected items. After selecting the desired vendor from the menu that is provided with the CD-ROM database, the user loads the vendor's software, which in turn sends the order file through a modem to the vendor's computer. This computer checks the availability of each title then reserves the order. Usually, the vendor provides the software and the communication dialing service free to the user. For example, *Books in Print Plus* can interface with Blackwell North America, Brodart, Ingram, and Baker & Taylor. Systems are expected to have the capability to dial local vendors as well. An edit screen is provided to format purchase orders for items not available in the database. There are two CD-ROM databases used by many libraries: *Anybook* from Library Corporation, and *Books in Print Plus* from Bowker. While Ingram's *LaserSearch* system uses *Anybook*, Baker & Taylor's BaTaSYSTEMS Order, Blackwell's PC Order Plus, Bowker, and Brodart PC Rose system use Bowker's CD-ROM *Books in Print Plus*.

There are some CD-ROM products that can be used for bibliographic verification, such as the *British Library General Catalogue of Printed Books to 1975 on CD-ROM, Cumulative Book Index, German Books in Print*, and all the *Plus* systems from Bowker. Many of the products listed in this category are helpful for collection development, for strengthening a specific subject area, or for supporting new courses offered by educational institutions.

The following are brief descriptions of some of the available products.

Anybook from Library Corporation provides information on the prices and publishers of more than 1.5 million English-language books in print or published in the last fifteen years from about 22,000 publishers. Annual subscription is $600 with quarterly update.

LaserSearch of Ingram Book Company is used in conjunction with the *Anybook* database. *LaserSearch* has the capability to print purchase orders to other publishers on 3-by-5-inch slips, interact with the budget and can handle up to 200 fund accounting. It also has a check-in system for orders received.

Bookbank, published by J. Whitaker and Sons, contains over 470,000 books in print from approximately 12,000 publishers. It uses BRS/SEARCH software to access the bibliographic information. Bookbank is based on the *British Books in Print* database. It includes a publisher file. The database is updated monthly. It supports PC-DOS. Supporting UNIX is in the planning. Price outside Europe is £1,015.

Bowker publishes the following products:

Books in Print Plus contains over 770,000 titles cross-referenced under 63,500 headings from *Books in Print, Subject Guide to Books in Print, Supplement to Books in Print, Forthcoming Books in Print*, and *Children's Books in Print*. A record of 21,000 publishers, approximately 70,000 LC subject headings, and 6,500 Sears and LC subject headings for children's fiction and nonfiction titles is also included. There are 22 different search categories—used alone or in combination—such as: author, title, subject, title key, audience, publisher, publication year, keyword, grade level, price, ISBN, LCCN, language, illustration, series title, and 4,4 author-title combination (the first four letters from the author's last name and the first four letters from the title). This product uses Boolean logic and truncation. It allows electronic transmission of purchase orders to Baker & Taylor, Blackwell North America, Brodart, and Ingram. The user can edit, print, and save citations as well as display them in any of five formats: standard, card catalog, MARC-tagged, customized, and detailed. Annual subscription price for the IBM or Macintosh version is $995.

Books in Print with Book Reviews Plus is necessarily the same as *Books in Print* in addition to book reviews from *Library Journal, Publishers Weekly, School Library Journal, Booklist*, and *Choice*. It has the same search criteria as *Books in Print Plus*. Annual subscription price for the IBM or Macintosh version is $1,395.

Books Out-of-Print Plus contains over 300,000 titles declared out of print or out of stock by publishers from 1979 to the present. It has the same search criteria as *Books in Print Plus*. Annual subscription is $395.

ULRICH'S Plus is based on *Ulrich's International Periodicals Directory, Irregular Serials and Annuals*, and *Bowker's International Serials Database Update*. It contains over 135,000 citations including 75,000 current periodicals in over 550 subject categories, 36,000 irregular serials and annuals, 14,000 former titles, over 6,000 new titles each year, title changes, and cessations. It has the same features as *Books in Print Plus* in addition to an ISSN index. Primary and secondary criteria include: Dewey Decimal, ISSN, subject, keyword, U.S. area code, media code, publishing code, status code, special index, year first published, country code, editor, publisher, title, circulation, frequency, online, price, special features, state, ZIP code, and 3,2,2,1 title. Annual subscription price is $395.

Variety's Video Directory Plus includes over 40,000 wide-ranging videos on the market and another 18,000 videos released every year. This reference and ordering system can be searched by eighteen search criteria to locate citations, such as title; performer/ director; other contributors; awards won; keyword within title or annotation; ISBN; manufacturer order number/UPC code; manufacturer/distributor; price; subject/genre; year produced; year released on video; MPAA rating; language; publication code; and status code. *Variety's Video Directory Plus* features nine quick-access indexes that allow browsing by title (including subtitle and series title); word within title; subject/genre; keyword; performer/director; other contributors; awards won; manufacturer/distributor; and order number/UPC code. Annual subscription price is $295.

BaTaSYSTEMS Order from Baker & Taylor is a free acquisitions system used with Bowker's *Books in Print Plus*. The system features electronic ordering, toll-free transmission, and electronic inventory confirmation. During a search, when each title is located in *Books in Print Plus*, the order system asks the user for quantity and binding desired, thus building an order file. At the end of the session, the file created may be transmitted into BaTaSYSTEM order. The same CD-ROM workstation will be used later to dial a toll-free inventory confirmation line. The service will send back to the workstation a status report of the ordered titles, such as which titles will be delivered, backordered, or are unavailable.

PC Order Plus from Blackwell is an acquisitions system that uses Bowker's *Books in Print Plus*.

Flash-Back from Ingram is another system that uses Bowker's *Books in Print Plus*. It enables the user to send orders to vendors and receive immediate confirmation. The user transmits the order file through a modem using Flash-Back software and a toll-free service. The software is provided free by Ingram along with documentation and a toll-free number for ordering. Annual subscription for the complete system including *Books in Print Plus* with weekly updates is $1,500; while *Books in Print Plus* with *Book Reviews Plus* and weekly updates is $1,900.

PC Rose from Brodart is an acquisitions system that utilizes Bowker's *Books in Print Plus.*

British Library General Catalogue of Printed Books to 1975 on CD-ROM is published jointly by Chadwyck-Healy and Saztec Europe. This catalog contains the largest collection of pre-1914 imprints in the world. It has the capability to create tailored bibliographies.

Cumulative Book Index, published by H. W. Wilson, contains bibliographic information on 60,000 English-language books published internationally. Includes paperbacks and foreign-language dictionaries, as well as information on publishers and distributors from 1982 to the present. One-year license is $1,295 with quarterly updates.

German Books in Print from Buchandler Vereinigung-GMBH is sold by Chadwyck-Healey.

The *Serials Directory* from EBSCO includes bibliographic information on over 114,000 international titles (journals, newspapers, and monographic series). Search capabilities include title, subject, ISSN, varying form of title, main entry, series, CONSER control number, index/abstract service, publisher, type of serial, editor, LC classification, Dewey decimal classification, universal decimal classification, CODEN designation, date of publication, language, frequency, price, country of publication, and keyword in editorial description. Data can be browsed by title and by subject classification, including cross-references. Searches can be stored for later use. The *Serials Directory* has the ability to place subscription orders. Boolean logic (AND, OR, NOT) and truncation are used. It has the ability to highlight only titles available in the library. Bibliographies and citations can be printed or copied to disc files ($495 plus updates).

Union Catalogs, Access Services, and Interlibrary Loan

CD-ROM can be used for interlibrary loan (ILL) applications, thus bringing together distant sites without telecommunication costs. An ILL system will tie individual libraries together, creating a local, regional, or statewide network for resource sharing. Libraries can communicate with other libraries through electronic mail or use the printed-form method. If the library is a participant on an electronic bulletin board, the result of a search can be stored on floppy diskettes, then sent to the online message system and distributed throughout the interlibrary loan network.

Access Pennsylvania is a union catalog database on CD-ROM disc and search software on floppy diskette. It is a joint effort of the State Library, the Pennsylvania Department of Education, and Brodart Company using LePac local access catalog software. It allows locating the records of all participating libraries or within a designated library collection. One of the goals of *Access Pennsylvania* is to bring school librarians into a statewide system of resource sharing. The system is based in school libraries and has resulted in a 68 percent increase in ILL transactions as well as a 300 percent to 500 percent increase in circulation of the libraries' own resources.[1]

BiblioFile Circulation from the Library Corporation is connected via serial cable to the intelligent catalog stations in the library. The system charges or discharges by optical scanning or manual keying of unique bar codes on the borrower's card and the item to be checked out. It handles renewals and fines, reserves/holds, recalls, and ILL tracking. The system features on-screen help messages and multiple-access levels and passwords to override due dates, fines, and blocks. Due dates and fines are calculated automatically and partial payments are allowed. Overdue items are automatically tagged as lost if not returned by a certain date. Notices are printed for overdues, fines, reserves, and recalls. Statistics on circulation activities are provided. Data are transferred between circulation systems during inactive periods. *BiblioFile Circulation* is a turnkey system that uses IBM's PC-LAN network operating system. The Videx hand-held, battery-powered bar-code wand can be used for inventory or remote check-out of materials. The charge for *BiblioFile Circulation* is $3,500, and $380 per year for updates and support per computer.

CD-CAT from Cooperating Libraries Automated Network (CLAN) is a backup for the CLAN online catalog that will be installed in member libraries.

HARLiC Union Catalog is being produced by Marcive. It will combine the collections of Houston Public Library, Texas A&M University, Texas Southern University, Prairie View A&M University, Houston Academy of Medicine–Texas Medical Center, and University of Texas Medical Branch at Galveston. When complete by fall 1989, the CD-ROM will contain approximately 2.1 million records.

1. Doris M. Epler and Richard E. Cassel, "*Access Pennsylvania*: A CD-ROM Database Project," *Library Hi Tech* 5(19): 81–92 (Fall 1987).

IMPACT from Auto-Graphics is a public access/union catalog. Searches can be narrowed based on location; thus, the user will be able to determine which libraries are included. Libraries' holdings can be displayed. (See Chapter 10 for more information.)

LaserCat is a product of Western Library Network (WLN). It holds three current years of LC MARC records and over two million records, holdings from more than 200 WLN member libraries on three CD-ROM discs. It covers books, films, serials, music, maps, and other formats. Retrieval can be done by author, title, subject, ISBN/ISSN/LCCN, or keyword. Truncation is allowed, and browsing can be done by author, title, or subject. These records can be searched to identify libraries owning specific materials and call numbers for ILL purposes. *LaserCat* prints bibliographies. It can be used for cataloging as it prints catalog cards and labels. It is a stand-alone system that runs on an IBM PC and compatibles. Annual subscription is $1,300 with quarterly updates.

Le Pac Interlibrary Loan from Brodart Automation allows the user to search Le Pac catalog for the desired item. When an item is located, Le Pac ILL automatically fills in the bibliographic information on the ILL request form. The user may add other information before sending it to the appropriate libraries. The printed request may be sent via the mail or facsimile machine to other libraries. *Le Pac Interlibrary Loan* offers a variety of request forms depending on types of material: audiovisual, serials, and monograph. A reference/subject form can be used if a specific title is not known. The system provides statistical reports on the number of materials by type and library name. It allows direct inquiry of the master request file, in order to answer questions about outstanding or filled requests. Pricing for the system varies depending on the method chosen, number of units, number of catalog copies, and options.

LOANet from Library Systems & Services, Inc. is an ILL system used by small libraries in Louisiana and Mississippi.

12 Other Applications

Full-Text Applications

A very small percentage of all CD-ROM products are published in full text. The problems associated with retrieval of text and graphics have affected the development of full-text products. Most of these full-text products do not provide graphics.

One available software package that does support the retrieval of full text and graphics is the KAware2 CD-ROM Image Management System from Knowledge Access International (Mount View, Calif.) KAware is designed to store and retrieve large databases that combine text and images (or feature images only). KAware can handle up to 5,000 color images and 50,000 black-and-white photos, with simultaneous display of text and images for CD-ROM and WORM applications.

Another program that can handle full text plus images in a hypertext application is the SearchExpress from Executive Technologies, Inc. (Birmingham, Ala.). Full-text products include the following (see Appendix A for more information):

Business

Business Periodicals Ondisc from UMI
Small Business Consultant from Microsoft Corporation

Chemistry

Kirk-Othmer Encyclopedia of Chemical Technology

Classical Works

PHI: Classical Latin Literature from Packard Humanities Institute
Papyri: Egyptian Papyri from Packard Humanities Institute (under development)
TLG discs A & B: Greek Literature from Thesaurus Linguae Graecae

Computer

Computer Library from Ziff Communications
The Sourcedisc from Diversified Data Resources

Education

Cross-Cultural CD from SilverPlatter
The International Encyclopedia of Education from Pergamon *Compact Solution*
Peterson's College Database from SilverPlatter
Peterson's Gradline from SilverPlatter
Texas State Education Encyclopedia from Quantum Access

Encyclopedias and Dictionaries

The Electronic Encyclopedia from Grolier Electronic Publishing
Merriam-Webster's Ninth New Collegiate Dictionary from Highlighted Data, Inc.

Engineering

Encyclopedia of Polymer Science and Engineering

Environment

EnFlex Info from ERM Computer Services

Legal

The Texas Attorney General Documents on CD-ROM from Quantum Access

Literature

Sherlock Holmes on Disc from CMC ReSearch

Medicine
AIDS

AIDS—Compact Library from the Medical Publishing Group
AIDS Information and Education Worldwide CD-ROM from CD Resources

Cancer

OncoDisc from J. B. Lippincott

Health Care

Drug Information Source from Compact Cambridge
The Nurse Library from Ellis Enterprises
Pediatrics on Disc from CMC ReSearch
Physician's Desk Reference from Medical Economics
The Physician Library from Ellis Enterprises
Scientific American Medicine Consult from Scientific American
Year Book on Disc from CMC ReSearch

News and Newspapers

Facts on File News Digest CD-ROM from Facts On File
Pravda on CD-ROM from Alde Publishing and Context Translations

Reference Works

Home Reference Library from Ellis Enterprises

Religion

The Bible Library from Ellis Enterprises
Luther Bible from Deutsche Bibelgeselschaft
Master Search Bible on Compact Disc from Tri Star Publishing

Science and Technology

Science and Technology Reference Set from McGraw-Hill

Government Publications: Census and Statistical Data

Government publications, census, and statistical data are available on
CD-ROM from different publishers. For instance, the SHIP disc collection from Slater Hall Information Products contains useful government
statistical data as released by the Census Bureau, the Bureau of
Economic Analysis, and other federal statistical agencies. Definitions

and documentation as prepared by the releasing agency are included. The user can print tables and create files for use in spreadsheets and other programs.

The SHIP collection includes *Business Indicators, County Statistics, Business Statistics 1929–85, 1982 Census of Agriculture,* and *Population Statistics.* Another developer, Space-Time Research Ltd., has published census data related to many countries including the United States, Sweden, New Zealand, Hong Kong, England, and Australia. Another useful database is *NTIS* (National Technical Information Service). *NTIS* contains citations and abstracts of the U.S. federal government–sponsored research, development and engineering studies, and reports prepared by federal agencies, their contractors, and grantees. It contains abstracts of unclassified, publicly available reports, software packages, and data files from more than 300 government agencies including NASA, DOD, DOE, EPA, DOT, and the Department of Commerce, which are produced by the National Technical Information Service, covering the years from 1983 to the present, in areas of aeronautics, engineering, communications, materials science, and physics. *NTIS* has been published on CD-ROM by at least three producers: Dialog Information Services, OCLC, and SilverPlatter.

The *Monthly Catalog* of U.S. government publications has been published by many publishers, including Information Access, Marcive, OCLC, H. W. Wilson, SilverPlatter, and Brodart.

Agriculture

Agribusiness U.S.A. DIALOG OnDisc from Dialog Information
AGRICOLA and CRIS-SilverPlatter from SilverPlatter
Agri/Stats from Hopkins Technology

Business

Business Indicators on CD-ROM from Slater Hall Information Products
Business Statistics 1929–85 from Slater Hall Information Products
Consu/Stats from Hopkins Technology
Labor/Stats from Hopkins Technology
STAT PACK from Microsoft

Census

Census of Australian Population & Housing, 1981 and 1986, (CDATA 86)
from Space-Time Research, Ltd.

Census: Australian Standardized Local Government Finance Statistics from Space-Time Research, Ltd.

1982 Census of Agriculture from Slater Hall Information Products

Census of England, Scotland and Wales, Small Area Statistics 1981 from Space-Time Research, Ltd.

Census of Hong Kong, 1981 and 1986 from Space-Time Research, Ltd.

Census of New Zealand, 1986 Census from Space-Time Research, Ltd.

Census of Sweden, 1970 to 1987 from Space-Time Research, Ltd.

Census Test Disc #1 from the U.S. Census Bureau

Census Test Disc #2 from the U.S. Census Bureau

Census: U.S. County Business Patterns, 1985 from Space-Time Research, Ltd.

Census: U.S. Data, 1980—Supermap from Space-Time Research, Ltd.

County Statistics from Slater Hall Information Products

POPLINE from SilverPlatter

Population Statistics on CD-ROM from Slater Hall Information Products

Economy

Econ/Stats from Hopkins Technology

Engineering/Construction

Construction Criteria Base from National Institute of Building Science

Environment

EnFlex Info from ERM Computer Services

Geology

CD-ROM Prototype Disc from U.S. Geological Survey

Government/Logos

Federal Logos Disc from Alde Publishing

Government Personnel

Personnet from Information Handling Services

Who Is in Washington from Alde Publishing

Government Procurement

CD-Fiche from USA Information Systems
Federal Procurement System Disc from Alde Publishing
Haystack: Logistics, Procurement, Engineering Files from Ziff Davis Technical Information
Parts-Master from National Standards Association
TLRN from Innovative Technology

Government Publications

Catalogue of United Kingdom Official Publications from Chadwyck-Healey and Her Majesty's Stationery Office
Congressional Information Service (CIS) from Congressional Information Service
GDCS Impact from Auto-Graphics
Government Publications Index from Information Access
GPO from Dialog Information Services
GPO from SilverPlatter
GPO Cat/PAC from Marcive
GPO Monthly Catalog & Index to Periodicals from H. W. Wilson
Le Pac: Government Documents Option from Brodart
Optext: Federal Regulations from VLS (Video Laser Systems)

Legal

The Texas Attorney General Documents on CD-ROM from Quantum Access

Medical and Health Care

Food/Analyst from Hopkins Technology

Real Estate

MetroScan from Digital Diagnostics

Science and Technology

NTIS—DIALOG OnDisc from Dialog Information
NTIS—OCLC from Online Computer Library Center
NTIS—SilverPlatter from SilverPlatter

Transportation

FORM41: Airline Carrier Filings from Data Base Products
International: Airline Traffic from Database Products
O&D Plus: Airline Traffic Origin/Destination from Data Base Products
O&D Plus Historical from Data Base Products
Onboard: Airline Traffic Data from Data Base Products

CD-ROM Applications for the Macintosh

The majority of CD-ROM discs and drives currently require an IBM PC or PC-compatible. Apple Computers has produced a SCSI-based CD-ROM drive that works with Macintosh and Apple II machines. The drive is supported by version 1.2 of Apple's HyperCard software. Most of the products that run on Apple computers are reference materials directed to vertical markets such as book lists, bibliographic databases, map collections, and art. Apple supports the High Sierra logical format. Its compact discs for the Macintosh computers use Hierarchical File System (HFS), a proprietary logical format that is incompatible with MS-DOS computers.

The CD-ROM drives that work with Macintosh computers include Apple CD SE, priced at $1,199, produced by Apple Computers. Toshiba America has developed the XM-2100A-MAC, featuring Toshiba's external XM-2100A player, which provides 680 megabytes of storage capacity and 400-millisecond access time, and audio output port for $995. All three drives require a Macintosh SE, Plus, or II, a SCSI port, and System 4.1 or higher.

SilverPlatter Information, Inc., has developed a Macintosh version of its search-and-retrieval software. In the meantime, OCLC (On-Line Computer Library Corporation) is planning a Macintosh version of Search CD-450 for many of its products for libraries and research, including resources for science, industry, agriculture, and education.

Of the more than 500 CD-ROM titles on the market, fewer than 8 percent are for the Macintosh computers. The following is a partial subject list of applications available for Macintosh computers.

Art

Art Room from Image Club
Comstock Desktop Photography from Comstock
Dark Room from Image Club
Graphics Lab from Alde Publishing

Kwikee Inhouse Graphics from Multi-Ad Services
Kwikee Inhouse Pal from Multi-Ad Services
Videoworks from MacroMind, Inc.
Wheeler Quick Art from Quanta Press

Bibliographic Tools

Books in Print Plus from Bowker Electronic Publishing
Books in Print Plus with Book Reviews Plus from Bowker Electronic
  Publishing

Computer

Club Mac from Quantum Access
The Educorp CD-ROM from Educorp
The MAC Guide USA CD-ROM from Mac Guide
MAK PAK from Alde Publishing
Manhole from Activision
PD-ROM from Berkeley Macintosh User Group
ProArt Trilogy I from Multi-Ad
Public Domain Software on File from Facts On File
QL Tech Mega-ROM from Quantum Leap Technologies
Universe of Sounds from Optical Media International

Directories

National Telephone Directory from Xiphias

Education

ESC Integrated Learning System from Education Systems
Time Table of History/Science & Innovation from Xiphias
The Whole Earth Learning Disc from Broderbund

Encyclopedias/Dictionaries

The Electronic Encyclopedia from Grolier Electronic Publishing
Merriam-Webster's Ninth New Collegiate Dictionary from Highlighted
  Data

Geography

Electronic Map Cabinet from Highlighted Data

Economics

Facts on File News Digest from Facts On File

Government

Fedstack from Highlighted Data
Seals of the U.S. Federal Government from Quanta Press
Statestack from Highlighted Data
The World Factbook from Quanta Press

Medicine

Medline Knowledge Finder from Aries Systems

Real Estate

Realscan Real Estate Information System from Laserscan Systems

Audio Applications

A number of products are aimed at audio users. The products that are designed to run on Macintosh computers have no problems. However, the PC version of any audio product needs a PC or compatible equipped with a speech synthesizer or special sampling adapter.

There are two types of speech synthesizers—internal circuit cards and external devices. The function of these adapters is to verbalize any text displayed on the screen or typed through the keyboard. There is no doubt that the audio feature adds dimension to training, education, reference, games, and entertainment. For instance, responses to the *BiblioFile Intelligent Catalog* of the Library Corporation are favorable. It seems that users tend to respond positively to a real voice that guides them through unknown territory. However, in the reference area, the sound level of a CD-ROM workstation might distract other library users unless a headset is hooked to the system. Audio capability is necessary for the sight-impaired as graphics and text is for the deaf. Voice has been added to a very small number of CD-ROM products.

An important factor that will increase the number of CD-ROM products that have audio capability is that government and state regulations favor buying products that support both the normal as well as the disabled communities. The following are examples of audio applications.

Apple Science CD from Apple Computer
CD-Audiofile from Compact Disc Products
CD-Capture from Compact Disc Products
CD-Companion-Beethoven Symphony No. 9 from Voyager
CD-Play from Compact Disc Products
Club Mac from Quantum Access
Intelligent Catalog from the Library Corporation
Merriam-Webster's Ninth New Collegiate Dictionary from Highlighted Data
16-Bit Sample Library: Sound Effects from Optical Media International
PD-ROM (MAC) from Berkeley Macintosh User Group
QL Tech Mega-ROM from Quantum Leap Technologies
Sound Designer from Optical Media International
Universe of Sounds from Optical Media International
Videoworks CD-ROM from MacroMind

APPENDIXES

A. CD-ROM Products (An Alphabetical List)

This list of CD-ROM products should by no means be considered complete. Every effort has been made to ensure the accuracy of information. Because prices change, they should be verified through vendors. Vendor addresses appear in Appendix C.

A-V ONLINE
Access Innovations, Inc.
SilverPlatter

A-V Online is a database of audiovisual materials from NICEM (National Information Center for Education Media, a division of Access Innovations, Inc.). *A-V Online* covers data from 1970 to the present. Includes videocassette titles, videotapes, disc records, overhead transparencies, 8mm motion cartridges, filmstips, sound recordings, and 16mm educational films. Coverage includes materials in Spanish, German, and French. Subject fields covered include vocational/technical AV, science and computer literacy, language arts, foreign languages, social studies, sports, health and fitness, travel, and special education. Provides information on producers and distributors. $795/year plus quarterly updates.

ABI/INFORM OnDisc
University Microfilms International

Provides access to business and management information with a comprehensive database of citations and abstracts to nearly 700 journals. Areas covered include accounting and auditing, banking and international trade, data processing and information management, economics, finance and financial management, general management, health care, human resources, insurance, law and taxation, management science, marketing, advertising and sales, real estate, and telecommunications. Annual subscription is $4,950.

About Cows
Quanta Press, Inc.

A reprint of the North Wood Press volume *About Cows* by Sara Roth. $29.95.

Academic Index
Information Access Co.

Indexes scholarly and general-interest journals for undergraduate research. Covers arts, education, history, anthropology, literature, computer,

religion, geography, psychology, and political science. It also includes African, Asian, Eastern European, Latin American, and Middle Eastern studies.
$4,000/year plus updates.

ACCESS Pennsylvania
Brodart Automation
See Chapter 11.

ADA ON CD-ROM
Alde Publishing
Public domain ADA programs, utilities, and source code from the SIMTEL
20 network. $99.

Agri/Stats
Hopkins Technology
U.S. agricultural statistics including crop estimates, grain stocks, county
estimates—crops and livestock, hog and pig estimates, cattle inventory, and
cattle on feed. Files date back to 1939. One foreign database is included:
Corn production in 42 African countries since 1966. $65.

Agribusiness USA
Pioneer Hi-Bred International
DIALOG Information Services
Agriculture database contains over 90,000 records covering a wide range
of the agricultural industry. Includes more than 300 prominent U.S. agricultural businesses. Trade and government publications are selectively indexed
and abstracted. It tracks competitors, locates statistical trends in agricultural
production and prices, monitors new products, obtains current agricultural
business news, and analyzes the global agricultural community. A number of
USDA narrative and statistical reports are included in their complete text, as
are many agricultural and statistical reports of the United Nations Food and
Agricultural Organization (FAO) and the European Economic Community
(EEC). This quarterly updated product covers the period from 1985 to the
present. $2,000/year plus updates.

AGRICOLA
Quanta Press, Inc.
Contains the National Agricultural Library's bibliographic database,
AGRICOLA. Covers the period from 1985 to the present. $99.

AGRICOLA and CRIS
OCLC
AGRICOLA database consists of citations to monographs, dissertations,
technical reports, journal articles, and selected chapters from over 5,000
serials and books as compiled by the National Agriculture Library. *CRIS*
(Current Research Information System) database cites abstracts and progress reports for current research in agriculture and related sciences. $795/year
plus updates. *AGRICOLA Retrospective File* (1979–1982) is listed for $350.

SilverPlatter
Contains descriptions of current publicly supported agriculture and
forestry research projects. *AGRICOLA* 1970 to present is $1,850, while
subscription for second year and subsequent years is $950/year plus updates.

Agriculture Library
  OCLC
  Compiled from OCLC union catalog. Contains over 300,000 bibliographic records on agriculture-related subjects. Represents agriculture materials in libraries, covering agriculture, food production, forestry, fisheries, and veterinary medicines in all formats. $350.

Agriculture Series
  OCLC
  Includes *AGRICOLA, CRIS,* and *Agriculture Library.* $1,095/year plus updates.

AIDS-Compact Library
  Medical Publishing Group
  Includes the *AIDS Knowledge Base* from San Francisco General Hospital, a special subset of *MEDLINE* containing citations related to AIDS, the *AIDS Database* from the Bureau of Hygiene and Tropical Diseases, and the full text of articles about AIDS from *Annals of Internal Medicine, Journal of Infectious Diseases, British Medical Journal, Lancet, Morbidity and Mortality Weekly Report, Nature, New England Journal of Medicine,* and *Science.* The *AIDS Knowledge Base* covers pathogenesis, diagnosis, and epidemiology of AIDS and discusses strategies for management and prevention. It includes sections on public health issues and social and psychological aspects of the disease. Updated quarterly and listed for $875.

AIDS Information and Education Worldwide CD-ROM
  CD Resources
  Includes materials from 230 publications and over 10,000 pages of core source materials on AIDS. It includes articles, technical reports, and case studies from over 230 full-text publications. Abstracts and bibliographic citations are also included. The database is in three volumes and covers AIDS literature from 1981 to the present. Purchase price is $1,295.

AIDS Supplement
  Digital Diagnostics, Inc.
  AIDS supplement consists of more than 40,000 citations included in *MEDLINE* covering six to eight years. This supplement contains the following medical subject headings (MeSH): Acquired Immunodeficiency Syndrome; HIV; HTLV-III; Immunologic Deficiency Syndrome; T Lymphocytes; Sarcoma, Kaposi's; Retrovirus; Cytomegalic Inclusion Disease; Cryptosporidiosis; Leukoviruses; Chancroid; Epidemiology; Homosexuality; Substance Use and Abuse; Candidiasis; Herpes; and Stomatitis. $395.

ALA CD-ROM Directory of Library & Information Professionals
  Knowledge Access International
  Includes biographical data on approximately 45,000 individuals in the information industry. Most entries include name, address, current employer, information on education, special areas of interest, and work experience. Features free text searching, cross tabulation, and statistical analysis. $495.

ALDE's $99 CD-ROM Disc
  Alde Publishing
  Public domain programs. $99.

American Authors on CD-ROM
    Electronic Text Corp.
    Published for WordCruncher and Library of America. Volume 1 contains a collection of the following ten authors: Henry David Thoreau, Ralph Waldo Emerson, Walt Whitman, Nathaniel Hawthorne, Henry James, Thomas Jefferson, Jack London, Herman Melville, Mark Twain, and Benjamin Franklin. $495.

Anybook
    Library Corporation
    Information on prices and publishers of English books in print. See Chapter 11.

Apple Science CD Volume 1
    Apple Computer, Inc.
    Designed to help science teachers and researchers in the classroom and lab. The disc includes scientific data, simulations, animations, and data analysis software. Designed for Macintosh Plus/SE/II.

Applied Science & Technology Index
    H. W. Wilson Co.
    Contains an index of 335 of the key English-language periodicals in applied science and technology, chemistry, computer technology, marine technology, geology, energy, and food (1983 to present). $1,495.

Aquatic Sciences and Fisheries
    Compact Cambridge
    The ASAF database is composed of literature published by the United Nations Department of International Economic and Social Affairs; the Food and Agriculture Organization of the United Nations (FAO); and the International Oceanographic Commission (OIC). Coverage includes all biological and ecological aspects of marine, freshwater, and brackish environments; pollution of aquatic environments; fisheries, aquaculture, and other living resources; selected descriptive works on the physical environment of aquatic organisms; aquatic communities; all aspects of oceanography; limnology; acoustics and optics of aquatic environments; marine meteorology and climatology; marine technology and engineering; related offshore operations and services; nonliving resources; and legal, economic, and sociological studies. Contains citations in more than 40 languages and corresponds to the monthly journal ASFA-1: Biological sciences and living resources; and ASFA-2: Ocean technology, policy and nonliving resources. $1,250/year plus updates.

Arctic and Antarctic Regions
    NISC
    Known also as the Cold Regions Database. Contains more than 147,000 citations compiled by the Science and Technology Division of the Library of Congress.

Art Index
    H. W. Wilson Co.
    Bibliographic database on articles from more than 230 domestic and

foreign periodicals, selected yearbooks, and museum bulletins covering art history, architecture, archeology, fine arts, crafts, and related subjects (1984 to present). $1,495/year.

ArtRoom
   Image Club Graphics, Inc.
   Includes clips for the Macintosh of more than 1,000 Postscript images and 100 laser advertising fonts for any publishing program that supports Postscript. $999.

ArtScan
   Newsreel Access

Associations: Global Access
   Gale Research, Inc.
   Knowledge Access, Inc.
   Includes Gale's *Encyclopedia of Associations International* and other related databases. Covers national organizations of United States; international organizations; state and local organizations in the United States; and approximately 11,000 association periodicals. Search fields are: basic index, association name, acronyms/keyword, primary keyword, subjects, city, state, ZIP code, area code, officer name, founding year, number of staff, budget size, descriptive text in abstract. Search results can be printed or saved on disc. There is an auto-dialer for telecommunications. A free demo disc is available for the IBM. Price is $2,195/year plus updates. An option is provided to print mailing lists and labels for $300.

Automated Facilities
   National Institute of Building Sciences

AVS+
   Information Update, Inc.
   National directory of addresses derived from ZIP+4 Directory. Updated quarterly. Annual subscription is $3,950.

BaTaSYSTEMS Order; Titles on CD
   Baker & Taylor
   An acquisitions system used with Bowker's *Books in Print Plus*. See Chapter 11.

Beilstein Handbook of Organic Chemistry
   Springer Verlag

BIB-BASE/CD-ROM
   Small Library Computing
   See Chapter 9.

Bible Library
   AIRS, Inc.
   Includes four translations of the Bible and some related works.

The Bible Library
   Ellis Enterprises, Inc.
   Includes several Bibles and twenty-one reference books integrated with

sixty word and phrase concordances. It contains the only Romanized Bible that is transliterated for Greek and Hebrew letters. It includes *A Bible Dictionary, Theological Dictionary, Edersheim's, The Life and Times of Jesus,* hymn stories, and over 3,000 nondenominational sermon outlines and illustrations. It uses the *New Morris Literal Translation* for biblical terms. Search can be done by topic, specific words, or word combinations. It features full-screen, side-by-side display of search results, index browsing of every word via a pop-up window, and recording of complex search requests for later use or modification, a hypertext feature. Updated periodically and listed for $595.

BiblioDisc
Online Computer Systems, Inc.
Contains approximately 300,000 titles distributed by the Canadian book trade. The disc was produced jointly by the National Library of Canada and the Canadian Telebook Agency.

BiblioFile Catalog Maintenance
Library Corp.
See Chapter 9.

BiblioFile Catalog Production
Library Corp.
See Chapter 9.

BiblioFile Circulation
Library Corp.
See Chapter 11.

Bibliographie Nationale Français depuis 1975 sur CD-ROM
Chadwyck-Healey, Inc.
Includes the French national bibliography.

BiblioMed
Digital Diagnostics, Inc.
$950/year plus updates.

Biography Index
H. W. Wilson Co.
Biographical database from periodical, books, critical studies, letters, autobiographies, diaries, and journals (1984 to present). $1,095/year plus updates.

Biological Abstracts
BIOSIS
Includes bibliographic citations and life science abstracts from more than 9,000 biological and biomedical journals worldwide.

Biological and Agricultural Index
H. W. Wilson Co.
Contains bibliographic information on articles covering agriculture, animal husbandry, biology, ecology, environmental sciences, forestry, soil science, zoology, and related subjects (1983 to present). $1,495/year plus updates.

Black Fiction Up to 1920
Cornell University

Blue Sail Library
Alde Publishing Co.
Contains public domain software that can be stored on approximately 1,000 floppy diskettes. $149.

Book Review Digest
H. W. Wilson Co.
Contains excerpts to reviews of current fiction and nonfiction books. Covers more than 6,000 English-language books (1983 to present). $1,095/year plus updates.

Bookbank
J. Whitaker
Based on the British *Books in Print*. See Chapter 11.

Books in Print Plus
Bowker Electronic Publishing
See Chapter 11.

Books in Print With Book Reviews Plus
Bowker Electronic Publishing
See Chapter 11.

Books Out of Print Plus
Bowker Electronic Publishing
See Chapter 11.

BPN/JR
Library Systems & Services, Inc.
Cataloging support.

BRIEF/CASE
JA Micropublishing, Inc.
Provides information on public, private, and nonprofit organizations. It also provides full-text information from annual reports, news releases, benefits, career and recruitment literature, company magazines and newspapers. Updated quarterly. $2,895 commercial enterprises; $1,250 academic institutions.

British Library General Catalogue of Printed Books to 1975 on CD-ROM
Chadwyck-Healey, Inc.
See Chapter 11.

British National Bibliography on CD-ROM
Chadwyck-Healey, Inc.
Includes records from the British National Library from 1950 to 1985 on two discs. $6900. Current disc covers records from 1986 to the present. $1,900/year plus quarterly updates. Prices will vary after November 1989.

Business Indicators
Slater Hall Information Products
An economic time series holding GNP Accounts from 1929, articles from

Blue Pages Survey of Current Business Statistics from 1929 to present; annual, quarterly, and monthly data; economic times series; income and employment data by industry for every state; and state personal income and employment from 1969 to present. Annual license $2,200 with monthly updates.

Business Periodicals Index
   H. W. Wilson Co.
A bibliographic index to more than 290 business magazines, with information on accounting, banking, building and construction, the chemical industry, marketing, and other related topics (1982 to present). $1,495/year plus updates.

Business Periodicals Ondisc (BPO)
   University Microfilms International
BPO is a full-text image system from UMI containing complete articles from nearly 300 business and management journals indexed in *ABI/INFORM*, covering 55 percent of all 1988 and 1989 *ABI/INFORM Ondisc* records. The 300 titles were selected by UMI according to a study of retrieval frequency in the *ABI/INFORM* online file. Retrospective coverage begins with 1987 material; the current collection contains sample titles (17 discs) from 1987, and more than 250 titles (65 discs) from 1988. The total of 50 to 60 discs contains approximately 5,500 article pages each. *BPO* is updated bimonthly, synchronized with *ABI/FORM Ondisc* subscription. As new records are added to *ABI/INFORM*, the corresponding articles are available through *BPO*. The system allows browsing through the table of contents of any periodical, or browsing through several issues to read relevant articles. Searching is done through *ABI/INFORM* first. Once a record is selected, a notation on the screen tells which disc holds the complete article. Upon insertion of the corresponding disc, the article appears on the screen. The user can move from page to page or zoom in on particular elements of the article. A laser printer is used to produce a high-quality photocopy.

The system is available as a turnkey package on a twelve-month subscription. It includes the *ABI/INFORM Ondisc* and *BPO* databases (a total of approximately 140 discs), and an image retrieval and output workstation, laser printer, application software, connector for debit card reader or coin box, and disc storage carousels. Free service is provided by UMI. If the user is an *ABI/INFORM* subscriber, the annual subscription of the *BPO* will cost $14,950; otherwise it is $19,900, including workstation and maintenance.

Business Statistics 1929–85
   Slater Hall Information Products
   Government statistics database. $1,200.

C CD-ROM
   Alde Publishing
   Source codes and utilities for C programming language. $99.

CAB Abstracts
   CAB International
CAB Abstracts is a comprehensive file of worldwide agricultural informa-

tion. Covers branches of agricultural science, including crop science and production, animal science and production, forestry, crop protection (pest control), machinery and buildings, biotechnology, economics, and sociology. Unique topics covered include veterinary medicine, human nutrition, developing countries, leisure, recreation, and tourism.

California Decisions
  ROM Publishers, Inc.
  $1,595.

California Music Directory
  Knowledge Access International
  Includes 1988 Who's Who in California Music Industry. $495.

Canadian Business and Current Affairs
  Micromedia Ltd.
  DIALOG Information Services
  Bibliographic database of articles from more than 200 business periodicals, 300 magazines, and 10 newspapers, including the *Globe and Mail, Toronto Star,* and *Montreal Gazette.* Covers the *Canadian Business Index, Canadian News Index, Canadian Magazine Index,* the *Bibliography of Works on Canadian Foreign Relations,* and the Ontario Securities Commission filings (1982 to present). $1,250/year plus updates (discount price available for Canadian schools).

Canadian Postal Codes
  SilverPlatter

Cancer-CD
  SilverPlatter
  Includes references, abstracts, and commentaries of the world's literature in cancer and related subjects from Elsevier Science Publishers, Year Book Medical Publishers, and the complete *CANCERLIT* file from the National Cancer Institute in conjunction with the National Library of Medicine. Covers current year plus five previous years (1983 to present). $1,750/year plus updates; $2,500 multiuser.

CancerLit
  Aries Systems Corp.

CancerLit
  CD Plus

CancerLit CD-ROM
  Compact Cambridge
  Includes citations and abstracts from over 3,000 biomedical journals worldwide. Includes papers presented at meetings, dissertations, and reports. $995/year.

Cancer on Disc: 1988
  CMC ReSearch
  Includes full text, images, and tables from *Cancer,* a journal of the American Cancer Society which is published by J. B. Lippincott Co. $195.

CAP
Computer Aided Planning, Inc.
Catalog and CAD libraries for twenty contract furniture manufacturers.
$1,500/year plus updates.

CASSIS CD-ROM
NISC
Published for the U.S. Patent Office. Two discs are published every two months. $465/year.

CAT CD450
OCLC
A cataloging system that enables users to search, create, edit, and print catalog records and spine labels offline. See Chapter 9.

Cataloger's Tool Kit
EBSCO
See Chapter 9.

Catalogue of United Kingdom Official Publications
Chadwyck-Healey, Inc.
800/year plus updates.

CCINFOdisc: OH&S Information (Series A)
Canadian Centre for Occupational Health & Safety (CCOHS)
Contains databases on material safety data sheets of trade-name chemical products; individual chemicals; Registry of Toxic Effects of Chemical Substances. $134/year plus updates.

CD-Audiofile
Compact Disc Products
$195.

CD Banking
Lotus Development Corp.
Commercial banks, holdings, and savings. $11,200/year.

CD-Capture
Compact Disc Products
Transfers audio data to computer's RAM. $100.

CD-CAT
Cooperating Libraries Automated Network (CLAN)
See Chapter 11.

CD-CATSS Current Cataloging
Utlas International
See Chapter 9.

CD-Companion. Beethoven Symphony No. 9
Voyager
HyperCard application using compact disc with Hans Schmidt-Isserstedt conducting the Vienna Philharmonic. $100.

CD-Fiche
USA Information Systems, Inc.
Includes the *Federal Supply Catalog*. Procurement history files cover price, quantity, and vendor information. Includes history files such as: Technical Characteristics, MIAPL; MCRL1,2, & 3; ML-C; H4/H8 CAGE Codes; AMDF: and P2300 Series. $3,995/year plus updates.

CD-GENE
Hitachi American Ltd.
Includes GenBank, EMBL, and Protein Identification Resource databases.

CD-Play
Compact Disc Products
Plays audio discs on CD-ROM drives. $95.

CD-ROM Developer's Lab
Software Mart, Inc.
A reference source on how to produce a CD-ROM disc. Provides information on design project management, programming, file formats, specifications, data preparation, premastering, and mastering for the IBM and Macintosh computers. $795.

CD-ROM Prototype Disc
U.S. Geological Survey
Geological information. $35.

CD-ROM Sampler
Discovery Systems
Multimedia free demo disc.

CD-ROM: The Conference Disc
PDO
2nd Microsoft Conference on CD-ROM. $20.

CD-ROM: The New Papyrus
Computer Access Corp.

CD/2000
OCLC
See Chapter 10.

CD/Biotech
PC-SIG, Inc.
Biotechnology database. $475/year plus update.

CD/Corporate
Lotus Development Corp.
Public companies, businesses, industries, and executives. $4,550/year.

CD/Corptech
Lotus Development Corp.
Public and private high-tech companies. $6,500/year.

CD/International
Lotus Development Corp.
Database of international companies. $13,650/year.

CD/Investment
Lotus Development Corp.
Bonds, Compustat, Compustat-Line of Business, Compustat-Research, Compustat-Utilities, daily stocks, Ford investors, Media General, Value Liner Estimates. $11,000–$18,000/year plus updates and system.

CD/Law: Illinois
CD/Law Reports, Inc.

CD/Newsline
Lotus Development Corp.
Dow Jones News Retrieval Service. $2,000/year.

CD/Private+
Lotus Development Corp.
Ward's Business Directory and *Macmillan Directory of Leading Private Companies*. $7,000/year.

CDID on Disc
Knowledge Access International
Includes consumer drug information on approximately 250 prescription drugs. $245.

CDMARC Bibliographic
Library of Congress
See Chapter 9.

CDMARC NAMES
Library of Congress
See Chapter 9.

CDMARC SUBJECTS
Library of Congress
See Chapter 9.

Census: Australian Standardized Local Government Finance Statistics
Space-Time Research, Ltd.
Includes the complete record of the Australian Bureau of Local Government Finance Statistics, such as expenditures by 1,000 local government areas.

Census Disc
U.S. Bureau of the Census
Includes agricultural data for counties, 1982; demographic data for ZIP codes, 1980; and population estimates for government units, 1984.

Census of Agriculture on CD-ROM (1982)
Slater Hall Information Products
Contains the complete Census Bureau county file of the 1982 Census of Agriculture as well as comparable data from the 1978 census for counties,

states, and U.S. totals. Data covers acreage, operating expenses, sales, productions, crops, livestock, farm loans, and others. $1,200.

Census of Australian Population & Housing, 1981 and 1986
Space-Time Research, Ltd.
Contains 50,000,000 pieces of information. $3,200.

Census of England, Scotland and Wales, Small Area Statistics 1981
Space-Time Research, Ltd.
Covers 1987 population estimates, boundary maps, and other census data.

Census of Hong Kong, 1981 and 1986
Space-Time Research, Ltd.
Contains information on the 21 tertiary planning units for 1981, 217 tertiary planning units for 1986, 19 district board election areas for 1981 and 1986, and map data for the tertiary planning units and district board election areas. $1,000.

Census of New Zealand, 1986 Census
Space-Time Research, Ltd.
Includes information and map boundary data for 1,400 area units. $3,200.

Census of Sweden, 1970 to 1987
Space-Time Research, Ltd.
Contains information and map boundary data for Sweden. $3,200.

Census Test Disc #1
U.S. Bureau of Census
Contains agricultural data from the 1982 Census of Agriculture and demographic data and population estimates data from the 1980 population estimates. $125.

Census Test Disc #2
U.S. Bureau of Census
Contains data from the 1982 Census of Agriculture, including final county file data from the 1982 Economic Census. $125.

Census: U.S. County Business Patterns, 1985
Chadwyck-Healey, Inc.
Space-Time Research, Ltd.
Contains complete record of the 1985 U.S. Bureau of Census County Business Patterns. Data include number of employees and expenditures, broken down by company size and SIC code. $990.

Census: U.S. Data, 1980—Supermap
Space-Time Research, Ltd.
Contains items from the 1980 U.S. census of population, housing, and other social and economic data. Contains tables and time series from 1960 to 1985. Supermap software retrieves, manipulates, and displays data subsets. Price varies depending on specific regions ($750–$1980).

CHEM-BANK
  SilverPlatter
  A collection of databanks of potentially hazardous chemicals, containing four complete major databanks: *Registry of Toxic Effects of Chemical Substances* (RTECS) from the National Institute for Occupational Safety and Health; *Oil and Hazardous Materials—Technical Assistance Data System* (OHMTADS); and *Toxic Substances Control Act* (TOSCA). Initial Inventory published June 1, 1979, both from the U.S. Environmental Protection Agency; and Chemical Hazard Response Information System (CHRIS), from the U.S. Department of Transportation (Coast Guard). $1,350/year plus updates; $1,050 for OSH-ROM subscribers.

Chrysler Parts Catalog
  Bell & Howell

CineScan
  Newsreel Access Systems
  Index to film and videotape archives. Prices vary.

Climatedata
  US West Optical Publishing
  Includes the National Climatic Data Center database. Provides information on daily rainfall, maximum temperature, etc. $495.

ClinMED-CD
  SilverPlatter
  A subset of the entire *MEDLINE* database focusing on clinical medicine and including journals, primarily in English, from the *Abridged Index Medicus,* the Brandon-Hill List from the *Bulletin of the Medical Library Association,* and the Library for Internists List recommended by the American College of Physicians. *ClinMED* will also include *AIDSLINE,* a new bibliographic file from the National Library of Medicine, which includes all AIDS-related citations from *MEDLINE,* and ten titles from the Year Book series, including *Year Book of Cardiology, Year Book of Critical Care Medicine,* and others. *ClinMED* will cover five years of data on a single disc. $850/year plus updates.

Clip Art 3-D
  NEC Home Electronics
  A collection of graphic images that can be rotated in three dimensions and converted to formats that allow inclusion into desktop publishing programs.

ClubMac
  Quantum Access, Inc.
  Club Mac, for the Macintosh, is a collection of public-domain software, "shareware," clip art, fonts, Hypercard stacks. Lists for $199 (single issue) and $350 (annual subscription with four quarterly issues).

Codice Tributario
  LaserData, Inc.

Compact Disclosure
Disclosure Inc.
Companies on U.S. Stock Exchange. $4,500/year plus updates.

Compact Disclosure Europe
Disclosure, Inc.
Covers financial information on 2,000 top European publicly held companies. Updated semiannually. $3,000/year; includes the CD drive.

Compact Med-Base
Online Research Systems, Inc.
$3,495/year plus updates.

Company Accounts & Register of Compustat PC Plus
Standard & Poors Compustat Services

Comprehensive Medline
EBSCO
$2,400/year plus updates.

Comptroller General Decisions
Information Handling Services

COMPU-INFO
SilverPlatter
See Computer—SPECS.

Compustat PC Plus on CD-ROM
Standard & Poor Compustat Services
Information on over 10,000 companies. $8,000–$45,000/year plus updates.

Computer Library
OCLC
Bibliographic database from the OCLC online union catalog. $300.

Computer Library
Ziff Communications
Full text and abstracted computer magazine articles. It contains the full text of the following computer magazines: *PC Magazine, PC Week, Lotus Magazine, Digital Review, MacUser, PC Tech Journal, Government Computer News, A+, Microsoft Systems Journal,* and *Communications of the ACM*. It also includes abstracts from more than 120 other publications, such as the *New York Times, ComputerWorld,* and *InfoWorld*. $695.

Computer—SPECS
GML Corp.
SilverPlatter
A database of 12,000 computer product listings that evolved from GML Corporation's popular REVIEW series of computer product references. It contains information about mainframes, microcomputers, minicomputers, operating systems, communications, display terminals, teleprinters, and other peripherals. It allows access by 300 specific categories as well as by name and model. $1,250/year plus updates.

Computerized Clinical Information Systems (CCIS)
Micromedex, Inc.
Includes the following databases: *Drugdex, Emergindex, Identindex, Poisindex, TOMES, Dosing and Therapeutic Tools,* and *Martindale.* $11,195.

Congressional Information Service
Congressional Information Service
Congressional Masterfile 1789–1969 includes the U.S. Serial Set (1789–1969), U.S. Congressional Committee Hearings (1833–1969), U.S. Congressional Committee Prints (1833–1969), and unpublished Senate hearings from 1824 to 1964.

Conquest: Consumer Information
Donnelley Marketing Information Services
$13,000–$30,000 plus system.

Constitution Papers
Optical Media International
24-Karat Gold Multimedia on the U.S. Constitution plus related topics. $29.95.

Construction Activity Locator
Knowledge Access International
CD Productions
Census data on building permits reported to the Bureau of the Census as of January 1987. Tracks more than 400,000 building permits and valuations for 17,000 cities. A "Top 50" category ranks the volume and growth of construction based on such indicators as single-unit residential and total residential units, plus residential, nonresidential, and total construction valuations. Features free text searching, cross-tabulation, and statistical analysis. $4,000/year.

Construction Criteria Base
National Institute of Building Sciences
Includes construction guides for selected government agencies. Data collected from the Bureau of Reclamation, Corps of Engineers, DOD, NASA, NAVFAC, and Veterans Administration. $550/year plus updates.

Consu/Stats
Hopkins Technology
Includes data files on 1984 surveys on consumer expenditures in different geographical areas. $65.

Core Medline
EBSCO
$1,400/year plus updates.

Corporate & Industry Research Reports
JA Micropublishing, Inc.
SilverPlatter
A cumulative index with abstracts to over 70,000 corporate and industry reports written by securities and investment banking firms from 1979 to present. $1,250/year plus updates.

County Statistics
Slater Hall Information Products
Includes county and metropolitan-area data. It is the Census Bureau's *COSTAT II* file and is a compendium of information for U.S. counties. Covers such topics as: population, housing, health, education, banking, retail and wholesale trade, and crime statistics. $1,200.

Cross-Cultural CD
SilverPlatter
Cross-Cultural CD, in collaboration with the *Human Relations Area Files* (HRAF), contains a series of full-text files designed for teaching in the social and behavioral sciences and the humanities. The texts are extracted from more than 1,000 anthropological, sociological, and psychological books and articles on life in sixty different societies around the world in the nineteenth and twentieth centuries. This database covers human sexuality. It is the first title in a series that will cover other topics including marriage, family life, crime and social problems, old age, death and dying, childhood and adolescence, socialization and education, religious beliefs, and religious practices. It is updated semiannually, and the annual license fee is $1,350.

CrossLink: Supply/Logistics Data
Information Handling Services, Inc.

Cumulative Book Index
H. W. Wilson Co.
See Chapter 11.

Current Cataloging Database
Utlas
See Chapter 9.

CUSIP Directory
Standard & Poor's Compustat Services

Daily Oklahoman
DataTimes
A database stored on CD-ROM, available for online search through Telenet. $1.40/minute.

Dark Room
Image Club Graphics Inc.
Dark Room for the Macintosh is a stock photo library with more than 500 professional, ready-to-use photos in four categories: sports, life-style, business, and travel. The photos can be used with any publishing program that uses the tagged image file format. $499.

Data Times Libraries System
DataTimes
A database stored on CD-ROM, available for online search through Telenet. $1.40/minute.

Decision Series
ROM Publishers, Inc.
Legal libraries by region. $3,500/year plus updates.

DECUS
　　Digital Decus Group
　　Composed of two discs: Disc 1, Fall 1986, includes VAX SIG Symposia
Collection. Disc 2, Spring 1987, includes Best of PC 8088 collections 1–8.
$100/disc.

Delorme's World Atlas
　　Delorme Mapping Systems
　　Worldwide vector-based atlas. Prices vary.

Desktop Photography
　　Comstock, Inc.
　　Comstock *Desktop Photography* for the Macintosh is a collection of almost
500 public-domain stock photographs from the Comstock photography
catalog used by magazine and agency art directors. The disc, which works on
a Macintosh II or SE, allows selection, sizing, and cropping of images on
screen, and requires Aldus Pagemaker or a comparable desktop publishing
program. The disc can be used with Pagemaker, QuarkXPress, or Ready-
Set-Go! software and any publishing program that uses the tagged image
file format. According to the licensing agreement, the disc-based photos
cannot be used as clip art. Also, the license limits the user to noncommercial
in-house usage. $500.

Desktop Sounds
　　Optical Media International
　　Contains over 400 digital sound effects such as crowds, household,
industry, human voice, weather, and many others. Requires HyperCard.
$149.

Deutsche Bibliographie-aktuell-CD-ROM
　　Chadwyck-Healey, Inc.
　　Includes the German national bibliography.

Dick's-Earth's Planes
　　Quanta Press, Inc.
　　The disc is a visual compendia of military aircraft worldwide. Includes a
detailed database of NATO and Warsaw Pact aircraft as well as those of
individual countries. Includes line drawings, black-and-white photographs,
and VGA color images. Includes information on origin, model, name,
manufacturer, service of use, crew, mission, wingspan, length, speed, range,
and ceiling. $249.95.

Disclosure Spectrum
　　Disclosure, Inc.

DisCon
　　Utlas International
　　See Chapter 9.

Discovery—DIALOG OnDisc
　　DIALOG Information
　　Contains brief descriptions of the following eight Dialog databases: *ERIC,
Medline, Agribusiness, NTIS, Canadian Business and Current Affairs, Standard and*

Poor's Public Companies, Poor's Private Companies, and *Poor's Executives.* Command language used in online service is included. $59.

Dissertation Abstracts OnDisc
University Microfilms International
Bibliographic references to doctoral and master's theses. $995/year.

Dosing and Therapeutic Tools
Micromedex, Inc.
Includes data support for diagnosis and therapy. $295.

Dover Clip Art Series
Alde Publishing
Clip art from Dover Publications, Inc., including images. $149.

Drug Information Center
Compact Cambridge
A full-text database covering three resources: (1) *American Hospital Formularly Services Drug Information*—the premier source for complete evaluative information on drug action, dosage, toxicity, interactions, pharmacokinetics, cautions, lab tests—with more than 935 full monographs relating to approximately 20,000 trade names, synonyms, and generic names, as well as drugs under investigation; (2) *Handbook on Injectable Drugs,* which includes compatibility and stability information for fixing drugs in solutions and syringes for almost 300 drugs, both commercially available and those under investigation; (3) *International Pharmaceutical Abstracts,* which includes approximately 50,000 citations and abstracts from over 700 international journals, covering almost any drug-related subject. Updated semiannually. $1950/year; $2145 overseas.

Drugdex
Micromedex, Inc.
Drug evaluations. $2,640; price includes quarterly updates.

Earth Science Series
OCLC
Includes *USGS Library, GEOINDEX,* and *Earth Science Data Directory.* $300/year.

EBook, Electronic Art Anthology
EBSCO Electronic Information Division
First volume is expected to include European paintings. Requires IBM PS/2 or compatibles and VGA graphics monitor.

Econ/Stats
Hopkins Technology
Comprises the following databases: *Capacity Utilization, Consumer Price Index, Export-Import Price Index, Industrial Production Index, Industry Employment Hours and Earning by State and Area, Money Stock, Producer Price Index,* and *Selected Interest Rate.* Some of the data date back to 1913. $65.

Education Index
H. W. Wilson Co.
Contains an index of more than 340 English-language periodicals, yearbooks, and monographs (1983 to the present). $1295/year plus updates.

Education Library
OCLC
Formerly EMIL—*Education Materials in Libraries*—compiled from the OCLC online union catalog, this database lists over 450,000 bibliographic records for materials pertaining to education ($350; member price $300).

Education Series
OCLC
Education Series comprises *ERIC* and the *Education Library.* Annual subscription is $1095; for OCLC members, $995.

Educorp CD-ROM
Educorp
Includes approximately 300 megabytes of public-domain "shareware" and "stackware" behind a Hypercard interface. $199.

EINECS Plus-CD
SilverPlatter
Jointly published with the European Community's Office for Official Publications, *EINECS Plus-CD* contains the advance edition of the *European Inventory of Existing Commercial Chemical Substances* (over 100,000), known as *EINECS*; together with the list of dangerous substances (now over 1,000) with labeling requirements as prescribed by European Community legislation. Information is indispensable to manufacturers, traders, administrators, and researchers, dealing with the twelve countries of the European Economic Community, the world's principal chemicals market. $1,400.

The Electronic Encyclopedia
Grolier Electronic Publishing Inc.
The entire text of the twenty volumes of the *Academic American Encyclopedia.* It contains almost 34,000 articles. Searches can be accomplished by any word or string in the ten-million-word database through the use of an electronic index. The encyclopedia is oriented to students from the higher elementary grades to college. It has a mouse support, an electronic bookmark, a notepad to save all or parts of articles, split-screen viewing to show more than one article at a time, and a menu. $299.

Electronic Map Cabinet
Highlighted Data, Inc.
A 600-megabyte database of U.S. geographic information, including detailed street maps for more than 300 major cities. It allows users to zoom in on any point in the country. Political boundaries can be designed and displayed. $199.95.

The Electronic Publishing Arts Disc
Network Technology Corp.
Contains desktop publishing clip art, fonts forms, templates, and software. $995.

Electronic Sweet's
McGraw-Hill

EMBASE (Excerpta Medica Abstract Journals on CD-ROM)
SilverPlatter
Excerpta, from Elsevier Science Publishers, contains approximately 150,000 abstracts a year about biomedical information taken from primary journals published in many different countries and languages.

Emergindex
Micromedex, Inc.
Includes critical care abstracts.

Encyclopedia of Polymer Science and Engineering
Wiley Electronic Publishing
Reflects the vast changes that have occurred in polymer science, including new topics such as natural and synthetic polymers, plastics, fibers, elastomers, and computer topics. It contains articles from 12 volumes (the paper edition is 19 volumes). The menu-driven database uses Boolean search features. The encyclopedia is updated annually. It lists for $3,200; customers who receive the printed edition may order it for $895.

Energy Library
OCLC
Materials from the OCLC online union catalog. $300.

Enflex Info
ERM Computer Services, Inc.
Contains the full text of the current federal and state environmental regulations and federal health and safety information. $2,500/year plus updates.

Engineering Information System
National Institute of Building Sciences

Enhanced BiblioFile
Library Corp.
See Chapter 9.

Environment Library
OCLC
Materials from the OCLC online union catalog. $300.

ERIC
The Educational Resources Information Center (ERIC) database, an educational research tool, is one of the most widely searched databases. It includes abstracts of articles published since 1966 in more than 750 educational journals and documents collected by the U.S. Department of Education. ERIC contains research reports, evaluation studies, curriculum guides, and lesson plans. The printed version of ERIC is composed of two major indexes: *Current Index to Journals in Education (CIJE),* handling the published journal articles; and *Resources in Education (RIE),* handling the document and report (fugitive) literature. ERIC is also available in printed form, on magnetic tape, and online. ERIC has been published on CD-ROM in three versions, DIALOG OnDisc, OCLC, and SilverPlatter. Each product offers

free-text searching, field qualifications, Boolean logic, expansion of search terms, truncation, nesting, proximity searching, index display, and downloading to disc. Each provides a toll-free telephone number and documentation. Only DIALOG includes a thesaurus, and it has sorting and online access capabilities. SilverPlatter provides on-disc tutorial. DIALOG features EASY MENU Search for the novice and COMMAND SEARCH for the experienced DIALOG searcher. All three products are compatible with other products from the same producer.

DIALOG Information Services, Inc.
DIALOG OnDisc ERIC (1966–present, $1,650; annual subscription $950.

OCLC
OCLC Search CD450 ERIC (ERIC 1982–present with quarterly updates $425; OCLC member price, $350); three ERIC retrospective files—CIJE 1969–1981, RIE 1977–1981, RIE 1967–1976—$900; OCLC member price $750.

SilverPlatter Information, Inc.
ERIC on SilverPlatter (1983–present, updated quarterly; annual license, $390); two archival discs—1966–1975, 1976–1982—purchase price, $900. (The complete starter set $1200, then second and subsequent annual subscriptions are available at $750.)

ESC Integrated Learning System
Education Systems Corp.
Includes 1,800 reading and math lessons for elementary ages. Features music, graphics, and animation capability for the Tandy, IBM, Apple IIgs, and Macintoch computers.

Essay and General Literature Index
H. W. Wilson
An index of English-language essays and anthologies. $695/year.

Exxon Corp. Basic Practices Manual
Amtec Information Services

FABS Electronic Bible
FABS International, Inc.
Allows the user to have access to all words in the following five translations of the English Bible: New International Version, Revised Standard Version, Good News Bible, King James Version, American Standard Version. Contains 390 concordances of each translation covering entire translation, Old Testament, New Testament, each book of the Bible, Pentateuch, historical books, wisdom, literature, poetry, prophets, Gospels, synoptic Gospels, words of Jesus, Pauline Epistles, non-Pauline Epistles. Includes a topical Bible, based on Nave's. $299.

FABS Reference Bible
FABS International, Inc.
Contains six English versions of the Bible: King James Version, American Standard Version, Revised Standard Version, New American Standard Bi-

ble, New International Version, New King James Version. Original-language texts include, Greek New Testament, Greek Septuagint, Hebrew Old Testament, Gospel Harmony, OT History Harmony, English Septuagint. $795.

Facts On File News Digest CD-ROM
Facts On File Publications
Includes more than 9,000 pages of the full text and more than 500 maps of any news items appearing in the original 1980–88 volumes of the printed *News Digest.* A free demonstration diskette from the vendor is available. To display maps, the user should use an enhanced *News Digest* CD-ROM. A special zoom function allows the user to magnify a map for specific detail. It features a date-limited search function to specific day, month, year, or range of days, months, or years; browsing through index headings; keyword Boolean search using logic (AND, OR, NOT) as well as nested and truncated Boolean logic; cross-referencing from article to article and from related subject to subject; and audit trail function keeps track of a researcher's search path; an electronic marking function allows researcher to mark an article and save it for later reference. The company offers customizing service to make the system available in public access areas. It runs on IBM PC computers and compatibles. Apple Macintosh II systems need 1megabyte of memory and a CD-ROM drive with a SCSI interface. Available for $695, while current subscribers to *News Digest*'s printed version pay $595.

Facts On File Visual Dictionary CD-ROM
Facts On File Publications
French/English version of *Visual Dictionary.* Primarily used in foreign language and instruction of English as a second language. Still in prototype version.

Fast Track: Nynex White Pages
Nynex Information Resources
An electronic telephone directory containing more than ten million published phone listings of residences and businesses. Material is taken from 300 phone directories in New York and New England areas. Search can be done by name, address, telephone number, or ZIP code. Search results can be printed; also, the system has a dialing capability to targeted phone listing if the computer is equipped with a modem. $10,000/year plus updates.

FBIS
Readex Microprint Corp.
Contains references to the Foreign Broadcast Information Service daily reports for all regions.

Federal Decisions
ROM Publishers, Inc.

Federal Logos Disc
Alde Publishing
Contains U.S. federal government logos, seals, and other devices used in the popular desktop publishing. $99.

Federal Procurement Package
  Alde Publishing
  U.S. federal supply and procurement information, holds three sets of federal government records. The *General Services Administration Supply Catalog* lists many of the products and tools used by the government, described with issue orders and price. Guiding the procurement of GSA items are the rules and regulations contained in the FAR database (Title 48 CFR Federal Acquisition Regulations). These are controls and policies for material procurement through the federal bureaucracy. The *Public Contracts and Property Management* database lists regulations governing public contracting through federal agencies. These policies, established by the GSA, are implemented through Title 41 CFR Public Contracts and Property Management regulations. Documentation is not supplied with the product. Listed for $199.

Fedstack
  Highlighted Data Inc.
  A hypercard directory with maps and ZIP codes of all federal government offices and personnel, including brief biographies and photos; updated quarterly.

FEDSTAT
  U.S. Statistics
  Volume 1 includes statistical data on the county level. Data derived from the following sources: *1988 Annual Demographic File, 1988 County and City Databook, 1988 Statistical Abstract, 1990 Census TIGER Prototype Files* (see below), *County Boundary File, County Business Patterns,* and *Regional Economic Information System.*

FEDSTAT/TIGER CD-ROM
  U.S. Statistics
  A map database of the United States, which can be used to develop maps at the county level or down to an individual city block showing the street name and address ranges. TIGER (Topologically Integrated Geographic Encoding and Referencing) will be used in the 1990 Census program. Maps may be produced using IMAGE (U.S. Statistics' Integrated Mapping and Geographic Encoding) system.

Film Literature Index
  H. W. Wilson
  An index to more than 200 international film periodicals and nonfilm periodicals. $695.

First National Item Bank and Test Development System
  Tescor, Inc.
  Database for testing and creating tests for grades K–12. $300–$800/month on lease.

Flash-Back/Books in Print Plus
  Ingram Book Company
  An acquisitions systems used with Bowker's *Books in Print Plus* with weekly updates. See Chapter 11.

Food/Analyst
   Hopkins Technology
   Analyzes food into specific components of calories, fat, protein, cholesterol, and vitamins. The data are based on the USDA's food composition database. $99.

FORM41: Airline Carrier Filings
   Data Base Products Inc.
   Includes products for aviation and aerospace industry. The product is useful for transportation study programs. Annual subscription is $7,000/year plus quarterly updates.

Gale Experimental Data Set
   University of Washington, Department of Atmospheric Sciences
   Includes meteorological data collected during Genesis of Atlantic Lows experiment during the period from January 15 to March 15, 1986. $100.

GDCS Impact
   Auto-Graphics, Inc.
   Includes the *Monthly Catalog of U.S. Government Publications.* Prices vary.

GE Aircraft Engines
   AMTEC Information Services

GEFAHRGUT CD-ROM — Dangerous Substances on CD-ROM
   Springer Verlag
   Contains information on dangerous materials, chemicals, and goods. Provides guidelines on how to handle hazardous materials. Data acquired from *HOMEL,* a manual of dangerous substances; *CHEMDATA* of Harwell Library; and *EINSATZAKTEN,* Swiss fire-service emergency advice. 6,500 DMark.

General Periodicals Index
   Information Access Co.
   A comprehensive InfoTrac database, available in two versions, the Academic Library Edition and the Public Library Edition. The Academic Library edition indexes approximately 1,100 general interest and scholarly publications. Subject areas covered include social sciences, general sciences, humanities, business, management, economics, and current affairs. The Public Library Edition indexes approximately 1,100 popular magazines and journals. Covers current events, consumer information, arts and entertainment, business, management, and economics. $7,500/year plus workstation.

General Science Index
   H. W. Wilson Co.
   An index to information in about 111 English-language science periodicals in areas such as astronomy, food and nutrition, botany, chemistry, biology, earth science, physics, and mathematics. $1,295/year plus updates.

GEOdisc: Florida Atlas
   GEOVISION, Inc.
   Contains a complete digital representation of the state of Florida at the 1:1,000,000 scale. $1,995.

GEOdisc: Georgia Atlas.
GEOVISION, Inc.
Contains a complete digital representation of the state of Georgia at the
1:1,000,000 scale. $1,995.

GEOdisc: U.S. Atlas
GEOVISION, Inc.
Contains a complete digital representation of the U.S. at the 1:2,000,000
scale. $990.

GEOdisc: Windows on the World
GEOVISION, Inc.
Provides geographic data on the U.S.

Geographic Locator
Network Technology Corp.
Includes digital mapping, ZIP code, longitude and latitude data.

German Books in Print
Buchandler Vereinigung-GMBH (sold by Chadwyck-Healey)
See Chapter 11.

GM Parts Catalog
Bell & Howell

Government Publications Index
Information Access Co.
An index to the monthly catalog of the Government Printing Office.
Includes indexing to public documents generated by legislative and execu-
tive branches of the U.S. government (1976 to present). $2,500/year plus
updates.

GPO Cat/PAC
Marcive Inc.
Includes *GPO Monthly Catalog.* Annual subscription is $995 including
bimonthly updates. Access is accomplished through author, title, subject, or
combined words and indexes using Boolean operators. Cross references are
used. Searching by SuDoc number allows users to browse through agencies'
publications. Patrons can search by stock number, including DMA (Defense
Mapping Agency) numbers, and the *Monthly Catalog* number and OCLC
number. It allows the user to create bibliographies by any access point and
print or download them to a disk.

GPO Laserfile
Library Systems & Services, Inc.
Includes the *Monthly Catalog of the U.S. Government Publications.* Updated
quarterly. $1,600.

GPO Monthly Catalog
OCLC
Contains over 250,000 bibliographic references to government agencies
publications on diverse subjects including agriculture, law, consumer issues,
health, nutrition, economics, and public affairs (1976 to present).

GPO Monthly Catalog Index to Government Periodicals
H. W. Wilson Co.
Contains a database of the printed *Monthly Catalog of the U.S. Government Publications* with public data on publications generated by federal government agencies from 1976 to the present. It covers information in 185 periodicals issued by more than 100 government agencies. $995/year.

GPO on SilverPlatter
SilverPlatter
Contains citations from 1976 to present for government publications, such as books, reports, studies, serials, maps, and other items from the *Monthly Catalog* published by the U.S. Government Printing Office. $950/year plus updates (no additional charge for multiuser).

Graphics Lab
Alde Publishing
Graphics files; desktop publishing in the GIF, MAC, and PIC graphic formats. $99.

The Guinness Disc of Records 1990
Pergamon Compact Solution
Includes Guinness records in full text, color photographs, animations, and music and sound effects. Used with an Apple Macintosh. £60/$99.

Harlic Union Catalog
Marcive
See Chapter 11.

Harrap's Multilingual Dictionary
Microinfo, Ltd
Includes 20 multilingual dictionaries from six publishers.

Haystack: Logistics, Procurement, Engineering Files
Ziff Davis Technical Information Co.

Health
CD Plus
This database is available online as Health Planning and Administration and in print as the *Hospital Literature Index*. It contains the entire database beginning in 1975. Updated monthly.

Health Index
Information Access Co.
$2,000.

HealthPLAN-CD
SilverPlatter
A bibliographic file covering the nonclinical aspects of health-care delivery, including, but not limited to, all aspects of administration and planning of health-care facilities, health insurance and financial management, licensing and accreditation, personnel management, staff, planning, quality assurance, health maintenance organizations (HMOs), and related topics. The file from 1975 includes over 420,000 citations supplied by the National Library

of Medicine, the American Hospital Association, and the National Health Planning Information Center. It also includes the entire *Hospital Literature Index.* $850/year plus updates.

HELECON on CD-ROM
Helsinki School of Economics Library
Includes the following five European management databases: *BISSE,* Business Information Sources and Services for Europe; *BLISS,* includes English and German abstracts; *FONDS QUETELET,* a major Belgian database; *SCANP,* a Scandinavian management database; and *SCIMP,* a selective index of major West European and American management journals. $2,000.

Home Reference Library
Ellis Enterprises, Inc.
Includes some encyclopedias, almanacs, and other reference works, as well as information from the Nurse Library, Physician's Library, and the Bible Library. List price, $895.

Honda Parts
Bell & Howell

Hoppenstadt Directory of Large Corporations
Dataware, Inc.

How to Become a U.S. Citizen
Quanta Press, Inc.
This United States Civics Disc is based on the U.S. Immigration and Naturalization Service's "Series of Federal Citizen Texts." The disc contains a full-text database that describes information for potential U.S. citizens. Also useful for persons researching the development of the United States and/or teaching American history. $99.

HP LaserROM
Hewlett Packard
Contains technical information for HP products, including reference manuals, application notes, and solutions to known product problems. Covers products such as HP 9000 business computers, including RISC-based Precision Architecture computers. $2,700.

Humanities Index
H. W. Wilson Co.
Contains an index of articles in more than 300 periodicals covering art, architecture, archaeology, area studies, film, folklore, and history (1984 to present). $1,295/year plus updates.

ICP Software Information Database
OCLC
ICP
A compilation of more than 15,000 software products and services. Each record contains a product description, hardware requirements, and operating system and source language specifications. The full-text disc is designed for software buyers and vendors, hardware vendors, researchers, and consulting firms. $1,350/year plus updates.

Identidex
Micromedex, Inc.
Provides tablet and capsule identification. $375.

Image Folio
NEC
Includes more than 4000 photographic images. $399.

Images Demo
Compact Discoveries, Inc.

Impact
Auto-Graphics, Inc.
See Chapter 10.

Index to Legal Periodicals
H. W. Wilson Co.
Contains an index to articles from more than 500 legal journals, year-books, institutes, university publications, law reviews and government publications (1981 to present). $1,495/year plus updates.

Infomark IV Laser PC System: Decision Support
National Decision Systems
Marketing decision support. $7,500–$17,800.

Intelligent Catalog
Library Corp.
See Chapter 10.

International: Airline Traffic
Data Base Products, Inc.
International origin and destination data. $10,000/year plus updates (discount rates for academic libraries).

International Books in Print
K. G. Saur

International Dictionary of Medicine and Biology
Wiley Electronic Publishing
$195.

The International Encyclopedia of Education
Pergamon Compact Solution
Includes the full text of all ten volumes of the printed version of the encyclopedia. This American Library Association Dartmouth Medal winner uses the Graphic Knowledge Retrieval System (Graphic KRS) software to search for any word or phrase contained in 1,448 articles. It can be used with a pointer device (such as a mouse). It includes cross-references to related topics. It tracks down the search path and allows the display of a list of all the articles that have been referred to by a specific article. The bookmark feature saves a place so that the user can refer back to same articles of interest. Tables, graphs, and other diagrams can be displayed alongside the text by using a split-screen feature. Diagrams can be magnified and panned for the user to examine a detail. $2150.

Intuition Expert
Telerate
Financial training. $850/month for two years plus system.

Iowa State Locator
Iowa State Library
Database of 400 state libraries. $55.

Italian Banking Legal and Technical Documentation
Eikon Sp A

Item Bank
Minnesota Department of Education
Includes approximately 90,000 test questions and answers in math, science, social science, and foreign languages. Updated annually.

Itineraries
Data Base Products, Inc.

Journal of Radiology
CMC ReSearch

King James Bible
Quantum Access

Kirk-Othmer Encyclopedia of Chemical Technology
Wiley Electronic Publishing
This CD-ROM edition contains more than 1,000 articles from 26 volumes, plus supplements, indexes, abstracts, and some 6,000 tables. The menu-driven database has Boolean search capability. $895.

Kwikee Inhouse Graphics Services
Multi-AD Services
Theme art library of 13,000 illustrations. $2,160/year plus updates.

Kwikee Inhouse Pal
Multi-AD Services
A library of professional-quality Postscript art for desktop publishers using the Macintosh. Includes more than 300 images in 12 categories: animals, careers, food, holidays, personal style, sports, around the house, education, hearts and flowers, leisure time, religion, and vacation. $149.95.

Labor/Stats
Hopkins Technology
Labor statistics from the following databases: *Employment Cost Index; Industry Employment and Earnings; International Labor and Price Trend Comparisons; Labor Force; Occupational Employment Statistics; Occupational Injury and Illness Incidence Rates; Productivity and Cost Indices; Productivity—Federal Government; Productivity—Industry.* $65.

Languages of the World
Network Technology Corp.
Multilingual dictionary of 12 languages: Chinese, Danish, Dutch, English, Finnish, French, German, Italian, Japanese, Norwegian, Spanish, and Swedish. $950.

Laser Disclosure: Commercial, Not for Profit, Wall Street
  Disclosure, Inc.
  Securities and Exchange Commission's annual reports and proxies.
$27,500–$97,000.

LaserCat
  Western Library Network
  See Chapter 11.

Lasergene CD-ROM
  DNAStar
  Includes biotechnology information on AIDS, Berlin RNA, GenBank, and
NBRF-PIR. Updated semiannually.

LaserGuide
  General Research Corp.
  See Chapter 10.

Laserlaw Series
  CD/Law Reports
  Includes legal reports.

LaserQuest
  General Research Corporation
  See Chapter 9.

LaserSearch/AnyBook
  Ingram Book Co.
  An acquisitions system used with Anybook of Library Corporation. See
Chapter 11.

Lasertrak Disc
  Lasertrack Corp.
  Navigation data: Jefferson Charts. $695.

LawMARC
  Utlas International
  See Chapter 9.

Le Pac
  Brodart Automation
  See Chapter 10.

Le Pac: Government Documents Option
  Brodart Automation
  Includes a catalog of documents printed by the U.S. Government Printing Office from 1976 to the present, containing about 230,000 records.
Documents can be searched by author, title, or subject, or by keyword
searching on any record field. Search can be done using Boolean logic and
truncation, in addition to the following search points: *Monthly Catalog* number, LCCN, and ISBN/ISSN. The catalog includes depository and nondepository
titles. $1,100/year plus updates.

Le Pac: Interlibrary Loan
  Brodart Automation
  See Chapter 11.

LegalTrac
Information Access Co.
Covers legal periodicals. $5,000/year plus updates, one workstation, $10,000/year plus updates, four workstations.

Library Literature
H. W. Wilson Co.
Covers international library periodicals, selected state journals, monographs and films (1984 to present). $1,095/year plus updates.

Life Sciences Collection
Compact Cambridge
Contains basic and applied scientific research information. Consists of 18 subject-oriented subfiles containing abstracts and citations from more than 5,000 core journals, books, international patents, and statistical publications. Coverage includes: *Animal Behavior; Cambridge Scientific Biochemistry: Amino Acids, Peptides and Proteins, Biological Membranes; Cambridge Scientific Biotechnology Research: Nucleic Acids; Calcified Tissue; Chemoreception; CSA Neuroscience; Ecology; Endocrinology* (from 1985); *Entomology; Genetic, Immunology; Microbiology: Algology, Bacteriology, Industrial and Applied Microbiology; Mycology and Protozoology; Toxicology;* and *Virology* (1982 to present). $4,750.

LISA
Library Association Publishing
SilverPlatter
Library and Information Science Abstracts of the world's literature in librarianship, information science, and related disciplines as compiled by the Library Association Publishing, Ltd. Covers the complete database from 1967. $995.

LOANet
Library Systems & Services, Inc.
See Chapter 11.

Lotus One Source
Lotus Development
Includes CD/Corporate, CD/Corp Tech, CD/Banking, CD/Private, and CD/International. $11,000–$30,000.

Luther Bible
Deutsche Bibelgeselschaft
Full text of Bible translated into German by Martin Luther.

LZ Services: (NAV/COM Terminal Charts)
Lasertrak Corp.
Navigational database, 13 discs. $945.

Mc Guide USA CD-ROM
Mac Guide
Allows users to view demonstrations of more than 4,000 types of available software and to read product reviews. In addition to the 450 megabytes of "shareware" available from Mac Guide, it provides a list of Macintosh user groups through the United States.

Macintosh Showcase
  Discovery Systems
  Multimedia demo; free disc.

Mack Electronic Parts Disc
  AMTEC Information Services

Magazine Article Summaries
  EBSCO
  Contains summaries of articles from over 200 general magazines since 1984, plus many other publications. *The New York Times* was added in 1989. Subscription prices vary depending on the number of updates as follows: Annual/$399, Quarterly/$799, Academic year/$1,199, Monthly/$1,599.

Magazine Index Plus
  Information Access Co.
  Indexes popular magazines plus the *New York Times*. $4,000/year plus updates.

MAK PAK
  Alde Publishing
  Contains more than 1,000 applications and programs for the MAC environment. $99.

Manhole
  Activision
  A journey to fantasy and wonder for children of all ages. Contains over 600 detailed interconnected graphic screens for the Macintosh. Magical characters, from dragons to dolphins, talk and move. A hypercard is required. $60.

MARCIVE/PAC
  Marcive Inc.
  See Chapter 10.

Martindale: The Extra Pharmacopoeia
  Micromedex, Inc.
  Includes information on drug products available in the United Kingdom. $550.

Master Search Bible on Compact Disc
  Tri Star Publishing
  Includes multiple versions of the Bible: New International Version (NIV), New American Standard Bible (NASB), King James Version (KJV). The following reference works are also included: *New Manners and Customs of Bible Times, Wycliffe Bible Commentary, Wycliffe Bible Encyclopedia, Wycliffe Historical Geography of Bible Lands* from Moody Press, *Handbook to Bible Study, NIV Scofield Study Bible* from Oxford University Press, *Expository Dictionary of Bible Words, New International Dictionary of Biblical Words, New International Dictionary of Biblical Archaeology, NIV Study Bible* from Zondervan, and *Strong's Exhaustive Concordance*. The text can be searched by word or phrase. Using windows, the user can compare translations of different Bibles, check definitions and identify quotes. The system includes a notepad. $695.

Material Safety Data Sheets
National Safety Data Corp.
$750/year plus updates.

Material Safety Data Sheets, Reference File
Occupational Health Services
Contains Material Data Safety Sheets on more than 10,000 of the most frequently used chemicals. $5,000/year plus updates.

MathSci Disc
American Mathematical Society
SilverPlatter
Contains the *MathSci* database of the American Mathematical Society. It comprises the *Mathematical Reviews* from 1985 through 1988 and more than 50,000 entries from current mathematical publications. Coverage includes the literature of mathematics and related fields such as statistics, computer science, and engineering. $3,510/year plus updates.

Medline—BiblioMed
Digital Diagnostics, Inc.
A subset of *MEDLINE,* containing abstracts of 450 major biomedical journals over a span of three to five years, chosen from select lists provided by leading universities and medical centers. It includes pop-up screens, while search can be done by words and phrases. It supports Boolean searching (AND, OR, NOT). Search results can be printed or downloaded. $950/year plus updates.

Medline—BiblioMed with AIDS Supplement
Digital Diagnostics, Inc.
A subset of *MEDLINE,* containing abstracts of 450 major biomedical journals over a span of five years, chosen from select lists provided by leading universities and medical centers. AIDS supplement consists of more than 40,000 citations included in *MEDLINE* covering six to eight years. This supplement contains the following medical subject headings (MeSH): Acquired Immunodeficiency Syndrome; HIV; HTLV-III; Immunologic Deficiency Syndrome; T Lymphocytes; Sarcoma, Kaposi's; Retrovirus; Cytomegalic Inclusion Disease; Cryptosporidiosis; Leukoviruses; Chancroid; Epidemiology; Homosexuality; Substance Use and Abuse; Candidiasis; Herpes; and Stomatitis. $1,150.

Medline—BRS Colleague Disc
BRS Information Technologies
Provides full citations from *MEDLINE* including foreign-language documents (1985 to the present). $995/year plus updates; $2,500 for the full package.

Medline—CD Plus
CD Plus
$3,495/initial year; $2,495/subsequent years.

Medline Clinical Collection
   DIALOG Information Services
   Covers five years of *MEDLINE* database related to clinical medicine. Includes all citations to articles from *Abridged Index Medicus,* plus citations from "A Library for Internists Recommended by the American College of Physicians" and Brandon and Hill's *Selected List of Books and Journals for the Small Medical Library.* Mostly used in public and hospital libraries and in group medical practices. $925/year plus updates.

Medline—Compact Cambridge
   Compact Cambridge
   $1,250/year plus updates.

Medline—DIALOG OnDisc
   DIALOG Information Services
   Includes references and abstracts from approximately 3,200 journals published in more than 70 countries. Includes data from the following National Library of Medicine databases: *Index Medicus, Index to Dental Literature,* and *International Nursing Index.* $950/year plus quarterly updates.

Medline Knowledge Finder
   Aries System Corp.
   A medical database containing 240,000 citations from *MEDLINE.* Features MeSH Explosions (groupings of synonymous or related terms); a MeSH thesaurus, covering most of the terms of the MeSH Blue Books including annotated MeSH, permuted MeSH, and tree structures. Covers five years of citations. $1,495/year plus updates; Network license, $2,295/year plus updates.

Medline on SilverPlatter
   SilverPlatter
   Contains the entire *MEDLINE* database of the National Library of Medicine from 1966 to the present. Contains bibliographic citations and abstracts of biomedical literature, including all foreign languages and all data elements, and is fully indexed. $950/year plus updates; complete database, $3,500.

Mega Rom
   Quantum Leap Technologies
   Contains more than 350 megabytes of public domain and shareware software collected from group users. $49.

Menu: International Software
   The Menu

Merriam-Webster's Ninth New Collegiate Dictionary
   Highlighted Data, Inc.
   The electronic version, with audio recorded pronunciation of the more than 160,000 entries and the full text and graphics of the printed version of the dictionary. $199.95.

MetroScan
Digital Diagnostics, Inc.
County real estate assessor's records. $600/year plus updates.

Microsoft Bookshelf
Microsoft Corporation
Contains the following ten commonly used reference works on a single disc: *The American Heritage Dictionary* (200,000 definitions); *Roget's Thesaurus; The World Almanac and Book of Facts; Bartlett's Familiar Quotations; The Chicago Manual of Style; Houghton Mifflin Spelling Verifier and Corrector; Forms and Letters* (more than 100 useful forms, letters, outlines, and checklists for business and personal use); *U.S. Zip Code Directory; Houghton Mifflin Usage Alert* (it alerts the user about common errors in word usage and common misspellings); and *Business Information Sources* (lists thousands of references—business journals, research reports, books, periodicals, and databases). The product interacts with many word processors. Electronic bookmarks let the user mark a location in the text of an article or entry then refer to it frequently. It is considered a writing tool that will help in checking for spelling, word usage and choice, punctuation, format, and style. $295.

Microsoft Office
Microsoft Corp.
This disc includes software marketed by Microsoft, such as Word, Excel, Mail, and PowerPoint. It also includes some Microsoft utility programs and related products from other vendors, as well as online documentation in Hypercard Format. $949.

Million Dollar Directory
Dun's Marketing Services

MLA International Bibliography
Modern Language Association
H. W. Wilson Co.
Covers bibliographical data on scholarship in modern languages, literature, and folklore from more than 3,000 journals and series, monographs, and book collections. $1,495/year plus updates.

Moody's 5000 Plus
Moody's Investors Service
Includes information on New York and American Stock Exchanges and companies from Moody's Manuals and News Reports. $2,500+

Moody's International Plus
Moody's Investors Service
A free demonstration disk is available from the company.

Multilingual Dictionary Database
Sansyusya Publishing Co., Ltd

Multilingual Dictionary of Science and Technology
Sansyusya Publishing Co. Ltd.

Mundocart/CD
Petroconsultants, Ltd.
Operational Navigational Charts covers coastline and drainage systems, international boundaries, and city outlines. $9,250/year.

Music Business Directory
Knowledge Access International
Includes 1988 record companies, distributors, and key executives. $495.

Music Radio Directory
Knowledge Access International
Includes information on approximately 4,200 radio stations. Lists stations by format, music director, and trade reporting status. $495.

NATASHA: National Archives on Sexuality, Health and Adolescence
Knowledge Access International
Includes 109 data sets and more than 40,000 identified variables from 82 major studies relevant to adolescence and sexuality. Includes SPSS-PC (Statistical Package for Social Sciences) for comparative analysis. $570.

National Directory of Addresses and Telephone Number
General Information, Inc.

National Meteorological Grid Data Point Set
University of Washington, Department of Atmospheric Sciences
Includes meteorological data of most of the Northern Hemisphere, 1940–80s. $100.

National Newspaper Index
Information Access Corp.
Indexes five major newspapers in one comprehensive source: the *New York Times* (late and national editions); *Wall Street Journal* (eastern and western editions); *Christian Science Monitor* (national edition); *Washington Post* (final edition); *Los Angeles Times* (home edition). Covers the most current four years of data. $4,000/year plus updates.

National Portrait Gallery, The Permanent Collection
Abt Books
Contains more than 3,000 portraits of famous Americans from the Smithsonian Institute's National Portrait Gallery in full color. Access is provided through indexes by names, subjects, and other criteria.

National Telephone Directory
Xiphias
Telephone numbers of major corporations and government agencies and institutions in North America. $150.

Natural Resources Database
NISC
Compiled from 45 intergovernmental databases such as: *Alaska Gas Pipeline Files, Aquatic Plant Database, Canadian Resource Family, Department of Energy, Energy Research and Development Administration, Federal Aid Database,*

Federal Aid Research in Progress Database, Land Management, National Wetlands Research Center, Natural Resource Expertise Database, Pacific Coast Ecosystems, and the *Smithsonian.* Updated semiannually. $495/year.

Navigational Geographic Maps
ETAK, Inc.

News Scan
Newsreel Access Systems

NewsBank Electronic Index
NewsBank
Prices vary.

Newspaper Abstracts Ondisc
University Microfilms International
All subscriptions include the *New York Times* plus any combination of the *Atlanta Constitution* (with selected articles from the *Atlanta Journal*), the *Boston Globe,* the *Chicago Tribune,* the *Christian Science Monitor, Los Angeles Times, Wall Street Journal,* and the *Washington Post.* $1,500; prices vary for additional titles.

1985 American Housing Survey
U.S. Bureau of the Census
National core file of housing data. $125.

NTIS
DIALOG Information Services
Includes U.S. National Technical Information Service research and engineering studies. Features include permuted subject terms, KWIC (Keywords in Context Index), EASY MENU, and EASY COMMAND. It is compatible with other DIALOG products and services. $2,750/year plus updates.

NTIS
OCLC
In addition to NTIS federal government reports, OCLC added materials on science and technology owned by OCLC member libraries. Covers 1983–85 on one disc and 1986 to the present on a second disc. $2,395/year plus updates.

NTIS
SilverPlatter
$2,250/year plus updates; multiuser subscription is expected to be higher.

Nurse Library
Ellis Enterprises, Inc.
The Nurse Library, sponsored by Oklahoma Nurse Association, contains a compilation of textbooks and manuals of nursing specialties and subspecialties and other medical textbooks. Updated periodically and listed for $895.

Nursing and Allied Health
SilverPlatter
This database is the *Cumulative Index to Nursing and Allied Health Literature.* It provides access to virtually all English language nursing journals, publications of the American Nurses' Association, the National League for Nursing,

and primary journals in more than a dozen allied health disciplines. It also includes selected articles from approximately 3,200 biomedical journals indexed in *Index Medicus*; from approximately 20 journals in the field of health sciences librarianship; and from educational, behavioral sciences, management, and popular literature. $950/year plus updates.

O&D Plus
Data Base Products Inc.
Includes Department of Transportation's Airline Traffic Origin/Destination for seven years for online local and online connecting O/D. $8,000/year plus updates (discount rates available for academic libraries).

O&D Plus Historical
Data Base Products, Inc.
$9,000.

OCLC/AMIGOS Collection Analysis CD
AMIGOS Bibliographic Council, Inc.
Using OCLC database subset, a library can perform interactive comparisons of its own collections. $2,500+

Officer's Bookcase—Terms
Quanta Press, Inc.
Includes military terms and acronyms from the Joint Chiefs of Staff's Military Terms Dictionary, the Defense Systems Management College's *Defense Acquisition Acronyms and Terms*, and the Soviet Military Thought Series volume *Soviet Terms Dictionary*. $149.

Onboard: Airline Traffic Data
Data Base Products, Inc.
Includes airline passenger statistics and traffic schedules from the Department of Transportation, corresponding to information taken from the filings of certified air carriers on the T-schedules of Form 41 and the domestic portions of filings under Economic Regulation 586 (1972 to present). Target markets include airports, airlines, investment analysts, transportation consultants, and transportation agencies (discount rates for academic libraries). $8,000/year plus quarterly.

OncoDisc
J. B. Lippincott Co.
A source for oncology information. It includes the full text from the following publications: *Physician Data Query, Cancerlit*, and other Lippincott books such as *Cancer: Principles and Practices of Oncology, Important Advances in Oncology 1985–1988*, and the *Beahrs' Manual for Staging Cancer.* Updated bimonthly. Annual license, $1,950.

Online Hotline News Service
Information Intelligence, Inc.
Includes the following five databases: *Joblines, Major Online Vendors, Online Hotline, Online Libraries and Microcomputers*, and *Online Newsletter.* $99 for subscribers for either the *Online Newsletter* or *Online Libraries and Microcomputers*; $199 for nonsubscribers.

ONTERIS (Ontario Education Resources Information System)
Reteaco, Inc.
The pilot CD-ROM disc of this database comprises research and reports generated in the province of Ontario by school boards, and curriculum documents and learning materials intended for elementary- and secondary-level schools.

Optext: Federal Regulations
VLS (Video Laser Systems), Inc.
Code of Federal Regulations, Optext Issue 101 (CFR Titles 28-50): 1985, Issue 104:1986 ($395); Code of Federal Regulations (Federal Register), Optext Issue 102:1986 ($395); Optext Code of Federal Regulations, Issue 103 (CFR Titles 1-27):1986 ($395).

OSH-ROM
SilverPlatter
A collection of occupational health and safety information. It contains four complete bibliographic databases: *NIOSHTIC*, database of the National Institute for Occupational Safety and Health (U.S.); *HSELINE*, database of the Health and Safety Executive (U.K.); *CISDOC*, database of the International Occupational Safety and Health Information Center of the International Labor Organisation (U.N.); and *MHIDAS*, the Major Hazard Incident Data Service, developed by the Major Hazards Assessment Unit of the British Health and Safety Executive. This product contains more than 300,000 citations taken from more than 500 journals and 100,000 monographs and technical reports. $900/year plus updates.

Oxford English Dictionary on CD-ROM
Tri Star Publishing
$950.

Oxford English Dictionary on CD-ROM
Oxford Electronics Publishing
$950.

The Oxford Textbook of Medicine—Electronic Edition
Oxford Electronic Publishing
Contains the complete text. It allows users to take notes on the screen and recall them as electronic bookmarks. $600.

PAHO Database
Pan American World Health Organization

PAIS on CD-ROM
Public Affairs Information Service
$1,795/year plus updates.

Papyri
Packard Humanities Institute
When complete, this full-text database will include Egyptian papyri from a 1,000-year period following the Greek conquest of 332 B.C. The project will bring together all extant classical Greek papyri.

Parts Master
National Standards Association, Inc.
A logistical support system for locating and retrieving purchasing information on more than 12 million parts procured or stocked by the U.S. government. Includes detailed item description and technical characteristics. $7,650/year plus hardware.

PC Order Plus
Blackwell North America, Inc.
An acquisitions systems used with Bowker's *Books in Print Plus*. See Chapter 11.

PC Rose System
Brodart Automation
An acquisitions system used with Bowker's *Books in Print Plus*. See Chapter 11.

PC-Blue: MS-DOS Public Domain Library
Alde Publishing
$199.

PC-PDF (Powder Diffraction File)
International Center for Diffraction Data
Contains the entire PDF-2 database and index files. $5,900 plus updates.

PC-SIG LIBRARY ON CD-ROM
PC-SIG, Inc.
$295.

PD-ROM
Berkeley Macintosh User Group (BMUG)
Includes more than 300 megabytes of public domain software, "shareware," clip art, and technical information for Macintosh users. Includes 50 educational programs, 100 function-key programs, 250 games, 500 stacks, 1,000 pictures, 30 telecommunications programs, 250 desk accessories, 500 fonts, 100 graphics programs, 200 Macintosh programs, 100 sounds, and 200 utilities. $100.

PDQ CD-ROM (Physicians' Data Query)
Compact Cambridge
SilverPlatter Information, Inc.
A database published by the National Cancer Institute, containing state-of-the-art treatment recommendations for 80 types of cancer, over 1,100 cancer treatment protocols, and directories listings 12,000 physicians and 1,500 organizations involved in cancer treatment. $850/year plus updates.

Pediatrics on Disc
CMC ReSearch
Contains the full text, tables, line art, and images from six years of the journal *Pediatrics*. A VGA monitor is required to display images. Purchase price for the period 1983 to 1988 is $395.

Periodical Abstracts
  University Microfilms, Inc.
  $1,175.

Personnet
  Information Handling Services, Inc.
  Federal personnel information. $3,950/year plus updates.

PEST-BANK
  SilverPlatter
  Covers approximately 45,000 U.S. registered pesticides used in agriculture, industry, and general commerce. It is the first in a series of SilverPlatter databases from the National Pesticide Information Retrieval System (NPIRS). The information in the database includes names and synonyms, registration dates and registering companies, compositions and formulation, sites and pests for which the pesticide is registered, and permissible residue levels. $2,850.

Peterson's College Database
  SilverPlatter
  Full-text database containing more than 3,000 profiles on all accredited colleges in the United States and Canada. Provides information such as enrollment, majors, SAT/ACT score ranges, expenses and financial aid, housing, campus life, and athletics. Annual license, $595.

Peterson's GradLine
  SilverPlatter
  Full-text database containing profiles of more than 26,000 graduate and professional programs offered by more than 1,400 colleges and universities in the United States and Canada. Provides information such as college name, address, degree levels, faculty and research specialties, and financial aid. Annual license, $695. Updated annually.

PHI: Classical Latin Literature
  Packard Humanities Institute
  Includes classical Latin literature through Tacitus. It also includes several biblical texts: the Vulgate Bible, the Septuagint, and two versions of the Greek New Testament. $100.

PHINET
  Prentice-Hall Information Network
  Private Letter Rulings Tax information on four discs. $2,500/disc.

Phone Disc
  Digital Directory Assistance
  This telephone directory includes approximately 10 million numbers from the white pages of New York State and New England. Updated monthly.

Photo Library
  Phillips Electronic Instruments (PEI)
  Stock photo catalog.

PhotoScan
Newsreel Access Systems

Physician Library
Ellis Enterprises, Inc.
Contains a compilation of complete textbooks and manuals of major medical specialties and subspecialties and other selected texts. $1,000.

Physician's Desk Reference
Medical Economics Co.
Contains the *Physician's Desk Reference, PDFR for Opthamology* and *Non-Prescription Drugs*. Also includes six indexes on drug interactions, side effects, generic active ingredients, therapeutic categories, manufacturers' names, and brand names. Updated three times per year. Annual license, $595.

Place-Name Index
Buckmaster Publishing
Place-names from quadrangle maps. $1,495; subscription, $295/year.

Plus 37
Philips Electronic Instruments
Diffraction parameters in Powder Diffraction File. $5,000.

Poisindex
Micromedex, Inc.
Toxicology database. $2,295.

POPLINE
SilverPlatter
A bibliographic database containing more than 150,000 citations on population family planning and related health care, law, and policy issues. The database reaches as far back as 1827 and includes citations and abstracts to journal articles, monographs, technical reports, and unpublished works. This database is maintained by the Population Information Program at John Hopkins University, in collaboration with the Center for Population and Family Health at Columbia University, Population Index at Princeton University, and the Carolina Population Center at the University of North Carolina at Chapel Hill. *POPLINE* production is funded primarily by the U.S. Agency for International Development and by the National Institute of Child Health and Human Development. The CD-ROM version of the database is funded by the United Nations Population Fund (UNFPA). $750/year plus updates.

Population Statistics on CD-ROM
Slater Hall Information Products
Contains detailed 1980 Census data for all places of 10,000 population or more—urbanized areas, metropolitan areas, congressional districts, counties, and states. The 1986 population and per capita income estimates for approximately 40,000 local areas are included. The 1982 and 1984 county population estimates by age, race, and sex; and state and metro area population projections to the year 2000 are tabulated. $1200.

Pravda on CD-ROM
Alde Publishing
Contains a fully indexed database for a full English translation of the Soviet newspaper *Pravda* for the years 1986 and 1987. Includes full text of the official speeches and announcements. Listed at $249.

ProArt Trilogy I
Multi-Ad
Includes 300 illustrations in three collections: business, holidays, and sports. Compatible with most desktop publishing software though designed for the Macintosh. $375.

Programmer's Library
Microsoft Corp.
Aimed at professional programmers. Includes many well-known technical references, including manuals for Microsoft's Basic, C, Pascal, Fortran, and Macro Assembler compilers; the OS/2 and windows 2.0 software development kits; the MS-DOS Encyclopedia; Inside OS/2; Proficient C; and many sample source codes. $395.

Programmer's ROM
Quanta Press, Inc.
Contains information and public domain source codes for various computer languages. These include ADA, Basic, C, Forth, Fortran, Modula2, PROLOG, and others. $149.

Prompt CD
Lotus Development Corp.
Includes ten technical support databases on Lotus products. Updated semiannually. $995.

PsycLIT
SilverPlatter
The American Psychological Association
Includes journal citations and abstracts in psychology and behavioral sciences from the PsycINFO department of the American Psychological Association (1974 to present). $3,995.

Public Domain Mac Programs
Educorp USA
Contains software ranging from spreadsheets to games. Hypercard retrieval is used. $199.

Public Domain Software On File
Facts On File Publications
Contains 200 programs for beginners to advanced users covering a broad spectrum of applications from business and personal finance to speed reading, entertainment, word processing, and home management. Each program is tested and debugged and menu-driven by topic. Updated annually. $195.

Publishers International Directory
K. G. Saur

QL Tech Mega-ROM
  Quantum Leap Technologies
  Contains hundreds of public domain software and many application programs, sound samples, graphics, and many others for the Macintosh. $49.

Rainbow the Connection: Businessbase
  Tetragon Systems, Inc.
  Canadian business addresses. $3,000/year (Canada).

Rainbow the Connection: Homebase II
  Tetragon Systems, Inc.
  Canadian residence addresses. $3,000/year (Canada).

RBBS-PC in a Box
  Quanta Press, Inc.
  Contains over 7,000 public domain, freeware, and shareware programs. The disc includes software for modem transfer. Program categories include databases, word processing, games, communications, and templates. $149.

Reader's Guide Abstracts
  H. W. Wilson Co.
  Indexes and abstracts more than 180 periodicals covered in the *Reader's Guide to Periodical Literature*. $1,995/year plus updates.

Reader's Guide to Periodical Literature
  H. W. Wilson Co.
  Indexes more than 180 of the most popular general-interest magazines covering news, current events, fashion, art, food, sports, politics, and education (1983 to present). $1,095/year plus updates.

Real Estate Transfer Database
  Abt Books, Inc.
  Massachusetts 1983–87, Connecticut 1987. The data are searchable by seller name, buyer name, street number or name, town, state, ZIP code, lot type, condo unit number, purchase price, mortgage lender, mortgage account, and transaction date. $4,640 for complete database.

Realscan Real Estate Information System
  LaserScan Systems, Inc.
  Includes information on all properties in selected Standard Metropolitan Statistical Areas (SMSAs) including ownership, property type, lot size, sale history, and building details. $1,500 plus cost of annual, quarterly, or weekly updates.

Reference Tool Kit
  EBSCO

Registry of Mass Spectral Data
  Wiley Electronic Publishing
  Designed by Fred McLafferty of Cornell University. It holds RMSD from 123,000 spectra records of over 90,000 compounds with CAS registry number. $2,895.

Resors: Satellite Remote Sensitivity Publications
PCI, Inc.
$1,100/year.

Resource/One
University Microfilms International
Ideal for small public or secondary school library, *Resource/One* indexes approximately 130 of the most frequently used general-interest periodicals and the *New York Times Current Events Edition* in one database. $795/year plus updates, plus a monthly backup microfiche edition of the database.

REX
FABS International
Contains all 30 volumes of religious and theological abstracts. Covers over 200 journals and includes over 65,000 abstracts in the area of religion and theology. Covers a period of 30 years. Search can be done by author, journal, year and/or keyword, or a combination of all of these fields. Updated quarterly. $895.

Right Stuffed
Quantum Leap Technologies
Contains over 600 megabytes of public domain and shareware software. Designed to be compatible with BBS host software programs. $100.

SchoolMatch
OCLC
The CD-ROM version of the SchoolMatch service offered by Public Priority Systems, Inc. It contains comprehensive information on more than 15,000 public school districts and private schools in the United States. The user can find the school that best meets specific needs based on an online questionnaire by matching personal profile to the school or school system. Annual update. $1,095.

Science & Technology Reference Set
McGraw-Hill Book Co.
Includes both a science and technology encyclopedia and a dictionary of scientific terms. Included are more than 7,000 articles from the *McGraw-Hill Concise Encyclopedia of Science and Technology* as well as about 99,000 terms and over 100,000 definitions from the *McGraw-Hill Dictionary of Science and Technical Terms*. Updated irregularly. $300.

Science Citation Index CD
Institute for Scientific Information
Each year this is published on two discs—one for citation access, the other for title access. The 1986 discs cost $2,550; 1987 discs cost $7,650; and the quarterly subscription to the 1988 discs cost $5,100.

Science Helper K–8
PC-SIG, Inc.
Includes almost 1,000 science and mathematics lesson plans for kindergarten through the eighth grade. Provides lesson plans from the following projects: Science: A Process Approach Project; Conceptually Oriented Pro-

gram for Elementary Science; Science Curriculum Improvement Study; Elementary Science Study Project; Unified Science/Math for Elementary Education; Minnesota Math/Science; and Elementary Science Study. Searching can be done by grade level, academic subject, words or strings, science processes, and content themes. $195.

Scientific American Medicine Consult
  Scientific American
  A full-text database. Includes some illustrations. Updated quarterly.

Seals of the U.S. Federal Government
  Quanta Press, Inc.
  Contains more than 500 federal and state government logos, seals, imprints, and other graphic devices. They can be imported into desktop publishing and other programs and used in official reports and documents. $69.95.

Selected Water Resources Abstracts
  OCLC
  Includes approximately 200,000 abstracts from 1967 to the present on two discs. $750/year plus quarterly updates.

Selected Water Resources Abstracts
  NISC
  Contains 21 years of water research from all across the globe. Includes data about water-related topics of both domestic and foreign origin. The database is compiled by the Water Resources Scientific Information Center of the U.S. Geological Survey and grouped into ten areas: nature of water, water supply conservation, water quality protection, resources data and grants, manpower and facilities, water cycle, water quality management and control, water resources planning, engineering works, and scientific and technical information. Updated every six months. $575.

Serials
  Library Corp.
  See Chapter 11.

Serials Directory
  EBSCO
  See Chapter 11.

Shareware Gold
  Quanta Press, Inc.
  Includes popular shareware programs in applications such as word processing, spreadsheets, telecommunications, special interest, database, financial programs, managers, utilities, and educational software. $79.95.

Shareware Grab Bag
  Alde Publishing
  Contains over 5,000 different software programs covering communications, editing and word processing, education, financial, games, graphs, Lotus and dBase templates, and programming. $99.

Sherlock Holmes on Disc
   CMC ReSearch
   Contains the complete full-text Holmes "canon," the *Medical Casebook of Dr. Arthur Conan Doyle* by Jack Key and Alvin Rodin; and medical poetry by Dr. George S. Bascom. $45.

Sigma-Aldrich Material Safety Data Sheets
   Aldrich Chemical Co.
   $1,300/year.

Small Business Consultant
   Microsoft Corp.
   Contains over 220 government publications from the Small Business Administration; Department of Commerce; Veterans Administration; Department of Defense; General Services Administration; and data from the accounting firm of Deloitte Haskins and Sells. Information covered includes planning and financing of small business, accounting and general management, marketing and advertising, doing business with the government, personnel management, crime and liability protection, importing and exporting information, and business information sources. Updated annually, $149.

Social Sciences Index
   H. W. Wilson Co.
   Includes more than 300 English-language periodicals covering areas of social science, anthropology, black studies, economics, urban studies, women's studies, and related areas. $1,295/year plus updates.

Sociofile
   SilverPlatter
   Contains abstracts of journal articles published in *Sociological Abstracts* since 1974 and the enhanced bibliographic citations for dissertations in sociology and related disciplines that have been added to the database since 1986. $1,950.

Software-CD
   SilverPlatter
   Database of Business Software Directory from Information Sources, Inc., of Berkeley, California. Contains more than 10,000 listings of software packages for the business, professional, and technical communities. Describes features and functions of the software package; lists the name, address, and telephone number of the manufacturer. Includes information on mini, micro, and mainframe computers, operating systems, programming languages, prices, potential users, date first available, installed base, related packages, and other services from the manufacturer. $1,250.

Software DuJour
   Alde Publishing

Software Information Database (SID)
   ICP Software Information
   Includes 15,000 software products on two discs. $3,900.

Software Library DataPlate
Reference Technology, Inc.
$195.

Sound Designer
Optical Media International
Sound effects and music samples. $595.

The Sourcedisc
Diversified Data Resources, Inc. (DDRI)
Contains descriptions and demonstrations of hundreds of CD-ROM titles currently available or under development within the United States and internationally. The *Sourcedisc* contains the full text from Microsoft Press's *CD-ROM: The New Papyrus* and *CD-ROM: Optical Publishing,* articles from the *CD Data Report,* plus a glossary and acronym list related to CD-ROM. $89.95.

Spectrum Clip Art
Alde
Includes accents, alphabets, borders, banners, corners, designs, headlines, humor, illustration, and letters. $299.

Spectrum 200
Gaylord Information Systems
See Chapter 10.

Sport Discus
SilverPlatter
This database is the CD-ROM version of *Sport Bibliography.* It contains the database of international sports from 1972 to present. It covers medicine, biomechanics, couching, counseling, psychology, sports medicine, and exercise physiology. The database is based on more than 2,000 international sources. Updated semiannually. $1,250/year.

Standard & Poor's Corporations
DIALOG Information Services
$4,250
Standard & Poor's Corporation
$4,250/year; $3,500/year for print subscribers.

This database provides access to corporate and financial information on a compact disc. It consists of data from *Standard & Poor's Corporate Descriptions, Standard & Poor's Register (Bibliographical and Corporate),* and *Standard & Poor's Compustat Services.* The data are organized in three files: public companies, private companies, and executives.

STAT Facts
Readex Microprint Corp.
Contains more than one-half million statistics and facts on all fifty states and the District of Columbia gathered from more than fifty sources.

STAT PACK
Microsoft Corp.
Statistical information provided by the U.S. government, including eco-

nomic, political, demographic agricultural, manufacturing, political subject areas, and business. It allows the user to load and manipulate statistics into applications such as Microsoft Excel and Lotus. $125.

State Income and Employment
Slater Hall Information Products
Covers personal income, earnings in each of approximately 90 industries and industry groups, employment by major industry group and transfer payments.

Statestack
Highlighted Data, Inc.
HyperCard directory with maps and ZIP codes of all state government offices and personnel, including brief biographies and photos. Updated quarterly.

SuperCAT
Gaylord Information Systems
See Chapter 9.

Supermap USA
Chadwyck-Healey, Inc.
U.S. Census information and county maps. Correlates census data with a national mapping system. Target applications include chain stores and franchises using map correlation to determine the best sites for new stores, city planners determining school sites, and real estate developers. $990.

Surface Data for North America, 1987
University of Washington, Department of Atmospheric Sciences

System George
Active English Information Systems, Inc.
Includes specifications, product sources, reviews for architects and facilities managers.

Tax Library
Tax Analysts
Contains U.S. federal tax information.

TELE-DIRECT
SilverPlatter
Contains all white- and yellow-pages telephone listings for Ontario and Quebec.

Termdok (Swedish Technical Terms — Multilingual)
Archetype Systems Ltd.
Walters Lexikon
A science and technology terminological database. Includes 25,000 single and multiword terms, complete with their synonyms in English, French, German, Danish, Norwegian, Finnish, Russian, and Spanish. $995.

Termium
Reteaco, Inc.
A computerized dictionary developed by the Canadian Translation Bureau

at the Secretary of State. When finished, *Termium* will contain about three million terms and their definitions and equivalents in English and French. It is expected to be distributed free of charge to government translation offices, research organizations, and international organizations, such as United Nations, NATO, and the Organization for Economic Cooperation and Development.

Texas Attorney General Documents on CD-ROM
Quantum Access, Inc.
Includes the full text of Opinions of the Attorney General's Office and Open Records Act decisions for Texas. The first issue of the disc includes all opinions of Mark White and Jim Mattox from 1979 through 1986. The plan is to include historical opinions through 1949. The update will include the Open Records Act Decisions, Letter Advisories, and Constitutional Convention Advisories. $600/year plus updates.

Texas State Education Encyclopedia
Quantum Access, Inc.
The *State Education Encyclopedia* is a product that is helpful to run a school district in Texas. It includes the full text of the Texas Education Code, Title 19; Texas Administrative Code Including Chapter 75; HB 72 "Encyclopedia"; letters "To the Administrator Addressed" since October 1984; all commissioner's decisions since 1978; all special education hearing decisions since 1978; federal statutes related to education; federal administrative regulations for education; amended guidelines for special programs; TASB policy reference manual; *Enhanced Texas School Directory and District Profiles*; state government directory; Accounting Bulletin 679; Texas property tax; family and election codes; TEA advisories on special programs; extracurricular activities; questions and answer updates; curriculum frameworks; teacher appraisal information; UIL Constitution and guidelines. The *Encyclopedia* is continually updated to incorporate all changes and additions. The yearly subscription fee is $2,000.

Time Table of History/Science and Innovation
Xiphias
Part of a planned series of products called *Time Table of History*; an interactive history of scientific development for the Macintosh. $150.

TLG Discs A & B: Greek Literature
Thesaurus Linguae Graecae
Includes all surviving Greek literature from 750 B.C. to 600 A.D. Byzantine Greek literature is expected to be added to this database. $200.

TLRN
Innovative Technology, Inc.
Access to almost 80 percent of the Technical Logistics Reference Network, Federal Catalog System. $5,160/year.

TOM
Information Access Co.
Designed exclusively for secondary school libraries. It indexes popular and general interest magazines.

TOMES (Toxic Occupational, Medical & Environmental Series)
Micromedex, Inc.
$1,495.

Toronto Globe & Mail
Info Globe
Newspaper. Works only with Phillips CM-100. $500 (Canadian).

TOXLINE
SilverPlatter
A collection of toxicological information from the National Library of
Medicine, containing references to published material and research in
progress in the areas of adverse drug reactions, air pollution, carcinogenesis
through chemicals, drug toxicity, food contamination, occupational hazards,
pesticides and herbicides, toxicological analysis, and water treatment.

Trademark Information Database
Tri Star Publishing
U.S. Federal trademarks with graphics.

U.S. City Map Atlas
Perceptronics

ULRICH'S Plus
Bowker Electronic Publishing
See Chapter 11.

United Nations Publications Index
Readex Microprint Corp.

Universe of Sounds, Volumes 1–2
Optical Media International
Includes more than 4,000 of digitized sound samples using Digidesign's
Sound Designer sound file format. Designed for the Macintosh; versions for
the IBM computers and compatibles require a special adapter. $595.

University of Guelph Catalog
University of Guelph
This catalog includes approximately two million book titles. $249.

USSR Source 21
Alde Publishing Co.
A reference library on Soviet history. Updated semiannually. $750.

Variety's Video Directory Plus
Bowker Electronic Publishing
See Chapter 11.

Videoworks CD-ROM
MacroMind, Inc.
Animations, clip art, sound for the Macintosh. $695.

Vietnam–USA War
Quanta Press, Inc.
Covers the U.S. involvement in the Vietnam conflict. $99.

Virginia Disk
Virginia Polytechnic Institute

Virginia State Legal Code
Michie Co.
Includes the 24 volumes of Virginia legal code. $700.

Voyager II: Images of Uranus
University of Colorado–LASP

Washington Post
DataTimes
A database stored on CD-ROM, available through Telenet. $1.40/minute.

West CD-ROM Bankruptcy Library
West Publishing Co.
Includes textbooks, cases, and bibliographic information relating to bankruptcy.

West CD-ROM Federal Civil Practice Library
West Publishing Co.
Includes textbooks, cases, and bibliographic information relating to federal civil practice.

West CD-ROM Government Contracts Library
West Publishing Co.
Includes textbooks, cases, and bibliographic information relating to government contracts.

West CD-ROM Libraries
West Publishing Co.
Includes all of West's CD-ROM products.

Wheeler Quick Art
Quanta Press, Inc.
Includes thousands of clip art images. The disc is a joint venture between Quanta Press and Wheeler Arts. $249.

Who Is in Washington
Alde Publishing
Federal personnel information. Contains a full-text database on the people in the federal government. Provides information such as names, addresses, phone numbers, positions, and salaries. $99.

Whole Earth Learning Disc
Broderbund Software
A CD-ROM version of *The Whole Earth Catalog*, a resource for self-education; uses Apple's hypercard software. $149.95.

WILSONDISC Demonstration Disc
H. W. Wilson
A demonstration disc containing six months of data from sixteen H. W. Wilson databases. $99.

World Atlas
Electromap, Inc.
Provides over 200 full-color maps. Includes comparative data for every country in both geographic and text format. Five subject areas complement maps: geography, economy, people, government, and communications. For instance, in the area of economy, information provided covers: GDP/GNP, inflation rate, natural resources, agriculture, fishing, major industries, exports, imports, electricity, and monetary conversion rate. The area of communications covers topics such as railroads, highways, inland waterways, pipelines, ports, civil aircraft, airfields, and telecommunications. $129.

World Currency Monitor
Meckler/Bank of America World Information Services
Presents the value of 100 currencies from 1976 to 1989. Searching is based on eight currencies (U.S. dollar, Canadian dollar, British pound sterling, West German Deutschmark, French franc, Swiss franc, Japanese yen, and Italian lira) against the value of 99 other world currencies. $995/year with annual updates; $1,495/year with quarterly updates.

The World Factbook CD-ROM
Quanta Press, Inc.
This full-text database of the Central Intelligence Agency's *World Factbook* is an annual world almanac that describes the political and foreign affairs of every territory and country in the world. Socioeconomic, demographic, and other country-specific data are provided in profiles of 248 countries based on unclassified CIA data. Includes a visual database including digitized map images of each country stored in tagged image file format. $99.95.

World WeatherDisc
University of Washington, Department of Atmospheric Sciences
WeatherDisc Associates, Inc.
Contains climatological records from thousands of weather stations around the world dating back to the eighteenth century. $295.

Worldscope Profiles
Wright Investors Service
Profiles on more than 4,000 leading worldwide companies (same as *CD/International*). Includes industrial, financial, and service company profiles.

X-RAY
DNAStar
Biotechnology information on 600 3D protein molecular structures from Brookhaven protein data bank. $1,500.

X-RAY Demo
National Library of Medicine

Yearbook
CMC ReSearch
Includes the full text, line art, and images from the following 1988 Medical Year Books: *Year Book of Medicine, Neurology/Neurosurgery, Drug Thera-*

py, Family Practice, Dermatology, Psychiatry, Obstetrics and Gynecology, Diagnostics Radiology, Emergency Medicine, and *Pediatrics.* $125.

Yellow Page Demo
Compact Discoveries

Your Marketing Consultant: Advanced Consumer
Knowledge Access International
Consumer buying power index. $249.

Your Marketing Consultant: Business-to-Business
Knowledge Access International
Sales territories and market shares. $249.

ZIP+4
Information Design, Inc.

B. CD-ROM Products (A Subject List)

Agriculture/Livestock

About Cows
Quanta Press

Agribusiness USA
DIALOG Information Services
Pioneer Hi-Bred International

AGRICOLA
Quanta Press

AGRICOLA and CRIS
OCLC
SilverPlatter

AGRICOLA Retrospective File (1979– 1982)
OCLC

Agriculture Library
OCLC

Agriculture Series
OCLC

Biological and Agricultural Index
H. W. Wilson Co.

CAB Abstracts
CAB International

Census of Agriculture on CD-ROM (1982)
Slater Hall Information Products

Art

Art Index
H. W. Wilson Co.

ArtRoom
Image Club Graphics, Inc.

ArtScan
Newsreel Access

Clip Art 3-D
NEC Home Electronics

Dover Clip Art Series
Alde Publishing

EBook Electronic Art Anthology
EBSCO Electronic Information Division

The Electronic Publishing Arts Disc
Network Technology Corp.

Graphics Lab
Alde Publishing

Images Demo
Compact Discoveries, Inc.

Kwikee Inhouse Graphics Services
Multi-AD Services

Kwikee Inhouse Pal
Multi-AD Services

National Portrait Gallery, The Permanent Collection
Abt Books

ProArt Trilogy I
Multi-AD Services

Spectrum Clip Art
Alde Publishing

Videoworks CD-ROM
MacroMind, Inc.

Wheeler Quick Art
Quanta Press, Inc.

Biographies

Biography Index
H. W. Wilson Co.

Biology

Aquatic Sciences and Fisheries
Compact Cambridge

Biological Abstracts
BIOSIS

Biological and Agricultural Index
H. W. Wilson Co.

International Dictionary of Medicine and Biology
Wiley Electronic Publishing

Life Sciences Collection
Compact Cambridge

Biotechnology

CD/Biotech
PC-SIG, Inc.

CD-GENE
Hitachi American Ltd.

Lasergene CD-ROM
DNAStar

X-RAY
DNAStar

Book Reviews

Book Review Digest
H. W. Wilson Co.

Business

ABI/INFORM OnDisc
University Microfilms International

Brief/Case
JA Micropublishing, Inc.

Business Indicators
Slater Hall Information Products

Business Periodicals Index
H. W. Wilson Co.

Business Periodicals Ondisc
University Microfilms International

Business Statistics, 1929–85
Slater Hall Information Products

Canadian Business and Current Affairs
DIALOG Information Services
Micromedia Ltd.

CD Banking
Lotus Development Corp.

CD/Corporate
Lotus Development Corp.

CD/Corptech
Lotus Development Corp.

CD/International
Lotus Development Corp.

CD/Investment
Lotus Development Corp.

CD/Newsline
Lotus Development Corp.

CD/Private+
Lotus Development Corp.

CD-ROM: The Conference Disc
PDO

Compact Disclosure
Disclosure, Inc.

Compact Disclosure Europe
Disclosure, Inc.

Company Accounts & Register of Compustat PC Plus
Standard & Poor's Compustat Services

Compustat PC Plus on CD-ROM
Standard & Poor's Compustat Services

Construction Activity Locator
Knowledge Access, Inc.

Corporate & Industry Research Reports
JA Micropublishing, Inc.
SilverPlatter

CrossLink: Supply/Logistics Data
Information Handling Services, Inc.

CUSIP Directory
Standard & Poor's Compustat Services

Disclosure Spectrum
Disclosure, Inc.

Exxon Corp. Basic Practices Manual
Amtec Information Services

Hoppenstadt Directory of Large Corporations
Dataware, Inc.

Infomark IV Laser PC System: Decision Support
National Decision Systems

The Intuition Expert
Telerate

Italian Banking Legal and Technical Documentation
Eikon Sp A

Laser Disclosure: Commercial, Not for Profit, Wall Street
Disclosure, Inc.

Lotus One Source
Lotus Development

Million Dollar Directory
Dun's Marketing Services

Moody's 5000 Plus
Moody's Investors Service

Moody's International Plus
Moody's Investors Service

PHINET
Prentice-Hall Information Network

Rainbow the Connection: Businessbase
Tetragon Systems, Inc.

Rainbow the Connection: Homebase II
Tetragon Systems, Inc.

Small Business Consultant
Microsoft Corp.

Standard & Poor's Corporations
DIALOG Information Services

Trademark Information Database
Tri Star Publishing

World Currency Monitor
Meckler/Bank of America Information Services

Worldscope Profiles
Wright Investors Service

Your Marketing Consultant: Advanced Consumer
Knowledge Access International

Your Marketing Consultant: Business-to-Business
Knowledge Access International

Catalogs—Parts

Chrysler Parts Catalog
Bell & Howell

GE Aircraft Engines
AMTEC Information Services

GM Parts Catalog
AMTEC Information Services

Honda Parts
Bell & Howell

Mack Electronic Parts Disc
AMTEC Information Services

Mercedes-Benz
Bell & Howell

Parts Master
National Standards Association,
Inc.

Chemistry

Beilstein Handbook of Organic Chemistry
Springer Verlag

CHEM-BANK
SilverPlatter

EINECS Plus-CD
SilverPlatter

GEFAHRGUT Chemdata
Springer Verlag

GEFAHRGUT Einsatzakten
Springer Verlag

GEFAHRGUT Hommel Chemdata
Springer Verlag

Kirk-Othmer Encyclopedia of Chemical Technology
Wiley Electronic Publishing

PC-PDF (Powder Diffraction File)
International Center for
Diffraction Data

Plus 37
Philips Electronic Instruments

Registry of Mass Spectral Data
Wiley Electronic Publishing

Classical Works

PHI: Classical Latin Literature
Packard Humanities Institute

Papyri: Egyptian Papyri
Packard Humanities Institute

TLG discs A & B: Greek Literature
Thesaurus Linguae Graecae

Computers

C CD-ROM
Alde Publishing

CD-Capture
Compact Disc Products

CD-Play
Compact Disc Products

CD-ROM Developer's Lab
Software Mart, Inc.

CD-ROM Sampler
Discovery Systems

CD-ROM Sourcedisc
Diversified Data Resources, Inc.

COMPU-INFO
SilverPlatter

Computer Library
OCLC

Computer Library
Lotus Development Corp.
Ziff Communications

Computer-SPECS (formerly
COMPU-INFO)
GML Corp.
SilverPlatter

Data Times Libraries System
DataTimes

HP LaserROM
Hewlett Packard

ICP Software Information Database
OCLC

Macintosh Showcase
Discovery Systems

MAK PAK
Alde Publishing

Manhole
Activision

Microsoft Office
Microsoft Corp.

Programmer's Library
Microsoft Corporation

Prompt CD
Lotus Development Corp.

Software Information Database
ICP Software Information

Software Library DataPlate
Reference Technology, Inc.

Software-CD
SilverPlatter

The Sourcedisc
Diversified Data Resources, Inc.

Dictionaries and Encyclopedias

The Electronic Encyclopedia
Grolier Electronic Publishing, Inc.

Harrap's Multilingual Dictionary
Microinfo Ltd.

Merriam-Webster's Ninth New Collegiate Dictionary
Highlighted Data, Inc.

Multilingual Dictionary Database
Sansyusya Publishing Co. Ltd.

The Oxford English Dictionary on CD-ROM
Oxford Electronics Publishing
Tri Star Publishing

TERMDOK (Swedish Technical Terms— Multilingual)
Archetype Systems Ltd.
Walters Lexikon

Termium
Reteaco, Inc.

Visual Dictionary CD-ROM
Facts On File Publications

Dissertations

Dissertation Abstracts OnDisc
University Microfilms International

Economics

HELECON on CD-ROM
Helsinki School of Economics Library

PAIS on CD-ROM
Public Affairs Information Service (PAIS)

Education

A-V ONLINE
Access Innovations, Inc.
SilverPlatter

Cross-Cultural CD
SilverPlatter

Education Index
H. W. Wilson Co.

Education Library
OCLC

Education Series
OCLC

ERIC
DIALOG Information Services
OCLC
SilverPlatter

ESC System
  Education Systems Corp.

First National Item Bank & Test Development System
  Tescor, Inc.

International Encyclopedia of Education
  Pergamon Compact Solution

Item Bank
  Minnesota Department of Education

ONTERIS
  Reteaco, Inc.

Peterson's College Database
  SilverPlatter

Peterson's GradLine
  SilverPlatter

SchoolMatch
  OCLC

Science Helper K–8
  PC-SIG, Inc.

Texas State Education Encyclopedia
  Quantum Access, Inc.

Time Table of History/Science & Innovation
  Xiphias

Whole Earth Learning Disc
  Broderbund Software

Energy

Energy Library
  OCLC

Engineering, Construction, and Architecture

Automated Facilities
  National Institute of Building Sciences

Construction Activity Locator
  Knowledge Access International
  CD Productions

Construction Criteria Base
  National Institute of Building Sciences

Encyclopedia of Polymer Science and Engineering
  Wiley Electronic Publishing

Engineering Information System
  National Institute of Building Sciences

System George
  Active English Information Systems, Inc.

Environment

Enflex Info
  ERM Computer Services, Inc.

Environment Library
  OCLC

Essays

Essay and General Literature Index
  H. W. Wilson

Film

CineScan
  Newsreel Access Systems

Film Literature Index
  H. W. Wilson

Furniture

CAP
  Computer Aided Planning, Inc.

Geography/Maps/Atlases

Arctic and Antarctic Regions
NISC

Delorme's World Atlas
Delorme Mapping Systems

Electronic Map Cabinet
Highlighted Data, Inc.

Fedstack
Highlighted Data, Inc.

GEOdisc Windows on the World
GEOVISION, Inc.

GEOdisc: Florida Atlas
GEOVISION, Inc.

GEOdisc: Georgia Atlas
GEOVISION, Inc.

GEOdisc: U.S. Atlas
GEOVISION, Inc.

Lasertrak Disc
Lasertrack Corp.

LZ Services (NAV/COM Terminal Charts)
Lasertrak Corp.

Navigational Geographic Maps
ETAK, Inc.

Place-Name Index
Buckmaster Publishing

Statestack
Highlighted Data, Inc.

Supermap
Chadwyck-Healey, Inc.

U.S. City Map Atlas
Perceptronics

World Atlas
Electromap, Inc

Geology

CD-ROM Prototype Disc
U.S. Geological Survey

Earth Science Series
OCLC

Hydrodata
U.S. West Optical Publishing

Hydropeak
U.S. West Optical Publishing

Surface Data for North America, 1987
University of Washington,
Department of Atmospheric
Sciences

Government Logos

Federal Logos Disc
Alde Publishing

Seals of the U.S. Federal Government
Quanta Press, Inc.

Government Personnel

Personnet
Information Handling Services,
Inc.

Who Is in Washington
Alde Publishing

Government Procurement

CD-Fiche
USA Information Systems, Inc.

Federal Procurement Package
Alde Publishing

Haystack: Logistics, Procurement, Engineering Files
Ziff Davis Technical Information
Co.

Parts Master
National Standards Association,
Inc.

TLRN (Technical Logistics Reference Network)
Innovative Technology, Inc.

Government Publications

Catalogue of United Kingdom Official Publications
Chadwyck-Healey, Inc.

CIS Congressional Masterfile 1789–1969
Congressional Service

GDCS Impact
Auto Graphics, Inc.

Government Publications Index
Information Access Co.

GPO Cat/PAC
Marcive, Inc.

GPO Laserfile
Library Systems & Services, Inc.

GPO Monthly Catalog
OCLC

GPO Monthly Catalog Index to Government Periodicals
H. W. Wilson Co.

GPO on SilverPlatter
SilverPlatter

Le Pac: Government Documents Option
Brodart Automation

Optext: Federal Regulations
VLS (Video Laser Systems), Inc.

History

Constitution Papers
Optical Media International

Humanities/ Popular Magazines

Academic Index
Information Access Co.

American Authors on CD-ROM
Electronic Text Corp.

Black Fiction Up to 1920
Cornell University

General Periodicals Index
Information Access Corp.

Humanities Index
H. W. Wilson Co.

Languages of the World
Network Technology Corp.

Magazine Article Summaries
EBSCO

Magazine Index Plus
Information Access Co.

MLA International Bibliography
H. W. Wilson Co.
Modern Language Association

Periodical Abstracts
University Microfilms, Inc.

Reader's Guide Abstracts
H. W. Wilson Co.

Reader's Guide to Periodical Literature
H. W. Wilson Co.

Resource/One
University Microfilms International

Sherlock Holmes on Disc
CMC ReSearch

TOM
Information Access Co.

WILSONDISC Demonstration Disc
H. W. Wilson Co.

Legal

California Decisions
ROM Publishers, Inc.

CD/Law: Illinois
CD/Law Reports, Inc.

Codice Tributario
LaserData, Inc.

Comptroller General Decisions
Information Handling Services

Decision Series
ROM Publishers, Inc.

Enflex Info
ERM Computer Services, Inc.

Federal Decisions
ROM Publishers, Inc.

Index to Legal Periodicals
H. W. Wilson Co.

Laserlaw Series
CD/Law Reports

LegalTrac
Information Access Co.

The Texas Attorney General Documents on CD-ROM
Quantum Access, Inc.

Virginia State Legal Code
Michie Co.

West CD-ROM Bankruptcy Library
West Publishing Co.

West CD-ROM Federal Civil Practice Library
West Publishing Co.

West CD-ROM Government Contracts Library
West Publishing Co.

West CD-ROM Libraries
West Publishing Co.

Libraries/Acquisitions/ Bibliographic Tools

Anybook
Library Corp.

BaTaSYSTEMS Order; Titles on CD
Baker & Taylor

Bibliographie Nationale Français depuis 1975 sur CD-ROM
Chadwyck-Healey, Inc.

Bookbank
J. Whitaker

Books in Print Plus
Bowker Electronic Publishing

Books in Print with Book Reviews Plus
Bowker Electronic Publishing

Books Out of Print Plus
Bowker Electronic Publishing

British Library General Catalogue of Printed Books to 1975 on CD-ROM
Chadwyck-Healey, Inc.

British National Bibliography on CD-ROM
Chadwyck-Healey, Inc.

Cumulative Book Index
H. W. Wilson Co.

Deutsche Bibliographie-aktuell-CD-ROM
Chadwyck-Healey, Inc.

Flash-Back/Books in Print Plus
Ingram Book Co.

German Books in Print
Buchandler Vereinigung-GMBH (sold by Chadwyck-Healey)

International Books in Print
K. G. Saur

LaserSearch/AnyBook
Ingram Book Co.

PC Order Plus
Blackwell North America, Inc.

PC Rose System/Bowker's Books in Print Plus
Brodart Automation

Publishers International Directory
K. G. Saur

Reference Tool Kit
EBSCO

Serials Directory
EBSCO

ULRICH'S Plus
Bowker Electronic Publishing

Variety's Video Directory Plus
Bowker Electronic Publishing

Libraries/Cataloging Support/Retrospective

BIB-BASE/CD-ROM
Small Library Computing

BiblioFile Catalog Maintenance
Library Corp.

BiblioFile Catalog Production
Library Corp.

BPN/JR
Library Systems & Services, Inc.

CAT CD450
OCLC

Cataloger's Tool Kit
EBSCO

CD-CATSS Current Cataloging
Utlas International

CDMARC Bibliographic
Library of Congress

CDMARC Names
Library of Congress

CDMARC Subjects
Library of Congress

Current Cataloging Database
Utlas International

DisCon
Utlas International

Enhanced BiblioFile
Library Corp.

LaserQuest
General Research Corp.

LawMARC
Utlas International

Serials
Library Corp.
Utlas International

SuperCAT
Gaylord Information Systems

Libraries/Circulation/ Interlibrary Loan/ Union Catalogs

ACCESS Pennsylvania
Brodart Automation

BiblioFile Circulation
Library Corp.

CD-CAT
Cooperating Libraries Automated
Network (CLAN)

Harlic Union Catalog
Marcive

LaserCat
Western Library Network

LePac: Interlibrary Loan
Brodart Automation

LOANet
Library Systems & Services, Inc.

Libraries/ Collection Analysis

OCLC AMIGOS Collection Analysis CD
AMIGOS Bibliographic Council,
Inc.

Libraries/Public Access Catalogs

CD/2000
OCLC

Impact
Auto-Graphics, Inc.

Intelligent Catalog
  Library Corp.

LaserCat
  Western Library Network

LaserGuide
  General Research Corp.

Le Pac
  Brodart Automation

MARCIVE/PAC
  Marcive, Inc.

Spectrum 200
  Gaylord Information Systems

University of Guelph Catalog
  University of Guelph

Library Science

ALA CD-ROM Directory of Library and Information Professionals
  American Library Association
  Knowledge Access International

BiblioDisc
  Online Computer Systems, Inc.

Iowa State Locator
  Iowa State Library

Library Literature
  H. W. Wilson Co.

LISA
  Library Association Publishers
  SilverPlatter

Mathematics

MathSci Disc
  American Mathematical Society
  SilverPlatter

Medicine/Aids

AIDS Information and Education Worldwide CD-ROM
  CD Resources

AIDS Supplement
  Digital Diagnostics, Inc.

AIDS—Compact Library
  Medical Publishing Group

Medline — BiblioMed with AIDS Supplement
  Digital Diagnostics, Inc.

Medicine/Cancer

Cancer-CD
  SilverPlatter

CancerLit
  Aries Systems Corp.
  CD Plus

CancerLit CD-ROM
  Compact Cambridge

Cancer on Disc: 1988
  CMC ReSearch

OncoDisc
  J.B. Lippincott Co.

PDQ CD-ROM
  Compact Cambridge
  SilverPlatter Information, Inc.

Medicine/Health Care

BiblioMed
  Digital Diagnostics, Inc.

CDID on Disc
  Knowledge Access International

ClinMED-CD
  SilverPlatter

Compact Med-Base
Online Research Systems, Inc.

Comprehensive Medline
EBSCO

Computerized Clinical Information Systems (CCIS)
Micromedex, Inc.

Core Medline
EBSCO

Dosing and Therapeutic Tools
Micromedex, Inc.

Drug Information Source CD
Compact Cambridge

Drugdex
Micromedex, Inc.

EMBASE (Excerpta Medica Abstract Journals on CD-ROM)
SilverPlatter

Emergindex
Micromedex, Inc.

Food/Analyst
Hopkins Technology

Health
CD Plus

Health Index
Information Access Co.

HealthPLAN-CD
SilverPlatter

Identidex
Micromedex, Inc.

International Dictionary of Medicine and Biology
Wiley Electronic Publishing

Journal of Pediatrics on Disc
CMC ReSearch

Journal of Radiology
CMC ReSearch

Martindale: The Extra Pharmacopoeia
Micromedex, Inc.

Medline—BiblioMed
Digital Diagnostics, Inc.

Medline—BRS/Colleague
BRS Information Technologies

Medline—CD Plus
CD Plus

Medline—Compact Cambridge
Compact Cambridge

Medline—Knowledge Finder
Aries System Corp.

Medline Clinical Collection
DIALOG Information Services

Medline DIALOG OnDisc
DIALOG Information Services

Medline on SilverPlatter
SilverPlatter

The Nurse Library
Ellis Enterprises, Inc.

Nursing and Allied Health
SilverPlatter

The Oxford Textbook of Medicine— Electronic Edition
Oxford Electronic Publishing

PAHO Database (Pan American World Health Organization)
PAHO

Pediatrics on Disc
CMC ReSearch

The Physician Library
Ellis Enterprises, Inc.

Physician's Desk Reference
Medical Economics Co.

Poisindex
Micromedex, Inc.

Scientific American Medicine Consult
Scientific American

TOMES (Toxic Occupational, Medical & Environmental Series)
Micromedex, Inc.

TOXLINE on SilverPlatter
SilverPlatter

X-RAY Demo
National Library of Medicine

Yearbook
CMC ReSearch

Meteorology

Climatedata
U.S. West Optical Publishing

Gale Experimental Data Set
University of Washington,
Department of Atmospheric
Sciences

National Meteorological Grid Data Point Set
University of Washington,
Department of Atmospheric
Sciences

World WeatherDisc
University of Washington,
Department of Atmospheric
Sciences
WeatherDisc Associates, Inc.

Military

Dick's-Earth's Planes
Quanta Press, Inc.

Officer's Bookcase—Terms
Quanta Press, Inc.

Vietnam—USA War
Quanta Press, Inc.

Music and Sound Effects

California Music Directory
Knowledge Access International

CD-Audiofile
Compact Disc Products

CD-Companion. Beethoven Symphony No. 9
Voyager

Desktop Sounds
Optical Media International

Music Business Directory
Knowledge Access International

Music Radio Directory
Knowledge Access International

Sound Designer
Optical Media International

Universe of Sounds
Optical Media International

Natural Resources

Natural Resources Database
NISC

News/Newspapers

Daily Oklahoman
DataTimes

Facts On File News Digest CD-ROM
Facts On File Publications

FBIS
Readex Microprint Corp.

National Newspaper Index
Information Access Corp.

News Scan
Newsreel Access Systems

NewsBank Electronic Index
NewsBank

Newspaper Abstracts Ondisc
University Microfilms
International

Online Hotline News Service
Information Intelligence, Inc.

Pravda on CD-ROM
Alde Publishing

Toronto Globe and Mail
Info Globe

Washington Post
DataTimes

Occupational Health and Safety

CCINFOdisc: OH&S Information
Canadian Centre for
Occupational Health & Safety

CHEM-BANK
SilverPlatter

Material Safety Data Sheets
National Safety Data Corp.

Material Safety Data Sheets, Reference File
Occupational Health Services

OSH-ROM
SilverPlatter

Sigma-Aldrich Material Safety Data Sheets
Aldrich Chemical Co.

TOMES (Toxic Occupational,
Medical & Environmental Series)
Micromedex, Inc.

TOXLINE
SilverPlatter

Patents

CASSIS CD-ROM
NISC

Pesticides

PEST-BANK
SilverPlatter

Photography

Dark Room
Image Club Graphics, Inc.

Desktop Photography
Comstock, Inc.

Photo Library
Phillips Electronic Instruments

Photo Scan
Newsreel Access Systems, Inc.

Psychology

PsycLIT
PsycINFO Services
SilverPlatter and the American
Psychological Association

Public Affairs

PAIS on CD-ROM
Public Affairs Information Service

Public Domain Software

ADA on CD-ROM
Alde Publishing

ALDE's $99 CD-ROM Disc
Alde Publishing

Blue Sail Library
Alde Publishing

ClubMac
Quantum Access, Inc.

DECUS
Digital Decus Group

Mega ROM
Quantum Leap Technologies

Menu: International Software
The Menu

PC-Blue: MS-DOS Public Domain Library
Alde Publishing

PC-SIG Library on CD-ROM
PC-SIG, Inc.

PD-ROM
Berkeley Macintosh User Group (BMUG)

Programmer's ROM
Quanta Press, Inc.

Public Domain Mac Programs
Educorp USA

Public Domain Software on File
Facts on File Publications

RBBS-PC in a Box
Quanta Press, Inc.

Right Stuffed
Quantum Leap Technologies

Shareware Gold
Quanta Press, Inc.

Shareware Grab Bag
Alde Publishing

Software DuJour
Alde Publishing

Real Estate

MetroScan
Digital Diagnostics, Inc.

Real Estate Transfer Database
Abt Books, Inc.

Realscan Real Estate Information System
LaserScan Systems, Inc.

Reference Works

Associations: Global Access
Gale Research, Inc.
Knowledge Access International

CD-ROM: The New Papyrus
Computer Access Corp.

Home Reference Library
Ellis Enterprises, Inc.

Microsoft Bookshelf
Microsoft Corp.

Religion

Bible Library
AIRS, Inc.

The Bible Library
Ellis Enterprises, Inc.

FABS Electronic Bible (FEB)
FABS International

FABS Reference Bible
FABS International

King James Bible
Quantum Access

Luther Bible
Deutsche Bibelgeselschaft

Master Search Bible on Compact Disc
Tri Star Publishing

REX (Religion Index)
FABS International

Science and Technology

Apple Science CD Volume 1
Apple Computer, Inc.

Applied Science & Technology Index
H. W. Wilson Co.

Electronic Sweet's
McGraw-Hill

Encyclopedia of Polymer Science and Engineering
Wiley Electronic Publishing

General Electric Jet Engine Division
Amtec Information Services

General Science Index
H. W. Wilson Co.

Multi-Lingual Dictionary of Science & Technology
Sansyusya Publishing Co. Ltd.

NTIS
Dialog Information Services
OCLC
SilverPlatter

Science and Technical Reference Set
McGraw-Hill

Science Citation Index CD
Institute for Scientific Information

Science Helper K–8
PC-SIG, Inc.

TERMDOK (Swedish Technical Terms —Multilingual)
Archetype Systems Ltd.
Walters Lexikon

Time Table of History/Science & Innovation
Xiphias

Virginia Disk
Virginia Polytechnic Institute

Social Sciences

How to Become a U.S. Citizen
Quanta Press, Inc.

NATASHA (National Archives on Sexuality, Health and Adolescence)
Knowledge Access International
Sociometrics Corp.

PAIS on CD-ROM
Public Affairs Information Service

POPLINE
SilverPlatter

Social Sciences Index
H. W. Wilson Co.

Sociofile
SilverPlatter

United Nations Publications Index
Readex Microprint Corp.

The World Factbook CD-ROM
Quanta Press, Inc.

Space

Resors: Satellite Remote Sensitivity Publications
PCI Inc.

Voyager II: Images of Uranus
University of Colorado—LASP

Sports, Games, and Recreation

The Guinness Disc of Records 1990
Pergamon Compact Solution

Sport Discus
SilverPlatter

Statistics

Agri/Stats
Hopkins Technology

Census Disc
U.S. Department of Commerce

Census of Australian Population & Housing, 1981 and 1986
Space-Time Research Ltd.

Census of England, Scotland and Wales, Small Area Statistics 1981
Space-Time Research Ltd.

Census of Hong Kong, 1981 and 1986
Space-Time Research Ltd.

Census of New Zealand, 1986 Census
Space-Time Research Ltd.

Census of Sweden, 1970 to 1987
Space-Time Research Ltd.

Census: Australian Standardized Local Government Finance Statistics
Space-Time Research Ltd.

Census: U.S. County Business Patterns, 1985
Chadwyck-Healey, Inc.
Space-Time Research Ltd.

Census: U.S. Data, 1980—Supermap
Space-Time Research Ltd.

Conquest: Consumer Information
Donnelly Marketing Information Services

Consu/Stats
Hopkins Technology

County Statistics
Slater Hall Information Products

Econ/Stats
Hopkins Technology

FEDSTAT
U.S. Statistics

FEDSTAT/TIGER CD-ROM
U.S. Statistics

Labor/Stats
Hopkins Technology

1985 American Housing Survey
U.S. Department of Commerce

Population Statistics on CD-ROM
Slater Hall Information Products

STAT Facts
Readex Microprint Corp.

STAT PACK
Microsoft Corp.

State Income and Employment
Slater Hall Information Products

Supermap
Chadwyck-Healey, Inc.

Taxes

PHINet Tax Resources
Prentice Hall Information Network

Tax Library
Tax Analysts

Telephone Directories

Fast Track: Nynex White Pages
Nynex Information Resources Co.

National Directory of Addresses & Telephone Numbers
General Information, Inc.

National Telephone Directory
Xiphias

Phone Disc
Digital Directory Assistance

TELE-DIRECT
SilverPlatter

Yellow Page Demo
Compact Discoveries

Training

Discovery—DIALOG OnDisc
Dialog Information Services

Transportation

FORM41: Airline Carrier Filings
Data Base Products, Inc.

International: Airline Traffic
Data Base Products, Inc.

Itineraries
  Data Base Products, Inc.

O&D Plus
  Data Base Products, Inc.

O&D Plus Historical
  Data Base Products, Inc.

Onboard: Airline Traffic Data
  Data Base Products, Inc.

USSR

Pravda on CD-ROM
  Alde Publishing

USSR Source 21
  Alde Publishing

Video Directories

Variety's Video Directory Plus
  Bowker Electronic Publishing

Videoworks CD-ROM·
  MacroMind, Inc.

Water Resources

Selected Water Resources Abstracts
  NISC (National Information
  Services Corp.)
  OCLC

ZIP Codes and Postal Services

AVS +
  Information Update, Inc.

Canadian Postal Codes
  SilverPlatter

ZIP + 4
  Information Design, Inc.

C. CD-ROM Distributors and Producers

Distributors

There are many CD-ROM distributors including:

ABT Books Inc.
146 Mt. Auburn St.
Cambridge, MA 02138
(617) 661-1300
Sells and rents some 60 CD-ROM databases including European.

Bureau of Electronic Publishing
P.O. Box 43131
Upper Montclair, NJ 07043
(201) 746-3031

CD One Stop
13 F. J. Clarke Circle
Bethel, CT 06801
(800) 826-0079
Wholesaler-compact discs.

Compact Disk Products, Inc.
223 E. 85th St.
New York, NY 10028
(212) 737-8400; FAX (212) 737-8289

EBSCO Publishing
P.O. Box 1943
Birmingham, AL 35201
(800) 826-3024, (205) 991-1182; FAX (508) 887-3923
A producer and distributor of CD-ROM products.

FAXON Co.
15 Southwest Park
Westwood, MA 02090
(800) 44-FAXON, (617) 329-3350; FAX (617) 326-5484
FAXON issues Access Faxon.

Jason
5459 Main St.
Williamsville, NY 14221
(716) 852-6711
Offers a wide variety of CD-ROM titles.

Ztek Co.
P.O. Box 1968
Lexington, KY 40593
(800) 247-1603, (606) 252-7276
CD-ROM products and videodiscs produced primarily for the education market.

Producers and Products

Abt Books, Inc.
146 Mt. Auburn St.
Cambridge, MA 02138
(617) 661-1300
Products: *Real Estate Transfer Database; National Portrait Gallery, The Permanent Collection*

Access Innovations, Inc.
P.O. Box 40130
4320 Mesa Grande S.E.
Albuquerque, NM 87196
(800) 421-8711, (505) 265-3591
Product: *A-V ONLINE*

Active English Information Systems, Inc.
P.O. Box 459
44 White Court
Canton, IL 61520
(309) 647-7668
Product: *System George*

Activision
2350 Bayshore Pkwy.
Mountain View, CA 94043
(415) 960-0410, (800) 227-6900
Product: *Manhole* (Mac)

AIRS, Inc.
Engineering Research Center
335 Paint Branch Dr.
College Park, MD 20742
(301) 454-2022
Product: *Bible Library*

Alde Publishing
4830 W. 77th St.
P.O. Box 35326
Minneapolis, MN 55435
(612) 835-5240; FAX (612) 835-3401
Products: *ADA on CD-ROM; Alde's $99 CD-ROM Disc; Blue Sail Library; C CD-ROM; The Dover Clip Art Series; Federal Logos Disc; Federal Procurement System Disc; Graphics Lab; MAK PAK; PC-Blue: MS-DOS Public Domain Library; Pravda on CD-ROM; Shareware Grab Bag; Software DuJour; Spectrum Clip Art; USSR Source 21; Who Is in Washington*

Aldrich Chemical Co.
1001 W. St. Paul St.
Milwaukee, WI 53233
(800) 231-8327
Product: *Sigma-Aldrich Material Safety Data Sheets*

American Library Association
Information Technology Publishing
50 E. Huron St.
Chicago, IL 60611
(800) 545-2433, (312) 944-6780
Product: *ALA CD-ROM Directory of Library and Information Professionals*

American Mathematical Society
P.O. Box 6248
Providence, RI 02940
(800) 556-7774, (401) 272-9500
Product: *MathSciDisc*

American Psychological Association
1400 N. Uhle St.
Arlington, VA 22201
(800) 336-4980, (703) 247-7829
Product: *PsycLit*

AMIGOS Bibliographic Council, Inc.
11300 N. Central Expressway, Suite 321
Dallas, TX 75243
(800) 843-8482, (214) 750-6130
Product: *OCLC/AMIGOS Collection Analysis CD*

Amtec Information Services
3700 Industry Ave.
Lakewood, CA 90714-6050
(213) 595-4756
Products: *Exxon Corp. Basic Practices Manual; GE Aircraft Engines; Mack Electronic Parts Disc*

Apple Computer
20525 Mariani Ave.
Cupertino, CA 95014
(408) 973-6025
Product: *Apple Science CD Volume 1*

Archetype Systems Ltd.
Boundary House
91-93 Charterhouse St.
London EC1M 6LN England
01-251-8644
Product: *Termdok*

Aries Systems Corp.
79 Boxford St.
North Andover, MA 01845-3219
(508) 689-9334
Products: *CancerLit; Medline—Knowledge Finder* (IBM & Mac)

Auto-Graphics, Inc.
3201 Temple Ave.
Pomona, CA 91768
(800) 325-7961, (714) 595-7204
Product: *GDCS Impact; Impact*

Baker & Taylor
50 Kirby Ave.
Somerville, NJ 08876
(800) 526-3811
(800) 352-4841 (in N.J.)
(800) 524-2486 (in Canada)
Product: *BaTaSYSTEMS Order*

Bell & Howell
5700 Lombardo Center
Suite 220
Seven Hills, OH 44131
(216) 642-9060
Products: *Chrysler Parts Catalog; GM Parts Catalog; Honda Parts Catalog; Mercedes-Benz*

Berkeley Macintosh User Group (BMUG)
2150 Kittredge 3B
Berkeley, CA 94709
(415) 549-2684
Product: *PD-ROM* (Mac)

BIOSIS
2100 Arch St.
Philadelphia, PA 19103-1399
(800) 523-4806, (215) 587-4800; FAX (215) 587-2016
Product: *Biological Abstracts*

Blackwell North America, Inc.
6024 SW Jean Rd.
Bldg. G
Lake Oswego, OR 97035
(503) 684-1140
Product: *PC Order Plus*

Bowker Electronic Publishing
245 W. 17th St.
New York, NY 10011
(800) 323-3288, (212) 337-6989; FAX (212) 645-0475
Products: *Books in Print Plus* (IBM/Mac); *Books in Print with Book Reviews Plus; Books Out of Print Plus; Ulrich's Plus; Variety's Video Directory Plus*

Brodart Automation
500 Arch St.
Williamsport, PA 17705
(800) 233-8467, (717) 326-2461
Products: *ACCESS Pennsylvania; LePac; LePac: Government Documents Option; LePac: Interlibrary Loan; PC Rose System*

Broderbund Software
17 Paul Dr.
San Rafael, CA 94903
(415) 479-1170
Product: *Whole Earth Learning Disc* (IBM/Mac)

BRS Information Technologies
919 Conestoga Rd.
Bldg. 1, Suite 301
Rosemont, PA 19010
(800) 468-0908, (215) 526-0128
Product: *Medline—BRS Colleague Disc*

Buchandler Vereinigung-GMBH
Grosser Hisxchgraben 17-21
Postfach 100442
6000 Frankfurt am Main 1, West Germany
Product: *Verzeichnis Lieferbarer Bucher* (*German Books in Print* sold by Chadwyck-Healey)

Buckmaster Publishing
Route 3
Box 56
Mineral, VA 23117
(800) 282-5628, (703) 894-5777
Product: *Place-Name Index*

C.A.B. International
Farnham House
Farnham Royal
Slough SL2 3BN England
Product: *CAB Abstracts*

Canadian Centre for Occupational Health & Safety
250 E. Main St.
Hamilton
Ont. L8N 1H6 Canada
(800) 263-8276 (Canada), (416) 572-2981; FAX (416) 572-2206
Product: CCINFOdisc: *OH&S Information*

CD/Law Reports, Inc.
305 S. Hale, Suite 1
Wheaton, IL 60187
(312) 668-8895
Products: *CD/Law: Illinois; Laserlaw Series*

CD Plus
2901 Broadway, Suite 154
New York, NY 10025
(212) 932-1485
Products: *CancerLit; Health; Medline—CD Plus*

CD Productions
1101 Amador Ave.
Berkeley, CA 94707
(415) 524-8450
Product: *Construction Activity Locator*

CD Resources
1123 Broadway, #902
New York, NY 10010
(212) 929-8044
Product: *AIDS Information and Education Worldwide CD-ROM*

Chadwyck-Healey, Inc.
1101 King St.
Alexandria, VA 22314
(800) 752-0515, (703) 683-4890
Products: *Bibliographie Nationale Français depuis 1975 sur CD-ROM; British Library General Catalogue of Printed Books to 1975 on CD-ROM; British National Bibliography on CD-ROM; Catalogue of United Kingdom Official Publications; Census: County Business Patterns; Deutsche Bibliographie-aktuel - CD-ROM; Supermap USA*

CMC ReSearch
7150 S.W. Hampton, Suite 120
Portland, OR 97223
(503) 639-3395
Products: *Cancer on Disc: 1988; Journal of Radiology; Pediatrics on Disc; Sherlock Holmes on Disc; Yearbook*

Compact Cambridge
Cambridge Information Group
7200 Wisconsin Ave.
Bethesda, MD 20814
(800) 227-3052, (301) 961-6700
Products: *Aquatic Sciences and Fisheries; CancerLit CD-ROM; Drug Information Center; Life Sciences Collection; Medline—Compact Cambridge; PDQ CD-ROM* (Physicians' Data Query)

Compact Disc Products
223 E. 85th St.
New York, NY 10028
(212) 737-8400, (800) 634-2998
Products: *CD-Audiofile; CD-Capture; CD-Play*

Compact Discoveries, Inc.
1050 S. Federal Highway
Delray Beach, FL 33444
(305) 243-1453
Products: *Images Demo; Yellow Page Demo*

Computer Access Corp.
26 Brighton St., Suite 324
Belmont, MA 02178
(617) 484-2412
Product: *CD-ROM: The New Papyrus*

Computer Aided Planning, Inc.
169-C Monroe N.W.
Grand Rapids, MI 49503
(616) 454-0000
Product: *CAP* (Computer Aided Programming)

Comstock, Inc.
30 Irving Pl.
New York, NY 10003
(212) 353-8686
Product: *Desktop Photography* (Mac)

Congressional Information Service, Inc.
4520 East-West Highway, Suite 800
Bethesda, MD 20814-1550
(301) 654-1550, (800) 638-8380
Product: *CIS Congressional Masterfile 1789–1969*

Cooperating Libraries Automated Network (CLAN)
Providence Public Library
Providence, RI 02903
(401) 521-8750
Product: *CD-CAT*

Cornell University Distribution Center
7 Research Park
Ithaca, NY 14850
(607) 255-2901
Product: *Black Fiction Up to 1920*

Data Base Products, Inc.
12770 Coit Rd., Suite 1111
Dallas, TX 75251-1314
(800) 345-2876, (214) 233-0595
Products: *FORM41: Airline Carrier Filings; International: Airline Traffic; Itineraries; O&D Plus; O&D Plus Historical; Onboard: Airline Traffic Data*

DataTimes
1400 Quail Springs Pkwy, #450
Oklahoma City, OK 73134
(405) 751-6400
Products: *Daily Oklahoman; Data Times Libraries System; Washington Post*

Dataware, Inc.
2 Greenwich Plaza, Suite 100
Greenwich, CT 06830
(203) 622-3908
Product: *Hoppenstadt Directory of Large Corporations*

Delorme Mapping Systems
P.O. Box 298
Freeport, ME 04032
(207) 865-4171
Product: *Delorme's World Atlas*

Deutsche Bibelgeselschaft
Balingerstrasse 31
7000 Stuttgart 80 East Germany
(49) 0711 71810
Product: *Luther Bible*

DIALOG Information Services
3460 Hillview Ave.
Palo Alto, CA 94304
(415) 858-3785, (800) 3-DIALOG
Products: *DIALOG OnDisc: Agribusiness USA DIALOG OnDisc; Canadian Business
and Current Affairs; ERIC; Medline; Medline Clinical Collection; NTIS; Standard
& Poor's Corporations*

Digital Decus Group
Boroughs' Plaza
219 Boston Post Rd.
Marlboro, MA 01752
(617) 480-3418
Product: *DECUS*

Digital Diagnostics, Inc.
601 University Ave.
Sacramento, CA 95825
(800) 826-5595, (916) 921-6629
Products: *AIDS Supplement; Medline—BiblioMed; Medline—BiblioMed with AIDS
Supplement; MetroScan*

Digital Directory Assistance
5161 River Rd.
Bethesda, MD 20816
(301) 657-8548
Product: *Phone Disc*

Disclosure
5161 River Rd.
Bethesda, MD 20816
(301) 951-1300, (800) 843-7747
Products: *Compact Disclosure; Compact Disclosure—Europe; Disclosure Spectrum;
Laser Disclosure: Commercial, Not for Profit, Wall Street*

Discovery Systems
47001 Discovery Blvd.
Dublin, OH 43017
(614) 761-2000
Products: *CD-ROM Sampler; Macintosh Showcase*

Diversified Data Resources, Inc.
6609 Rosecroft Pl.
Falls Church, VA 22043-1828
(202) 237-0682
Products: *The Sourcedisc*

DNAStar
1801 University Ave.
Madison, WI 53705
(608) 233-5525, (608) 251-9685
Products: *Lasergene CD-ROM; X-RAY*

Donnelley Marketing Information Services
70 Seaview Ave.
P.O. Box 10250
Stamford, CT 06904
(800) 527-3647, (203) 353-7474
Product: *Conquest: Consumer Information*

Dun's Marketing Service
49 Old Bloomfield Rd.
Mountain Lakes, NJ 07046
(800) 526-0651, (201) 299-0181
Product: *Million Dollar Directory*

EBSCO Electronic Information
P.O. Box 325
Topsfield, MA 01983
(800) 221-1826, (508) 887-6667
Product: *Cataloger's Tool Kit; Comprehensive Medline; Core Medline; Reference Tool Kit; The Serials Directory*

Education Systems Corp.
6170 Cornerstone Court East, Suite 300
San Diego, CA 92121-3170
(619) 587-0087
Product: *ESC Integrated Learning System*

Educorp USA
531 Stevens Ave., Suite B
Solana Beach, CA 92075
(800) 843-9497, (619) 259-0255
Product: *Public Domain Mac Programs* (Macintosh)

Eikon Spa
Lungotevere Raffaello Sanzio, 9
Roma 00153 Italy
39-6-5809920
Product: *Italian Banking Legal and Technical Documentation*

Electromap, Inc.
P.O. Box 1153
Fayetteville, AR 72702-1153
Product: *World Atlas*

Electronic Text Corporation
2500 N. University Ave.
Provo, UT 84604
(801) 226-0616
Product: *American Authors on CD-ROM*

Ellis Enterprises, Inc.
225 N.W. 13th St.
Oklahoma City, OK 73103
(405) 235-7660
Products: *The Bible Library; Home Reference Library; The Nurse Library; The Physician Library*

ERM Computer Services, Inc.
Environmental Resources Management
1309 Vincent Pl.
McLean, VA 22101
(703) 448-0966
Product: *EnFlex Info*

ETAK, Inc.
1455 Adams Dr.
Menlo Park, CA 94025
(408) 328-3825
Product: *Navigational Geographic Maps*

FABS International
Foundation for Advancing Biblical Study
P.O. Box 427
DeFuniak Springs, FL 32433
(800) 782-6257, (904) 892-6257
Products: *FABS Electronic Bible; FABS Reference Bible; REX* (Religion Index)

Facts On File Publications
460 Park Ave. South
New York, NY 10016
(800) 322-8755, (212) 683-2244, (416) 441-2992 (Canada); FAX (212) 213-4578
Products: *Facts On File News Digest CD-ROM* (IBM/Mac); *Public Domain Software On File* (IBM/Mac); *Visual Dictionary CD-ROM*

Gale Research, Inc.
835 Penobscot Bldg.
Detroit, MI 48226
(313) 961-2242
Product: *Associations: Global Access*

Gaylord Information Systems
7272 Morgan Rd.
Liverpool, NY 13088
(800) 634-6304, (315) 457-5070
Products: *Spectrum 200; SuperCAT*

General Information, Inc.
401 Park Pl., Suite 305
Kirkland, WA 98033
(206) 828-4777
Product: *National Directory of Addresses & Telephone Number*

General Research Corporation
5383 Hollister Ave.
Santa Barbara, CA 93111
(800) 235-6788, (805) 964-7724
Products: *LaserGuide; LaserQuest*

GEOVISION
270 Scientific Dr., Suite 1
Norcross, GA 30092
(404) 448-8224
Products: *GEOdisc: Florida Atlas; GEOdisc: Georgia Atlas; GEOdisc: U.S. Atlas; GEOdisc: Windows on the World*

GML Corp.
594 Marrett Rd.
Lexington, MA 02173
(617) 861-0515
Product: *Computer-SPECS*

Grolier Electronic Publishing, Inc.
Sherman Turnpike
Danbury, CT 06816
(800) 356-5590, (203) 797-3500
Product: *The Electronic Encyclopedia* (IBM/Mac)

Helsinki School of Economics
Library
Runeberginkatu 22-24
00100 Helsinki, Finland
Product: *HELECON on CD-ROM*

Hewlett-Packard Co.
19310 Pruneridge Ave.
Cupertino, CA 95014
(800) 752-0900
(415) 857-1501
Product: *HP LaserROM*

Highlighted Data, Inc.
P.O. Box 17229
Washington, DC 20041
(703) 533-1939
Products: *Electronic Map Cabinet* (IBM & Mac); *Fedstack* (Mac); *Merriam Webster's Ninth New Collegiate Dictionary* (Mac); *Statestack* (Mac)

Hitachi American Ltd.
Software Sales & Support Dept.
950 Elm Ave.
San Bruno, CA
(415) 872-1902
Product: *CD-GENE*

Hopkins Technology
421 Hazel Lane
Hopkins, MN 55343-7117
(612) 931-9376
Products: *Agri/Stats; Consu/Stats; Econ/Stats; Food/Analyst; Labor/Stats*

ICP Software Information
9100 Keystone Crossing, Suite 200
Indianapolis, IN 46040
(317) 844-7461; FAX (317) 574-0571
Product: *Software Information Database (SID)*

Image Club Graphics, Inc.
19th St. NE, Suite 206-2915
Calgary, Alta. T2E 7A2 Canada
(800) 661-9410, (403) 250-1969
Products: *ArtRoom* (IBM/Mac); *Dark Room* (Mac)

Info Globe
444 Front St. West
Toronto, Ont. M5V 2S9 Canada
(416) 585-5250; FAX (416) 585-5249
Product: *Toronto Globe and Mail*

Information Access Co. (IAC)
362 Lakeside Dr.
Foster City, CA 94404-9888
(800) 227-8431, (415) 378-5200
Products: *Academic Index; General Periodicals Index* (Academic Library Edition);
General Periodicals Index (Public Library Edition); *Government Publications
Index; Health Index; LegalTrac; Magazine Index Plus; National Newspaper Index;
TOM* (popular magazine for secondary school libraries)

Information Design, Inc.
P.O. Box 7130
1300 Charleston Rd.
Mountain View, CA 94039-7130
(415) 969-7990
Product: *ZIP+4*

Information Handling Services
15 Inverness Way East
Englewood, CO 80112
(800) 241-7824, (303) 790-0600
Products: *CrossLink: Supply/Logistics Data; Personnet; Comptroller General Decisions*

Information Intelligence, Inc.
P.O. Box 31098
Phoenix, AZ 85046
(800) 228-9982, (602) 996-2283
Product: *Online Hotline News Service*

Information Update, Inc.
1190 Saratoga Ave., Suite 210
San Jose, CA 95129-3433
(408) 236-3297; FAX (408) 247-1108
Product: *AVS +*

Ingram Book Company
347 Reedwood Dr.
Nashville, TN 37217-9989
(800) 251-5902, (800) 468-9464 (in Tennessee), (615) 793-5000
Products: *Flash-Back/Books in Print Plus; LaserSearch/Any-Book*

Innovative Technology, Inc.
7927 Jones Branch Dr.
McLean, VA 22102
(800) 327-6154, (703) 734-3000
Products: *Technical Logistics Reference Network* (TLRN)

Institute for Scientific Information
3501 Market St.
Philadelphia, PA 19104
(800) 523-1850, (215) 386-0100
FAX (215) 386-6362
Product: *Science Citation Index CD*

International Center for Diffraction Data
1601 Park Lane
Swarthmore, PA 19081-2389
(215) 328-9400
Product: *PC-PDF* (Powder Diffraction File)

Iowa State Library
Networking Dept.
E. 12th & Grand
Des Moines, IA 50319
(515) 281-4118, (515) 281-4499
Product: *Iowa State Locator*

JA Micropublishing, Inc.
271 Main St., Box 218
Eastchester, NY 10707
(800) 227-2477, (914) 793-2130
Products: *BRIEF/CASE; Corporate & Industry Research Reports* (CIRR)

Knowledge Access International
2685 Marine Way, Suite 1305
Mountain View, CA 94043
(800)2-KAware, (415) 969-0606
Publisher of KAware2 CD-ROM/ Management System Image
Products: ALA CD-ROM *Directory of Library & Information Professionals; Associations: Global Access; California Music Directory; CDID on Disc; Construction Activity Locator; Music Business Directory; Music Radio Directory; NATASHA:* (National Archives on Sexuality, Health and Adolescence); *Your Marketing Consultant: Advanced Consumer; Your Marketing Consultant: Business-to-Business*

LaserData, Inc.
10 Technology Dr.
Lowell, MA 01851
(617) 937-5900
Product: *Codice Tributario*

LaserScan Systems, Inc.
10481 N. Kendall Dr., Suite D203
Miami, FL 33176
(305) 595-3640
Product: *Realscan Real Estate Information System* (Mac)

Lasertrak Corporation
6235-B Lookout Rd.
Boulder, CO 80301
(800) 255-TRAK, (303) 530-2711
Products: *Lasertrak Disc; LZ Services* (NAV/COM Terminal Charts)

Library Association Publishing
7 Ridgmount St.
London, WC1E 7AE England
01-36-7543
Product: *LISA*

Library Corporation
P.O. Box 40035
Washington, DC 20016
(800) 624-0559, (304) 229-0100
Products: *Anybook; BiblioFile Catalog Maintenance; BiblioFile Catalog Production; Bibliofile Circulation; Enhanced BiblioFile; The Intelligent Catalog; Serials*

Library of Congress
Cataloging Distribution
Customer Services Section
Washington, DC 20541
(202) 707-6167
Products: *CDMARC Bibliographic; CDMARC Names; CDMARC Subjects*

Library Systems & Services, Inc.
20251 Century Blvd.
Germantown, MD 20874-1162
(800) 638-8725, (301) 258-0200
Products: *BPN/JR; GPO Laserfile; LOANet*

J. B. Lippincott Co.
E. Washington Sq.
Philadelphia, PA 19105-9961
(800) 523-2945, (215) 238-4200
Product: *OncoDisc*

Lotus Development Corporation
55 Cambridge Pkwy.
Cambridge, MA 02142
(800) 554-5501, (617) 577-8500; FAX (617) 255-1293
Products: *CD Banking; CD/Corporate; CD/Corptech; CD/International; CD/Investment; CD/Newsline; CD/Private+; Lotus One Source; Prompt CD*

Mac Guide
550 S. Wadsworth Blvd., Suite 500
Lakewood, CO 80226
(303) 935-8100, (800) 877-9100
Product: *The Mac Guide USA CD-ROM*

MacroMind, Inc.
1028 W. Wolfram St.
Chicago, IL 60657
(312) 871-0987
Product: *Videoworks CD-ROM*

Marcive, Inc.
P.O. Box 47508
San Antonio, TX 78265-7508
(800) 531-7678, (512) 646-6161
Products: *GPO Cat/PAC; Harlic Union Catalog; MARCIVE/PAC*

McGraw-Hill Book Co.
11 W. 19th St.
New York, NY 10011
(800) 262-4729, (212) 337-5907; FAX (212) 512-2821
Products: *CD-ROM Science & Technical Reference Set; Electronic Sweet's*

Medical Economics Co.
680 Kinderkamack Rd.
Ordell, NJ 07649
(201) 262-3030, (800) 526-4870
Product: *Physician's Desk Reference*

Medical Publishing Group
1440 Main St.
Waltham, MA 02154
(800) 342-1338, (617) 893-3800; FAX (617) 647-5785
Product: *AIDS—Compact Library*

Medical Publishing Group
Saxon Way, Melbourn
Royston, Herts SG8 6NJ England
07-636-2368; FAX (07) 636-2040
Product: *AIDS—Compact Library*

The Menu
1520 S. College Ave.
Fort Collins, CO 80504
(303) 482-5000, (800) THE-MENU
Product: *Menu: International Software*

Michie Co.
P.O. Box 7587
Charlottesville, VA 22906
(804) 295-6171
Product: *Virginia State Legal Code*

Microinfo Ltd.
P.O. Box 3
Omega Park
Alton, Hants GU24 2PG England
(44) 420 868 48
Product: *Harrap's Multilingual Dictionary*

Micromedex, Inc.
6600 Bannock St., Suite 300
Denver, CO 80204
(800) 525-9083, (303) 623-8600
Products: *Computerized Clinical Information Systems (CCIS); Dosing & Therapeutic Tools; Drugdex; Emergindex; Identidex; Martindale: Extra Pharmacopoeia; Poisindex; TOMES* (Toxic Occupational, Medical & Environmental Series)

Micromedia Ltd.
158 Pearl St.
Toronto, Ont. M5H 1i3 Canada
(800) 387-2689 (Canada), (416) 593-5211; FAX (416) 593-1760
Product: *Canadian Business and Current Affairs*

Microsoft Corporation
16011 N.E. 36th Way
Redmond, WA 98073-9717
(800) 426-9400, (206) 882-8080
Products: *Microsoft Bookshelf; Microsoft Office; Programmer's Library; Small Business Consultant; Stat Pack*

Minnesota Dept. of Education
733 Capital Sq. Bldg.
550 Cedar St.
St. Paul, MN 55101
(612) 296-6005
Product: *Item Bank*

Modern Language Association
10 Astor Pl.
New York, NY 10003-6981
(212) 614-6304
Product: *MLA International Bibliography*

Moody's Investors Service
99 Church St.
New York, NY 10007
(800) 342-5647, (212) 553-0858
Products: *Moody's 5000 Plus; Moody's International Plus*

Multi-AD Services
1720 W. Detweiller Dr.
Peoria, IL 61615-1695
(800) 447-1950, (309) 692-1530
Products: *Kwikee Inhouse Graphics Services; Kwikee Inhouse Pal* (Mac); ProArt
Trilogy I

National Decision Systems
539 Encinitas Blvd., Box 9007
Encinitas, CA 92024
(800) 882-6200, (619) 942-7000
Product: *Infomark IV Laser PC System: Decision Support*

National Information Center for Educational Media
Div. of Access Innovations, Inc.
P.O. Box 40130
Albuquerque, NM 87196
(800) 421-8711, (505) 265-3591
Product: *A-V ONLINE*

National Information Services Corp. (NISC)
P.O. Box 828
335 Paint Branch Dr.
College Park, MD 20742
(301) 454-8040; FAX (301) 454-8061
Products: *Arctic and Antarctic Regions; CASS CD-ROM; Natural Resources
Database; Selected Water Resources Abstracts*

National Institute of Building
Sciences
1015 15th St., N.W., Suite 700 W
Washington, DC 20005
(202) 347-5710
Products: *Automated Facilities; Construction Criteria Base; Engineering Information
System*

National Library of Medicine
National Institutes of Health
8600 Rockville Pike
Bethesda, MD 20894
(301) 496-6531
Product: *X-RAY demo*

National Safety Data Corp.
259 West Rd.
Salem, CT 06415
(203) 859-1162
Product: *Material Safety Data Sheets*

National Standards Association, Inc.
5161 River Rd.
Bethesda, MD 20816
(800) 638-8094
Product: *Parts-Master*

NEC Home Electronics, Inc.
1255 Michael Dr.
Wood Dale, IL 60191
(312) 860-9500
Products: *Clip Art 3-D; Image Folio*

Network Technology Corp.
P.O. Box 6069
Alexandria, VA 22306-0069
(703) 768-3327
Products: *The Electronic Publishing Arts Disc; Geographic Locator; Languages of the World*

NewsBank, Inc.
58 Pine St.
New Canaan, CT 06840
(800) 243-7694, (800) 223-4739; FAX (203) 966-6254
Product: *NewsBank Electronic Index*

Newsreel Access Systems
150 E. 58th, 35th Floor
New York, NY 10155
(800) 242-2463, (212) 826-2800
Products: *ArtScan; CineScan; News Scan; PhotoScan*

Nynex Information Resources Co.
195 Market St.
Lynn, MA 01901
(617) 581-4674, (617) 581-4972
Product: *Fast Track: Nynex White Pages*

Occupational Health Services
450 Seventh Ave., Suite 2407
New York, NY 10123
(800) 445-6737, (212) 967-3974
Product: *Material Safety Data Sheets, Reference File*

OCLC (Online Computer Library Center)
6565 Frantz Rd.
Dublin, OH 43017-0702
(614) 764-6000, (800) 848-5878
Products: *AGRICOLA* and *CRIS; AGRICOLA Retrospective File (1979–1982); Agriculture Library; Agriculture Series; CAT CD450; CD/2000; Computer Library; Earth Science Series; Education Library; Education Series; Energy Library; Environment Library; ERIC; GPO Monthly Catalog; ICP Software Information Database; NTIS; OCLC/AMIGOS Collection Analysis CD; SchoolMatch; Selected Water Resources Abstracts*

Oklahoma Nurse Association
6414 N. Santa Fe
Oklahoma City, Ok 73160
(405) 840-3476
Products: *The Nurse Library; The Physician Library*

Online Computer Systems, Inc.
20251 Century Blvd.
Germantown, MD 20874
(800) 922-9204, (301) 428-3700
Product: *BiblioDisc*

Online Research Systems, Inc.
2901 Broadway, Suite 154
New York, NY 10025
(212) 408-3311
Product: *Compact Med-Base*

Optical Media International
495 Alberto Way
Los Gatos, CA 95032
(408) 395-4332; FAX (408) 395-6544
Products: *Constitution Papers; Desktop Sounds; Sound Designer; Universe of Sounds* Vol. 1–2 (Mac)

Oxford Electronic Publishing
Oxford University Press
200 Madison Ave.
New York, NY 10016
(212) 889-0206
Products: *The Oxford English Dictionary on CD-ROM; The Oxford Textbook of Medicine—Electronic Edition*

Packard Humanities Institute
300 2nd St., Suite 200
Los Altos, CA 94022
(415) 948-0150; FAX (415) 948-5793
Products: *PHI; Papyri*

Pan American Health Organization
525 23rd St., N.W.
Washington, DC 20037
(202) 861-3200
Product: *PAHO Database*

PC-SIG, Inc.
1030-D E. Duane Ave.
Sunnyvale, CA 94086
(408) 730-9291; FAX (408) 730-2107
Products: *CD/Biotech; Science Helper K–8; PC-SIG Library on CD-ROM*

PCI, Inc.
50 West Wilmot St., Unit #1
Richmond Hill, Ont. L4B1M5
Canada
(416) 764-0614
Product: *Resors: Satellite Remote Sensitivity Publications*

PDO
1402 Foulk Rd., Suite 200
Wilmington, DE 19803
(302) 479-2500
Product: *CD-ROM: The Conference Disc*

Perceptronics
1911 N. Ft. Myer Dr.
Arlington, VA 22209
(703) 525-0184
Product: *U.S. City Map Atlas*

Pergamon Compact Solution
Headway House
66–73 Shoe Lane
London EC4P 4AB England
(01) 377-4918; FAX (01) 583-3887
Products: *The Guinness Disc of Records 1990; The International Encyclopedia of Education*

Philips Electronic Instruments
85 McKee Dr.
Mahwah, NJ 07430
(201) 529-3800
Products: *Photo Library; Plus 37*

Pioneer Hi-Bred International
11153 Aurora Ave.
Des Moines, IA 50322
(800) 826-5944, (515) 253-5848
Product: *Agribusiness USA*

Prentice-Hall Information Network
1 Gulf & Western Plaza
New York, NY 10023
(212) 373-8600
Product: *PHINet Tax Resource*

PsycINFO Services
American Psychological Association
1400 N. Uhle St.
Arlington, VA 22201
(800) 336-4980, (703) 247-7829; FAX (703) 524-1205
Product: *PsycINFO*

Public Affairs Information Service
521 W. 43rd St.
New York, NY 10036-4396
(800) 288-7247, (212) 736-6629; FAX (212) 643-2848
Product: *PAIS on CD-ROM*

Quanta Press, Inc.
2239 Carter Ave.
St. Paul, MN 55108-9928
(612) 641-0741; FAX (612) 644-8811
Products: *About Cows; AGRICOLA; Dick's-Earth's Planes; How to Become a U.S. Citizen; Officer's Bookcase—Terms; Programmer's CD-ROM; RBBS-PC in a Box; Seals of the U.S. Federal Government; Shareware Gold; Vietnam—USA War; Wheeler Quick Art; The World Factbook CD-ROM*

Quantum Access, Inc.
1700 W. Loop South, Suite 1460
Houston, TX 77027
(713) 622-3211, (800) 822-4211
Products: *ClubMac* (Mac); *King James Bible; Texas State Education Encyclopedia; Texas Attorney General Documents on CD-ROM*

Quantum Leap Technologies
314 Romano Ave.
Coral Gables, FL 33134-7246
(305) 446-2477
Products: *Mega Rom; QL Tech Mega-ROM; Right Stuffed*

Readex Microprint Corp.
58 Pine St.
New Canaan, CT 06840
(800) 223-4739, (203) 966-5906
Products: *FBIS; STAT Facts; United Nations Publications Index*

Reference Technology, Inc.
5700 Flatiron Pkwy.
Boulder, CO 80301
(800) 642-4947, (303) 449-4157; FAX (303) 442-1816
Product: *Software Library DataPlate*

Reteaco, Inc.
716 Gordon Baker Rd.
Toronto, M2H 3B4
Ontario, Canada
(800) 387-5002, (416) 497-0579
Products: *ONTERIS; Termium*

ROM Publishers, Inc.
1033 O St., Suite 300
Lincoln, NE 68508
(402) 476-6234
Products: *California Decisions; Decision Series: Northwest Legal Libraries; Federal Decisions*

Sansyusya Publishing Co. Ltd.
1-5-34 Taito-ku
Tokyo 110, Japan
Products: *Multi-Lingual Dictionary of Science & Technology; Multilingual Dictionary Database*

K. G. Saur
245 W. 17th St.
New York, NY 10011
(212) 645-9700, (800) 521-8110, (800) 537-8416 (in Canada)
Products: *International Books in Print; Publishers International Directory*

Scientific American
415 Madison Ave.
New York, NY 10017
(212) 754-0801
Product: *Scientific American Medicine Consult*

SilverPlatter
37 Walnut St.
Wellesley Hills, MA 02181
(800) 343-0064, (617) 239-0306
Products: *A-V ONLINE; AGRICOLA* and *CRIS; Canadian Postal Codes; Cancer-CD; CHEM-BANK; ClinMED-CD; COMPU-INFO; Computer-SPECS* (formerly COMPU-INFO); *Corporate & Industry Research Reports* (CIRR); *Cross-Cultural CD; EINECS Plus-CD; EMBASE* (Excerpta Medica Abstract Journals on CD-ROM); *ERIC ; GPO on SilverPlatter; HealthPLAN-CD; LISA; MathSci Disc; Medline on SilverPlatter; NTIS; Nursing & Allied Health CD* (CINAHL); *OSH-ROM; PEST-BANK; Peterson's College Database; Peterson's GradLine; POPLINE; PsycLIT; Sociofile; Software-CD; Sport Discus; TELE-DIRECT; TOXLINE on SilverPlatter*

Slater Hall Information Products
1522 K St., NW, Suite 1112
Washington, DC 20005
(202) 682-1350
Products: *Business Indicators; Business Statistics 1929–85; Census of Agriculture on CD-ROM* (1982); *County Statistics; Population Statistics on CD-ROM; State Income and Employment*

Small Library Computing
619 Mansfield Rd.
Willow Grove, PA 19090
(215) 657-8472
Products: *BIB-BASE/CD-ROM*

Sociological Abstracts, Inc.
Database Services
P.O. Box 22206
San Diego, CA 92122-0206
(619) 565-6603
Product: *Sociofile*

Sociometrics Corp.
685 High Street, 2E
Palo Alto, CA 94301
(415) 321-7846
Product: *NATASHA* (National Archives on Sexuality, Health and Adolescence)

Software Mart, Inc.
4131 Spicewood Springs Rd., Suite I3
Austin, TX 78759
(512) 346-7887
Product: *CD-ROM Developer's Lab*

Space-Time Research Ltd.
668 Burwood Rd.
Hawthorn East
Victoria 3123 Australia
03-813-3211
Products: *Census of Australian Population & Housing, 1981 and 1986* (CDATA
86); *Census: Australian Standardized Local Government Financial Statistics; Census
of England, Scotland and Wales, Small Area Statistics 1981; Census of Hong Kong,
1981 and 1986; Census of New Zealand, 1986; Census of Sweden, 1970 to 1987;
Census: U.S. County Business Patterns, 1985; Census: U.S. Data, 1980* — Supermap
USA

Springer Verlag
P.O. Box 105280
D-6900 Heidelberg 1
West Germany
011 49 6221 4870
Tx: 74506, TA: Springerbuch Wien
Products: *Beilstein Handbook of Organic Chemistry; GEFAHRGUT Chemdata;
GEFAHRGUT Einsatzakten; GEFAHRGUT Hommel Chemdata*

Standard & Poor's Compustat Services
1221 Ave. of the Americas
New York, NY 10020
(212) 512-4900
Products: *Compustat PC Plus on CD-ROM; CUSIP Directory*

Standard & Poor's Corp.
25 Broadway
New York, NY 10004
(800) 233-2310, (212) 512-4900
Product: *Standard & Poor's Corporations*

Tax Analysts
400 N. Washington St.
Falls Church, VA 22046
(703) 532-1850
Product: *Tax Library*

Telerate Systems, Inc.
1 World Trade Center
New York, NY 10048
(212) 938-5200
Product: *The Intuition Expert*

Tescor, Inc.
461 Carlisle Dr.
Herndon, VA 22070
(800) 842-0077, (703) 435-9501
Product: *First National Item Bank & Test Development System*

Tetragon Systems, Inc.
5445 Pare St., Suite 102-2
Montreal, Que. H4P 1R1 Canada
(800) 363-2372, (514) 737-3550 (Montreal), (416) 479-2000 (Toronto)
Products: *Rainbow the Connection: Homebase II; Rainbow the Connection: Businessbase*

Thesaurus Linguae Graecae
(TLG) Project
University of California
Irvine, CA 92717
(714) 856-6404
Product: *TLG Discs A & B: Greek Literature*

Tri Star Publishing
475 Virginia Dr.
Fort Washington, PA 19034
(800) 872-2828, (215) 641-6000
Products: *Master Search Bible on Compact Disc; Trademark Information Database;
The Oxford English Dictionary on CD-ROM*

University Microfilms International
300 N. Zeeb Rd.
Ann Arbor, MI 48106
(800) 521-3044, (800) 343-5299 (Canada), (313) 761-4700; FAX (313) 665-5022
Products: *ABI/INFORM OnDisc; Business Periodicals Ondisc* (BPO); *Dissertation
Abstracts OnDisc; Newspaper Abstracts Ondisc; Periodical Abstracts; Resource/One*

University of Colorado—LASP
Campus Box B10
Boulder, CO 80309
(303) 492-6867
Product: *Voyager II: Images of Uranus*

University of Guelph
Chief Librarian
Guelph, Ont. N1G2W1 Canada
(519) 824-4120 x2181
Product: *University of Guelph Catalog*

University of Washington
Dept. of Atmospheric Sciences
AK-40
Seattle, WA 98195
(206) 545-0910
Products: *Gale Experimental Data Set; National Meteorological Grid Data Point Set; Surface Data for North America, 1987; World WeatherDisc*

U.S. Bureau of the Census
Data Users Service Division
Washington, DC 20233
(202) 763-4100
Products: *1985 American Housing Survey; Census Disc; Census Test Disc #1; Census Test Disc #2*

U.S. Geological Survey
804 National Center
Reston, VA 22092
(703) 648-4000
Product: *CD-ROM Prototype Disc*

U.S. Statistics
1101 King St., Suite 601
Alexandria, VA 22314
(703) 979-9699
Products: *FEDSTAT; FEDSTAT/TIGER CD-ROM*

U.S. West Optical Publishing
90 Madison St., Suite 200
Denver, CO 80206
(800) 222-0920, (303) 370-1460
Product: *Climatedata*

USA Information Systems, Inc.
3303 Duke St.
Alexanderia, VA 22314
(800) 872-8830, (703) 370-7800
Product: *CD-Fiche*

Utlas International
8300 College Blvd.
Overland Park, KS 66210
(913) 451-3111, (800) 33-UTLAS
Products: *CD-CATSS Current Cataloging; DisCon; LawMARC*

Video Laser Systems, Inc.
310 S. Reynolds Rd.
Toledo, OH 43615-5995
(419) 536-5820
Product: *Optext: Federal Regulations*

Virginia Polytechnic Institute
Blacksburg, VA 24061
(703) 231-6000
Product: *Virginia Disk*

Voyager Co.
1351 Pacific Coast Hwy.
Santa Monica, CA 90401
(213) 451-1383
Product: *CD Companion-Beethoven Symphony No. 9*

Walters Lexicon Co.
Sodermalmstrong 8,
17800 Stockholm, Sweden
Product: *Termdok*

WeatherDisc Associates, Inc.
4584 N.E. 89th St.
Seattle, WA 98115
(206) 524-4314
Product: *World WeatherDisc*

West Publishing Co.
P.O. Box 64526
St. Paul, MN 55164-0526
(612) 228-2497
Products: *West CD-ROM Bankruptcy Library; West CD-ROM Federal Civil Practice Library; West CD-ROM Government Contracts Library; West CD-ROM Libraries*

Western Library Network
Washington State Library
Mail Stop AJ-11W
Olympia, WA 98504-0111
(206) 459-6518; FAX (206) 459-6341
Product: *LaserCat*

J. Whitaker & Sons Ltd.
BookBank on CD-ROM
12 Dyott St.
London WC1A 1Df, England
(44) 1-836-8911
Product: *BookBank*

Wiley Electronic Publishing
605 Third Ave.
New York, NY 10158-0012
(212) 850-6509
Products: *Encyclopedia of Polymer Science and Engineering; International Dictionary of Medicine and Biology; Kirk-Othmer Encyclopedia of Chemical Technology; Registry of Mass Spectral Data*

H. W. Wilson Co.
950 University Ave.
Bronx, NY 10452
(212) 588-8400
Products: *Applied Science & Technology Index; Art Index; Biography Index; Biological and Agricultural Index; Book Review Digest; Business Periodicals Index; Cumulative Book Index; Education Index; Essay and General Literature Index; Film Literature Index; General Science Index; GPO Monthly Catalog Index to Government Periodicals; Humanities Index; Index to Legal Periodicals; Library Literature; Modern Language Association Index; Reader's Guide Abstracts; Reader's Guide to Periodical Literature; Social Science Index; WILSONDISC Demonstration Disc*

Wright Investors' Service (WIS)
10 Middle St.
Bridgeport, CT 06604
(203) 333-6666
Product: *Worldscope Profiles*

Xiphias
Helms Hall
875 Venice Blvd.
Los Angeles, CA 90034
(213) 821-0074
Products: *National Telephone Directory* (Mac); *Time Table of History/Science & Innovation* (Mac)

Ziff Communications
1 Park Ave.
New York, NY 10016
(212) 503-4400
Product: *Computer Library*

Ziff Davis Technical Information Co.
80 Blanchard Rd.
Burlington, MA 01830
(617) 273-5500
Product: *Haystack: Logistics, Procurement, Engineering Files*

D. Manufacturers of CD-ROM Drives

Amdek Corp.
1901 Zanker Rd.
San Jose, CA 95112
(408)636-8570
Model: Laserdek 1000*; Laserdek 2000*

*Original equipment manufacturer

Apple Computer
20525 Mariani Ave.
Cupertino, CA 95014
(408)745-2000
Model: AppleCD SC (Sony drive, $1,199)

Chinon America, Inc.
660 Maple Ave.
Torrance, CA 90503
(213) 533-0274
Model: CDS-430*

Denon
222 New Rd.
Parsippany, NJ 07054
(201)575-7810
Model: DRD-250 (Sony drive*); DRD-251 (Sony drive*); DRD-253 (Sony drive*); DRD-550 (Denon drive*)

Digital Equipment Corp.
10 Tara Blvd.
Nashua, NH 03062
(603) 884-2166
Model: RRD50-AA ($1,000); RRD50-EA ($1,200); RRD50-QA ($1,200)

Hitachi
401 W. Artesia Blvd.
Compton, CA 90220
(213) 537-8383, (800) 262-1502
Model: CDR-1502S ($899); CDR-1503S ($899); CDR-1553S ($1,199); CDR-2500 ($899); CDR-3500 (Sony $875)

JVC
41 Slater Dr.
Elmwood Park, NJ 07407
(201) 794-3900
Model: XR-R100*; XR-R1001*

Laser Magnetic Storage International (MSI)
4425 Arrows West Dr.
Colorado Springs, CO 80907
(303) 593-4269, (303) 593-4270
Model: CM121 (Philips, $820); CM131 (Philips, $1,130); CM132 (Philips, $1,190); CM201 (Philips*); CM210 (Philips*)

NEC Home Electronics
1255 Michael Dr.
Wood Dale, IL 60191
(312) 860-9500
Model: Intersect CDR-77 ($999); Intersect CDR-80 ($899)

*Original equipment manufacturer

Panasonic
1 Panasonic Way
Secaucus, NJ 07094
(201) 392-4602
Model: SQ-D1 ($999); SQ-D101 ($1,149)

Philips Information Systems, Inc.
2111 Wilson Blvd., Suite 435
Arlington, VA 22201
(703) 875-2222
Model: CM100; CM110; CM121; CM201; CM210

Reference Technology
5700 Flatiron Pkwy.
Boulder, CO 80301
(303) 449-4157
Model: Clasix 500 ($990)

Sanyo
51 Joseph St.
Moonachie, NJ 07074
(201) 440-9300
Model: ROM-300*; ROM-2500*

Sony
Computer Peripheral Division
1 Sony Dr.
Park Ridge, NJ 17656
(201) 930-7071, (408) 432-0190
Model: CDU-510 ($895); CDU-6100*; CDU-6101*; CDU-6110*; CDU-6111*;
CDU-7101 ($1,095)

Toshiba
9740 Irvine Blvd.
Irvine, CA 92680
(714) 583-3117
Model: XM-2000A*; XM-2000B*; XM-2100A*; XM-3100*

E. Manufacturers of WORM Drives

Alcatel Thompson Gigadisc, Inc.
400 W. Cummings Park
Woburn, MA 01801
(617) 890-0801
Model: GM1001/1 Gb/12″ ($13,000)

*Original equipment manufacturer

Cherokee
1880 S. Flatiron Court, Suite H
Boulder, CO 80301
(303) 449-8850
Model: M600Mb/5.25″; Tracker/520Mb/5.25″

Corel Systems
333 W. Wacker Dr.
Chicago, IL 60606
(312) 444-2770
Model: S200/200Mb/5.25″ ($2,800); S800/800Mb/5.25″ ($4,395)

Digital Equipment Corp.
2 Mount Royal Ave.
Marlboro, MA 01752
(617) 480-4816
Model: RV20 subsystem/2Gb/12″ ($30,000)

Eastman Kodak Co.
Kodak Mass Memory Division
460 Buffalo Rd.
Rochester, NY 14611
(716) 588-0452
Model: 6800/6.8Gb/14″ ($47,000)

Hitachi Sales Corporation
2 Lincoln Center, Suite 865
5420 LBJ Freeway
Dallas, TX 75240
(214) 991-7983
Model: OD301-1/1.311Gb/12″

IBM
Information Systems Group
900 King St.
Rye Brook, NY 10573
(914) 934-4000
Model: A01 (PC's & PS/2-30)/200Mb/5.25″ ($2,950);   A11 (PS/2 External)/
200Mb/5.25″ ($2,950);   8700 (PS/2 Internal)/200Mb/5.25″ ($2,700)

Information Storage, Inc.
2768 Janitell Rd.
Colorado Springs, CO 80906
(303) 579-0460
Model: 525WC/488Mb/5.25″ ($1,888 Internal, $2,088 External);   525Gb/
1.2Gb/5.25″   ($5,988 Internal, $6,188 External);   525GbX2/600/1200Mb/5.25″
($9,488)

Laser Magnetic Storage International
4425 Arrowswest Dr.
Colorado Springs, CO 80907
(303) 593-4269
Model: LaserDrive 1200/1Gb/12″ ($8000); LaserDrive 1200 Jukebox model/
1Gb/12″ ($8000)

Laserdrive Ltd.
1101 Space Park Dr.
Santa Clara, CA 95050
(408) 970-3600
Model: 810 Subsystem/400Mb/5.25″ ($5,495, single drive; $7,995, dual drive)

LMSI
4425 Arrows West Dr.
Colorado Springs, CO 80907
(303) 593-7900
Model: 510/650Mb/5.25″ ($2,880);   1200-1250/2Gb/12″*

Maximum Storage
5025 Centennial Blvd.
Colorado Springs, CO 80919
(303) 531-6888
Model: APX-4000/488Mb/5.25″ ($3,175)

Micro Design International
6985 University Blvd.
Winter Park, FL 32792
(305) 677-8333
Model: Laserbank 800/800Mb/12″ ($9,995)

N-Hance
908 Providence Hwy.
Dedham, MA 02026
(800) 286-9676
Model: 525/488Mb/5.25″ ($2,388)

Optimem
297 N. Bernardo Ave.
Mountain View, CA 94043
(415) 961-1800
Model: OM-1000/1.024Gb/12″ ($13,000); OM-2400/2.4Gb/12″ ($14,900);
OM-600Mb/5.25″ ($3,295)

Optotech, Inc.
740–770 Wooten Rd.
Colorado Springs, CO 80915
(719) 570-7500
Model: 5984/400Mb/5.25″ ($2,950)

Panasonic
Computer Products Division
2 Panasonic Way, 7G-0
Secaucus, NJ 07094
(201) 392-4263
Model: LF5000/200Mb/5.25″ ($2,595)

---

*Original equipment manufacturer

Pioneer Communications of America
600 E. Crescent Ave.
Upper Saddle River, NJ 07458
(201) 327-6400
Model: DD-55001/654Mb/5.25"* ($3,100)

Ricoh Systems, Inc.
2071 Concourse Dr.
San Jose, CA 95121
(408) 432-8800
Model: RS9200/800Mb/5.25"*

Sanyo
51 Joseph St.
Moonachie, NJ 07074
(201) 440-9300
Model: DF-8061-11/860Mb/12"

Sony Corp. of America
Sony Dr.
Park Ridge, NJ 07656
(201) 930-1000
Model: WDD-2000/375Mb/8" ($2,495)

Toshiba America
Disk Products Division
9740 Irvine, CA 92718
(714) 583-3150
Model: WM-D050/800Mb/5.25"; WM-D070/900Mb/5.25"; WM-S500/5Gb/12"
($13,995)

F. Manufacturers of Erasable Drives

Advanced Graphics Applications
90 Fifth Ave.
New York, NY 10011
(212) 337-4200
Model: Discus—Internal ($4,995); External ($5,495). ISO Standard. 650Mb.
Average access time is 80 milliseconds (ms). Disc costs $250.

Alphatronix
P.O. Box 13687
Research Triangle Park
Durham, NC 27709-3687
(919) 544-0001
Model: Infinity—External single drive ($9,995); dual drive ($14,950). ISO
Standard. 650Mb. Disc costs $250.

---

*Original equipment manufacturer

Canon, U.S.A., Inc.
1 Canon Plaza
Lake Success, NY 11042
(516) 488-6700
Model: OM-500D. Not compatible with ISO Standard. Works with two
discs, 256Mb and 512Mb. 80ms access time. Disc costs $200.

Maxtor Corp.
211 River Oaks Pkwy.
San Jose, CA 95134
(408) 432-1700
Model: Tahiti 1. 1Gb. ISO Standard. $5,995. Disc costs $250.

Pinnacle Micro, Inc.
15625 Alton Pkwy.
Irvine, CA 92718
(800) 553-7070, (714) 553-7070 (in CA)
Model: REO-650Mb. $5,995.

Sony Corp. of America
Technology Operations Center
5665 Flatiron Pkwy.
P.O. Box 17186
Boulder, CO 80301
Model: Internal SMO-D501; External SMO-S501. Both $4,650. ISO Standard.
80ms access time. Disc costs $250.

G. Retrieval Software Developers

This partial list includes developers of retrieval software tool kits, service
bureaus, specialists, and retrieval software vendors. Also included is a list of
Macintosh retrieval software vendors.

Access Innovations, Inc.
P.O. Box 40130-4314
4320 Mesa Grande S.E.
Albuquerque, NM 87196
(800) 421-8711, (505) 265-3591

Borland International
4585 Scotts Valley Dr.
Scotts Valley, CA 95066
(408) 438-8400
Retrieval software: PARADOX

Box Co.
63 Howard St.
Cambridge, MA 02139
(617) 576-0892
Retrieval software: WindoBook

Computer Access Corp.
26 Brighton St., Suite 324
Belmont, MA 02178-4008
(617) 484-2412
Retrieval software: BlueFish

Creative Index, Inc.
3325 N. University Ave., Suite 250
Provo, UT 84601
(801) 374-8600
Retrieval software: FastFind

Dataware, Inc.
2 Greenwich Plaza, Suite 100
Greenwich, CT 06830
(203) 622-3908
Retrieval software: CD Author/
CD Answer

Del Mar Group, Inc.
722 Genevieve, Suite M
Solana Beach, CA 92075
(619) 259-0444
Retrieval software: SmarTrieve

Dialog
3460 Hillview Ave.
Palo Alto, CA 94043
(415) 858-4088
Retrieval software: DIALOG OnDisc

Digital Equipment Corp.
CD Publishing Group
12 Crosby Dr.
Bedford, MA 01730
(613) 276-1345
Software: VAX VTX

Digital Library Systems
5161 River Rd., Bldg. 6
Bethesda, MD 20816
(301) 657-2997

Executive Technologies, Inc.
2120 16th Ave. South
Birmingham, AL 35205
(205) 933-5494
Software: Search Express

Fulcrum Technologies
560 Rochester St.
Ottawa, Ont., K1S 5K2 Canada
(613) 238-1761
Retrieval software: FULCRUM
Ful/Text

Group L Corp.
481 Carlisle Dr.
Herndon, VA 22070
(703) 471-0030
Retrieval software: DELVE

Information Dimensions, Inc.
655 Metro Pl. South
Dublin, OH 43017-1396
(800) 328-2648, (614) 761-7300
Retrieval software: MicroBASIS

Intechnica
2810 Parklawn Dr., Suite 402
Midwest City, OK 73110
(405) 737-9639

Knowledge Access
2685 Marine Way
Mountain View, CA 94043
(415) 969-0606
Retrieval software: KAware

KnowledgeSet Corp.
60 Garden Court, Building A—3rd
floor West
Monterey, CA 93940
(408) 357-2638
Retrieval softwares: KRS (Knowledge
Retrieval System); Graphic KRS (for
the Macintosh)

Marnick Associates, Inc.
101 Chestnut Hill Rd.
Chestnut Hill, MA 02167
(617) 566-0860

Online Computer Systems, Inc.
20251 Century Blvd.
Germantown, MD 20874
(800) 922-9204

Personal Library Software
15215 Shady Grove Rd., Suite 204
Rockville, MD 20850
(301) 926-1402
Retrieval software: Personal
Librarian

Publishers Data Service Corp.
2511 Garden Road, Building C
Monterey, CA 93940
(408) 371-2812

Quantum Access, Inc.
1700 W. Loop South, Suite 1460
Houston, TX 77027
(713) 622-3211
Retrieval software: The Quantum
Leap CD-ROM System

Reference Technology, Inc.
5700 Flatiron Pkwy.
Boulder, CO 80301
(303) 449-4157
Retrieval softwares: Full Text
Manager; Key Record Manager

Reteaco
716 Gordon Baker Rd.
Willowdale, Ont. M2H 3B4 Canada
(416) 497-0579
Retrieval software: FindIT

Space-Time Research Ltd.
27–31 King St.
Melbourne, 3000 Victoria Australia
(011) 613614-2871

Taunton Engineering
505 Middlesex Turnpike, Suite 11
Billerica, MA 01821
Retrieval software: Silversmith

TMS, Inc.
7840 Computer Ave.
Minneapolis, MN 55435
(612) 835-4399
Retrieval softwares: TMS Research;
Disc Architecture Software

Macintosh Retrieval Software Vendors

ACIU
20300 Stevens Creek Blvd. #495
Cupertino, CA 95014
(408) 252-4444

KnowledgeSet Corp.
60 Garden Court, Building A—3rd
floor West
Monterey, CA 93940
(408) 357-2638
Retrieval software: Graphic KRS
(for the Macintosh)

Odesta Corp.
4084 Commercial Ave.
Northbrook, IL 60062
(312) 498-5615

OMNIS
Blyth Software, Inc.
2929 Campus Dr.
San Mateo, CA 94403
(415) 571-0222

Virginia Systems Software Services,
Inc.
5509 W. Bay Court
Midlothian, VA 23113
(804) 739-3200

Basic Sources

Associations

Optical Publishing Association, 1880 Mackenzie Drive, Suite 111, Columbus, OH 43220; (614) 442-1955. The aim of OPA is to promote digital optical publishing and educate the public and serve as an industry forum. The organization provides information about CD-ROM, CD-I, and other optical publishing technologies including WORM and erasable optical media.

Bibliographies

Ali, S. Nazim. "A Selected Bibliography on Optical Disc Publishing," *Electronic and Optical Publishing Review* 6(4): 210–13 (Dec. 1986). Supplement 1 was published in same journal 7(2): 78–83 (June 1987).

Elshami, Ahmed. *CD-ROM: An Annotated Bibliography.* Englewood, Colo.: Libraries Unlimited, 1988. 138p. $24.50. Available on diskettes for the IBM ($20), Macintosh in Microsoft Works format ($21), and Apple II family in AppleWorks format ($20.50). Items in this bibliography are arranged alphabetically under broad topics.

Motley, Susan A. "Optical Disc Technology and Libraries: A Review of the 1988 Literature." *CD-ROM Librarian,* 4(5): 8–30 (May 1989).

National Technical Information Service. *Compact Optical Disc Technology—CD-ROM, April 1979–1986.* Springfield, Va.: NTIS, Dec. 1986 (PB87-852885/XAB). 154p. (Rept. for Apr. 79–1986. Supersedes PB86-853439.)

National Technical Information Service. *Erasable Optical Disks, 1975–January 1986.* Springfield, Va.: NTIS, Jan. 1986. (PB86-856408). 55p. (Rept. for Jan. 75–1986).

National Technical Information Service. *Optical Memory Data Storage, 1975–February 1986.* Springfield, Va.: NTIS, Feb. 1986 (PB86-858248). (Rept. for Feb. 75–1986. (Supersedes PB85-855039.)

Rechel, Michael. "How to Keep Up Absolutely Essential CD-ROM Reading." *Wilson Library Bulletin* 62(4): 41–42 (Dec. 1987).

Rechel, Michael. "Laser Disc Technology: A Selective Introductory Bibliography." *CD-ROM Librarian* 3(7): 16–18, 20–24 (July/Aug. 1987)

Directories and Guides

Access Faxon, a printed guide to more than 250 CD-ROM products, is published by the Faxon Press (15 Southwest Park, Westwood, MA 02090). It provides descriptions for more than 170 titles. Each entry includes a description of the CD-ROM product, required hardware and software, price, ordering number, and frequency of publication. This one-stop distributor is helpful especially when it is difficult to acquire enough information on a specific product. *Access Faxon* is priced at $24/year, with a charter subscription rate of $12.

AIIM Buying Guide: The Official Registry of Information and Image Management Products and Services. Silver Spring, Md.: Association for Information and Image Management, 1985–

Ali, S. Nazim. "Directory of Databases on Optical Discs," *Electronic and Optical Publishing Review* 6(4): 198–208 (Dec. 1986).

Bowers, Richard A. *Optical Publishing Directory.* Medford, N.J.: Learned Information, 1987. 200p. $45. Includes only CD-ROM titles that are actually in the market. The 1988 edition covers about 200 titles. A description for each product is provided along with producer's name, address, telephone number, and price.

Brandt, Richard. *Videodisc Training: A Cost Analysis* (A Guide and Workbook for Choosing Your Courseware Delivery). Falls Church, Va.: Videodisc Monitor, 1988. $49.95.

The CD-ROM Directory is a British publication listing information on most of the British CD-ROM products and the European marketplace, giving price in British pounds. Published by TFPL Publishing, 76 Park Rd., London NW1 4SH, England.

CD-ROM Yearbook. Published by Microsoft Press, 16011 NE 36th Way, Redmond, WA 98073. 960p. $79.95. Includes information on compact disc technology and products as well as lists companies, conferences, consultants, products, and publications.

CD-ROMS in Print, from Meckler Corporation (11 Ferry Lane W., Westport, CT 06880), is published annually and resembles Bowers' *Optical Publishing Directory.* It provides an alphabetical list of CD-ROM products currently in print, including information such as description of product, producer, technical specifications, and price. Includes other lists by producers, vendors, title, and CD-ROM players in addition to a subject listing. Listed price, $37.50.

Computer-Readable Databases: A Directory and Data Sourcebook. Edited by Kathleen Young Maracaccio. 1188p. $160. Available from Gale Research, Inc., Book Tower, Detroit, MI 48226; (800) 223-4253. The CD-ROM product index contains more than 200 databases.

"Directory of WORM (Write-once, Read-many) Companies and Organizations." *Optical Information Systems* 7(3): 185–92 (May/June 1987).

Educational Videodisc Directory. Available from Systems Impact, Inc., 4400 MacArthur Blvd., Suite 203, Washington, DC 20007. Free.

Gale, John. *State of the CD-ROM Industry: Applications, Players, and Products.* Alexandria, Va.: Information Workstation Group, 1987–

Gale, John; Lynch, Clifford; and Brownrigg, Edward. *Report on CD-ROM Search Software.* Alexandria, Va.: Information Workstation Group, 1987.

Guide to Producing Videodiscs in NTSC and PAL. Available from Philips and DuPont Optical Co., 1409 Foulk Rd., Wilmington, DE 19803; (800) 433-DISK; (302) 479-2500. 1989. Free.

Helgerson, Linda and Ennis, Martin. *The CD-ROM Sourcedisc.* Falls Church, Va.: Diversified Data Resources, Inc., 1987.

Information and Image Management: The State of the Industry 1989. Published by the Association of Information and Image Management, 1100 Wayne Ave., Suite 1100, Silver Spring, MD 20910; (301) 587-8202. $695 ($495 for AIIM members).

Interactive Videodiscs for Education. Available from Ztek Co., P.O. Box 1968, Lexington, KY 40593; (800) 247-1603. Free.

Laser-Optical Storage: The New Dimension in Information Automation. Prepared by Dan Costigan, published by Avedon Associates, 14 Accord Court, Potomac, MD 20854; (301) 983-0604. 1988. $250. The package includes text and 77 color slides.

"Library Vendor Directory." *Wilson Library Bulletin* 62(4): 21–22 (Dec. 1987).

Micrographic and Optical Recording Buyers Guide. Published by Spectrum Publishing, Unit 3A, Aston Road, Cambridge Road Estate, Bedford MK42 OLJ England. 1989.

Nelson, Nancy Melin. *Library Applications of Optical Disk and CD-ROM Technology* Westport, Conn.: Meckler 1987. 252p. $19.95. An entry in the Essential Guide to the Library IBM PC series (V.8).

Nihei, Wes. "CD-ROM Resource Guide." *PC World* 5(4): 256–59 (Apr. 1987).

1988 Medicaldisc Directory. Published by Stewart Publishing, Inc., 6471 Merritt Court, Alexandria, VA 22312; (703) 354-8155. 1988. $90. Includes more than 300 commercial videodiscs and CD-ROM projects developed for the health sciences.

"1989 Buyer's Guide & Consultant Directory," a special issue of *Optical Information Systems,* 8, no. 6 (Nov.–Dec. 1988), is a listing of hundreds of products and services in the following areas: Interactive Videodisc, WORM Optical Disk, Erasable Optical Disk, CD-ROM Technologies, and Optical Memory Card.

Optical Disk Storage and Document Image Processing: Buyer's Guide to Products and Systems. Published by Cimtech, Hatfield Polytechnic, College Lane, Hatfield, Herts AL10 9AB England. 1989. £18.

"Optical Disk Storage Systems." *Computerworld* 2(49): S13 (Dec. 7, 1987).

Schwier, Richard. *Interactive Video.* Published by Educational Technology Publications. 1987. 202 p. Distributed by the Videodisc Monitor, P.O. Box 26, Fall Church, VA 22046. $36.95.

The Summer 1989 Product Guide. Published by the Bureau of Electronic Publishing, Upper Montclair, N.J. (201) 746-3031.

Tiampo, Janet M. "Buyers Guide to CD-ROM Drives." *CD-ROM Review,* 1987–

Videodisc in Health Care: A Guide to the Industry. Published by Stewart Publishing, Inc., 6471 Merritt Court, Alexandria, VA 22312; (703) 354-8155. 1988. $249.

Videodiscs for Education: A Directory. Available from Minnesota Educational Computing Corp., Special Products, 3290 Lexington Ave. North, St. Paul, MN 55126. Free.

Videodiscs in Museums: A Project and Resource Directory. Published by the Videodisc Monitor, P.O. Box 26, Falls Church, VA 22046; (800) 323-3472. 1987. $70.

Who's Who in Optical Memories and Interactive Videodisks. San Francisco, Calif.: Rothchild Consultants, 1983–

Glossaries

Becker, Karen A. "CD-ROM: A Primer." *College & Research Libraries News* 48(7): 388–90, 392–93 (July/Aug. 1987).

"CD-ROM Glossary." *CD-ROM Review* 2(1): 55–58, 60–61 (Mar./Apr. 1987).

Glossary in CD-ROM: The Basics, published by Hewlett-Packard, 1987.

"Glossary" in *CD-ROM, Volume Two: Optical Publishing: A Practical Approach to Developing CD-ROM Applications.* Ed. by Suzanne Ropiequet and others (Redmond, Wash.: Microsoft, 1987).

"Glossary of CD-ROM-Related Technical Terms and Acronyms." *Optical Information Systems* 6(3): 230–34 (May/June 1986).

Law

A Guide to Database Distribution: Legal Aspects and Model Contracts. Prepared by attorneys Joseph Bremner and Peggy Miller, this guide helps in the negotiating of contracts with database owners. It details commercial database distribution issues such as legal relationships between involved parties, contracts, and licensing. It describes aspects of agreements, limitations of liability, and the legal positions of the licensee and licensor. (NFAIS: National Federation of Abstracting and Information Services, 112 South 16th St., Philadelphia, PA 19102; (215) 563-2406. $160.)

Legality of Optical Storage (1988), ed. by Robert F. Williams, includes "Introduction to Optical Storage," "Introduction to Evidentiary Law," "Analysis of How to Overcome the Hearsay and Best Evidence Rule Objections," "Compendium of Current Laws," and "Guidelines for Enhancing the Admissibility of Optically Stored Information." Researched by the law firm of Nixon, Hargrave, Devans & Doyle. (Distributed by Cohasset Associates, Inc., 3808 Lake Point Tower, 505 N. Lake Shore Dr., Chicago, IL 60611; (312) 527-1550. $230.)

Periodicals and Newsletters

CD-Computing News. 1988. Monthly, $150 (foreign $165). W V Publishing Co., Box 138, Babson Park, Boston, MA 02157; (617) 449-1603. ISSN 0893-4843.

CD Data Report. Monthly newsletter covering the CD-ROM industry and related optical storage technologies. 1984. 12 issues, $225. Langley Publications, 1350 Beverly Rd., Suite 115-324, McLean, VA 22102; (703) 241-2131. ISSN 8755-5727.

CD-I News. Issued for the consumer electronics, entertainment, publishing, information, and education industries. 1986. Monthly. Free. Link Resources Corp., 79 Fifth Ave., New York, NY 10003-2025; (212) 627-1400.

CD Publisher News. Free. Meridian Data, Inc., 4450 Capitola Rd., Suite 101, Capitola, CA 95010; (408) 476-5858.

CD-ROM Access Newsletter. Free. Compact Cambridge. 7200 Wisconsin Ave., Bethesda, MD 20814; (301) 961-6700.

CD-ROM Librarian. 1986. 10 issues, $65. Meckler Corp., 11 Ferry Lane W., Westport, CT 06880-5808; (203) 226-6967. ISSN 0893-9934.

CD-ROM Review. 1986. Ceased publication with the December 1988 issue. IDG Communications, 80 Elm St., Peterborough, NH 03458; (603) 924-9471. ISSN 0891-3188.

DATABASE. 1975. Bimonthly. $85. Online, Inc., 11 Tannery Lane, Weston, CT 06883; (203) 227-8466.

Electronic and Optical Publishing Review. Quarterly. $75. Reports on the online and videotex industries and the emerging fields of desktop publishing and optical disc technology. Learned Information Ltd., 143 Old Marlton Pike, Medford, NJ 08055-8707; (609) 654-4888. ISSN 0360-6650.

Electronic Information Report. 1979. $295. Link Resources Corp., c/o International Data Corp., 79 Fifth Ave., New York, NY 10003; (212) 627-1400.

The Electronic Library. 1983. Bimonthly. $79. For librarians and information center managers interested in microcomputers and library automation. Learned Information Ltd., 143 Old Marlton Pike, Medford, NJ 08055-8707; (609) 654-4888. ISSN 0264-0473.

Electronic Publishing. Semiannually. John Wiley & Sons, 605 Third Ave., New York, NY 10158; (212) 850-6000. ISSN 0894-3982.

Electronic Publishing Abstracts. 1983. Monthly. $440. Pergamon Press, Inc., Journals Division, Maxwell House, Fairview Park, Elmsford, NY 10523; (914) 592-7700. ISSN 0739-2907.

Electronic Publishing Business. 1983. Monthly (except August). $95. Provides information on current computer systems available for use by publishers and booksellers. Electronic Publishing Ventures, Inc., 885 N. San Antonio Rd., Los Altos, CA 94022. ISSN 0888-0948.

IDP Report. 1980. Biweekly newsletter for information industry personnel. $315. Knowledge Industry Publications, Inc. 701 Westchester Ave., White Plains, NY 10604; (914) 328-9157. ISSN 0197-0178.

Inform (formerly *Journal of Information and Image Management*). 1987. Monthly. $55. Association for Information and Image Management, 1100 Wayne Ave., Suite 1100, Silver Spring, MD 20910; (301) 587-8202.

Information Market. 1976. Irregular, 5 issues/year. Free. Contains European news of new online and CD-ROM products as well as user problems and European policies toward the information market. Commission of European Communities, Euronet Diane, 177 Route d'Esch, L-1471 Luxembourg, Luxembourg. ISSN 0250-5789.

Information Media and Technology. 1967. Bimonthly. £40 CIMTECH, P.O. Box 109, Hatfield Polytechnic, College Lane, Hatfield, Herts. AL10 9AB, England. ISSN 0266-6969.

Information Standards Quarterly. Published by the National Information Standards Organization, P.O. Box 1056, Bethesda, MD 20817; (301) 975-2814. $40. 4 issues/year.

Information Today. 1983. 11 issues, $27.50. Learned Information, 143 Old Marlton Pike, Medford, NJ 08055; (609) 654-6266.

Interactive Update. Bimonthly. $110. Available from the National Interactive Video Center, 24 Stephenson Way, London NW1 2HD England; 01-387-2233.

The Laserdisk Professional. 1988. Bimonthly. $78. Pemberton Press, 11 Tannery Lane, Weston, CT 06883; (800) 248-8466. ISSN 0896-4149.

Library Hi Tech Journal. 1983. Quarterly. $55. A comprehensive current guide to all forthcoming and available technologies applicable to libraries and information centers. Concentrates on reporting on the selection, installation, maintenance, and integration of systems and hardware. The Pierian Press, Inc., P.O. Box 1803, Ann Arbor, MI 48106. ISSN 0737-8831.

Library Hi Tech News. 1984. Monthly. $65. Pierian Press, Inc., P.O. Box 1803, Ann Arbor, MI 48106; (313) 434-6409. ISSN 0741-9058.

NewLaser. Published by Laser Learning Technologies, 3114 37th Place South, Seattle, WA 98144; (206) 722-3002.

ONLINE. 1977. Bimonthly. $85. Online, Inc., 11 Tannery Lane, Weston, CT 16883; (302) 227-8466.

Online Review. The international journal of online information systems. 1977. Bimonthly. $85. Learned Information Ltd., 143 Old Marlton Pike, Medford, NJ 08055-8707; (609) 654-6266. ISSN 0309-314X.

Optical Information Systems. Bimonthly. $95. Meckler Corp., 11 Ferry Lane W., Westport, CT 06880-5808; (203) 226-6967. ISSN 0886-5809.

Optical Memory News. 1982. 11 issues, $295. The journal of record of the optical memory industry. (Rothchild Consultants, 256 Laguna Honda Blvd., San Francisco, CA 94116-1496; (415) 681-3700.

Solutions. A newsletter published by FileTek, Inc., 6100 Executive Blvd., Rockville, MD 20852; (301) 984-1542.

T.H.E. Journal (Technological Horizons in Education Journal). 10 issues/year. Free; $29 for nonqualifying subscriptions. Includes a section on optical disc technology. T.H.E. Journal, P.O. Box 15126, Santa Ana, CA 92705-0126. ISSN 0192-592X.

Videodisc Monitor. 1983. Monthly. $247. Future Systems, Inc., Box 26, Falls Church, VA 22046; (703) 241-1779.

Wilsonlines. Free. The H. W. Wilson Co., 950 University Ave., Bronx, NY 10452-9978; (800) 367-6770.

Index

Ahmed M. Elshami is the reference librarian at the Instructional Materials Center, Temple University Library, Philadelphia, Pennsylvania. His recent publications include *CD-ROM: An Annotated Bibliography* (Englewood, Colo.: Libraries Unlimited, 1988). He is co-author of the *Encyclopedic Dictionary of Library and Information Science Terms: English-Arabic* (Riyadh: Mars Publishing House, 1988).